"Tom did a masterful job of staying very honest and evenhanded in a way that very few could do.... It is an intriguing read, and readers not familiar with the roots of the Boston/ICOC movement will find this book absolutely captivating. It deserves to become a best seller."

—Gordon Ferguson,
Author, Elder
Phoenix Valley Church of Christ

"I am deeply grateful for Tom's work on this and feel it will be of benefit to many people—inside and outside of the International Churches of Christ fellowship."

—Dr. Douglas A. Foster
Associate Dean, Graduate School of Theology
Abilene Christian University

"Riveting. I couldn't put it down."

—Ed Anton
Author, Evangelist
Hampton Roads Church

"This book is an excellent and needed addition to our history in the Restoration Movement."

—Chuck Lucas
Evangelist, Cornerstone Church
Thomasville, GA

"*In Search of a City* is a touching story, and a much needed one. Everyone in the family of the Churches of Christ or Christian Churches will benefit from the Joneses' story, although it will also resonate with outsiders to this fellowship. A fast-moving work, it is well conceived, affably shared, ably worded, and succinctly presented."

—Dr. Douglas Jacoby
Author, Director
Athens Institute of Ministry

"Tom's book inspired me to have a new vision of reaching the world from my local congregation. It gave me an understanding of how God has worked through the years to bring about the fellowship I now know. Men of faith went after their dreams and acted on their convictions. That is exactly what we need to be doing now as we move forward."

–Keith Davis
Minister
Nashville Church

"Tom Jones' story is a must read for those with personal struggles as a disciple. But it is more than that. It is an account of one family's responses to numerous challenges over four decades as members of the International Church of Christ."

–Dr. Thomas H. Olbricht
Distinguished Professor Emeritus of Religion
Pepperdine University

"I found Tom's book very interesting and thoughtful. I especially like his recommended path forward for ICofC folks toward the end of the book."

–Bob Harrington
Director of Church Planting Networks
Stadia

"I appreciate the fresh view Tom delivers from his own personal experience as simply a Christian, but also the unique lens he's able to provide with being part of the leadership in the ICOC."

–Damien Charley
Youth Minister
Nashville Church

"Tom's autobiographical survey has filled in the blanks on some key questions giving context for the tensions between the "mainline" churches and the discipling movement that I could never have otherwise known. He helped recreate the drama to give us in the ICOC the behind the curtain insight into this great and complex epic that we have witnessed and participated in."

–Steve Staten
Teacher
Chicago Church of Christ

In Search of a

City

Other Books by Thomas A. Jones

No One Like Him: Jesus and His Message

Strong in the Grace: Reclaiming the Heart of the Gospel

God's Perfect Plan for Imperfect People: The Message of Ephesians

Letters to New Disciples:
Practical Advice for Those Who Have Decided to Follow Jesus

The Prideful Soul's Guide to Humility
(co-authored with Michael Fontenot)

To Live Is Christ: An Interactive Study of Philippians
(co-authored with Sheila Jones)

Mind Change: A Biblical Path to Overcoming Life's Challenges

In Search of a

City

An Autobiographical Perspective on a Remarkable but
Controversial Movement

THOMAS A. JONES

www.dpibooks.org
www.insearchofacity.net

In Search of a City
©2007 by DPI Books
5016 Spedale Court #331
Spring Hill, TN 37174

All Scripture quotations, unless indicated, are taken from
the NEW INTERNATIONAL VERSION.
Copyright ©1973, 1978, 1984 by the International Bible Society.
Used by permission of Zondervan Publishing House.
All rights reserved.

The "NIV" and "New International Version" trademarks
are registered in the United States Patent Trademark Office
by the International Bible Society.
Use of either trademarks requires the permission of
the International Bible Society.

Printed in the United States of America

ISBN: 978-1-57782-221-9

Cover Design: Brian Branch, Full Sercal Graphix
Interior Design: Thais Gloor

To Sheila

I could not possibly dedicate a book that covers these forty years to anyone but you, the one who has been my friend, and then lover and partner during this time.

Acknowledgments

My goal in writing this book was to communicate accurately, openly, humbly, faithfully and with an attitude shaped by Scripture in order that the most people might be enlightened, instructed, warned and inspired. I knew very well that in order to even approximate this goal, I would need the help of others. I was blessed to receive it.

Thirty people read my manuscript and offered input that was encouraging and corrective. If it takes a village to raise a child, it seems to have taken a "house church" to make a book. Everyone who gave me feedback made suggestions that were helpful. A book can always be improved, and even in its present form this one is not the exception. However, it is far better because of my wife, my children, long-time friends, teachers, elders and new friends in scholarly circles outside my own church culture. I am indebted to you all, but must single out my wife, Sheila, who was my chief advisor and editor, and our daughters—Amy, Bethany and Corrie—who probably gave the most extensive input. I am grateful for the way you all invested yourselves with me in this project.

There were others I could have consulted with great benefit. However, at some point one has to draw a line and finish the work. Knowing that still more people will read this and think of things they would like to add to the story I tell, a Web site can be accessed at this address: www.insearchofacity.net. There readers will be able to send their own recollections, and the work of understanding a movement that has affected many over the last forty years will prayerfully be advanced.

Again, I am grateful for each one who took the considerable amount of time needed to read this work and offer me your encouragement and advice. May God bless you and bless all of us as we strive to learn, understand, mature, speak and advance the gospel.

Of course, my greatest thanks goes to Jesus the Messiah, whose message captivated me, caused me to start this journey and stays with me on it. He is still the *archegos*—captain pioneer, trailblazer, author and champion of my faith (Hebrews 12:2). To him I humbly give praise.

Table of Contents

Introduction

Understanding Backward

By faith Abraham, when called to go to a place he would later receive as his inheritance, obeyed and went, even though he did not know where he was going. By faith he made his home in the promised land like a stranger in a foreign country; he lived in tents, as did Isaac and Jacob, who were heirs with him of the same promise. For he was looking forward to the city with foundations, whose architect and builder is God.

Hebrews 11:8–10

For here we do not have an enduring city, but we are looking for the city that is to come.

Hebrews 13:14

History has always fascinated me. Though my primary goal in college was to get a degree in accounting, I added a second major in history which made little sense to my advisors, but was done because I so thoroughly enjoyed it.

Typical of the way my mind works, after hearing so much about the destruction of the World Trade Center in the September 11 attack, I found myself later absorbed by a *New York Times* piece on the history of those buildings. From the initial idea in 1955 to the opening in 1973, the design and construction of this American icon passed through many twists and turns. I was intrigued by the opposition that was mounted to the project, by the maneuvering it took to overcome that opposition, by the hundred-plus architectural plans that were rejected, and most of all, by the bold and innovative engineering that made the twin towers possible.

For almost forty years I have been an observer of and participant in the movement that culminated in the group known as the International Churches of Christ (ICOC). As God would have it, my wife and I are among just a few people who have been connected almost continuously with this movement from its earliest days to the present day. That does not give us an infallible perspective, but it would seem to give us a special responsibility.

I have often been asked by younger disciples, who are as fascinated by history as I am, to tell them more about how things developed and came to the present point. As I have shared orally some of the things you will find here, I have found people to be very surprised to learn some of the facts. They generally had heard only one version of this history—a version that likely was driven by a particular agenda. Their questions, and gaps in their knowledge, often caused me to see the need to put my memories and observations in print.

More recently, conversations have begun again between those in the ICOC and believers in other groups—a development I have welcomed. With that has come a need to explain how this movement developed as it did and why some of us made the choice to align ourselves with something that has resulted in unprecedented growth, fierce controversy and eventually, serious reevaluation.

> If you would understand anything, observe its beginning and its development.
>
> —Aristotle

The more I worked on this, the more I realized it was also a good personal exercise for me as I sought to sort out the good and the bad, and to understand the various ways God has worked in my life through an assortment of transitions. I certainly don't have my arms around it all, but feel I am better for the attempt.

For some time I have thought about publishing my own recollections. I think I have hesitated to do this because I understand some of the perils and risks of writing history. Several years ago I shared an early draft of this book with several friends and got responses similar to those John Bunyan got before he published *Pilgrims Progress*. A more recent distribution of my updated manuscript brought a bit more of the same. In what was called "The Author's Apology for This Book" placed right after the title page, Bunyan included these words in his rhyming text:

> Some said, John, print it; others said, Not so.
> Some said, It might be good, others said, No.
> Now was I in a straight, and did not see
> Which was the best thing to be done by me:
> At last I thought, Since you are thus divided,
> I print it will; and so the case was decided.

While I didn't make my final decision quite as Bunyan did, I seemingly did it with a good deal more angst than he indicates, and don't expect my work to become the classic his became, I do know the feeling of having some say *print it* and others, *not so*.

Somewhere I read that history is not an account of what actually happened, but our effort to report what happened based on the best information we have. I am quite sure that I don't have all the information and just as sure that I cannot be completely objective about the events that I will describe. I will be tempted to portray things in a way that makes me look better than I am. Though I will pray to resist that temptation, I cannot guarantee my readers how successful I will be. Though I was personally involved in various developments and an eyewitness to others, there were many things that I was never privy to, resulting undoubtedly in some flawed analysis.

In some cases, my own memory of situations that I *was in* is less than perfect. As is always the case, there were certainly a variety of psycho-social factors affecting me and everyone else—factors we often become aware of, if at all, only with the passage of time.

As I write, I will try to be personally self-revealing, but that of course, is only possible to the extent of my own self-awareness, which is never complete, but hopefully ever-growing. For the most part, I will leave it to others to reveal relevant aspects of their own lives.

With all the limitations, perils and challenges in mind, I have decided that there is still something worthwhile about the testimony of one eyewitness. Soren Kierkegaard once wrote, "We live forward but we can only think backward." I have heard that last part rephrased to say, "But we can only understand backward." I hope that this look back will bring about a bit more understanding.

It is also my great hope that my modest efforts will encourage others to write and publish their stories and their memories. As I think about that possibility, I know I will be the first in line to buy those accounts, for I am eager to know what others experienced, what the view was from their perspective as well as what they learned. Maybe I can motivate some of my peers to put in the sweat needed to make this happen by saying, "If nothing else, write for your children and grandchildren." But perhaps I can give even a greater motivation by sharing with you some reasons I felt it was important for me to write this book.

First, I believe that we always can learn valuable lessons from history. Most are familiar with George Santayana's famous quote that "Those who cannot learn from history are bound to repeat it." While we need to spend plenty of time looking forward, we need to be informed by what we can see—good and bad—in a look through the rear view mirror. Santayana was thinking mostly about our mistakes (and sometimes that is far too kind a word for what we have done). As painful as it is, we must not forget those. In seems unthinkable, but we could repeat some of the awful past. That is why Jewish people today put so much emphasis on remembering the holocaust and why African-Americans insist we not forget the two hundred years of slavery or the hundred years of discrimination that followed a great civil war.

There are some things about the last forty years those of us in the ICOC fellowship would rather forget, but we must not. But we can also learn from looking back to victories, and by the grace of God, there were victories. There can be more.

Second, I write because I believe we all need a conviction that the story of both Testaments and the story of God's work today are the story of the divine working through the human with all the frailties and weaknesses of the latter. When God chose to put treasure in jars of clay, like the Jews, and then, like us, he knew that the result would be less than pristine. As Rabbi Lionel Blue once said: "The Jews are just like everybody else, only more so."[1] The same can be said of the church, but God's work in our flaws still bears great witness to his touch and his power.

It is no surprise that we who follow Jesus make plenty of mistakes and even commit foolish sins. Did we not learn that from Peter? What is surprising is how God still uses us and gives victories. It was once said about my favorite team that they "win ugly," but they won a national championship "winning ugly." When God's people win, it is not always pretty. But if it is a win for God, it is worth celebrating, and all the more because his power is demonstrated in our weakness. I pray this effort to remember will show that clearly.

Recently I heard an intriguing interview with a young physician who had written a book reflecting on medical students' work in the anatomy lab. The doctor shared that she stood in awe of and marveled at those individuals who had donated their bodies to advance medical understanding. Perhaps it is not the best analogy, but it is my hope that in "donating" my story for public "dissection" (have mercy please!) that I will in some way advance our understanding of the way God works among us—in, through and in spite of our humanity and help us to take some righteous steps forward.

Third, I write not only with the hope of having some effect on the church and movements within the church, but with a hope to give heart and encouragement to individuals who may be all too focused on their own weakness, wondering if God can still use them. I have a special place in my heart for such as these. By sharing openly about my own weakness, I hope others will find the courage that God has given me to continue the journey even when tempted to fall into what Bunyan called, in one of his most vivid phrases, the "Slough of Despond."

Finally, I write hoping to contribute to a developing body of writing that

---

1. Quoted in N.T. Wright, *Simply Christian* (New York: HarperSanFrancisco, 2006), 75.

will give us all a greater understanding of some of God's work in our day. Many of you have, no doubt, heard the old story of the blind men and elephant. John Godfrey Saxe (1816–1887) published a rhyming version of it that may be best known. In the story, six blind men go to examine an elephant to determine what it is like. Saxe's version begins this way:

> It was six men of Indostan,
> To learning much inclined,
> Who went to see the Elephant
> (Though all of them were blind),
> That each by observation
> Might satisfy his mind.

Of course, each man came away from the experience with a different conclusion based on his own perspective. One thought an elephant was like a wall, one a spear, one a snake, one a fan, one a rope, and one a tree. Near the end Saxe has these lines:

> And so these men of Indostan
> Disputed loud and long,
> Each in his own opinion
> Exceeding stiff and strong,
> Though each was partly in the right,
> And all were in the wrong!

What this group needed was a meeting where they combined their different perspectives to get the larger picture. In writing this book, I realize I am just one of the "blind men" trying to tell what I have experienced. If others would join me in an enterprise like this, there is the possibility that someone much later who is trained in historical disciplines may be able to study what a number of us have written and more carefully analyze the events that led to an amazing movement—one that eventually revealed both our capacity to catch and be stirred with a vision from God, and yet, slip at times toward the dark side.

My desire is that somehow through this exercise, the grace of God might be more fully appreciated, conviction about his work in our weakness might increase, commitment to the body of Christ might deepen, and hearts longing to fulfill God's purpose might multiply.

When I first wrote the preceding paragraph, I was thinking mostly of encouraging others in my church fellowship to reflect and to write. However, since that was written three months ago, I have seen that our reflections alone will limit our understanding. We need to hear the stories of others who are also in the Body of Christ.

As a sort of memoir, by its nature this book will tell you a lot about me and my wife—where we were, what we thought, what we felt and why we made decisions as we did. I hope, however, that as you read you will be asking a question about someone else. I hope you will be asking "What was God doing?" (And "What is he doing now?") I hope this work will not only cause you my reader to look for that in my life or the lives of those I describe, but will cause you to look for that in your own life and those you know. The fact that the answer will not always be obvious does not keep this from being an important question to ask.

Though I didn't realize it forty years ago, in my first few steps toward Jesus I was beginning to look for that eternal city "whose architect and builder is God." This book is the account of one man's journey toward that city and of the companions I chose to travel with. My hope and prayer is that it will cast some light on the nature of the expedition and the One whose life causes us to make the trip. I pray it will encourage others to join us as pilgrims, and like Christian in Bunyan's classic, to never give up when difficulty comes.

As I was finishing this book, I happened to look back over the little volume that I recently revised: *Letters to New Disciples*.[2] As I browsed through the chapters (or letters) of that work, it occurred to me that the topics parallel the progression of my convictions as I share them in this book. Along the way these truths were either first learned or became especially meaningful to me. So at the close of each chapter you will find a short excerpt from that book that fits quite well, I think, with the chapter you will have just read. It describes some conviction that was most important to me and to us at that time in our history. By including these I hope to keep the focus also on God's message and not just the experiences of our life. Beyond that it is good for all of us to remember afresh the things that need to be said to new believers, for those are the simpler truths that help ground us when we tend to over-complicate our lives.

---

2. Thomas Jones, *Letters to New Disciples: Revised Edition* (Spring Hill, TN: DPI, 2007).

1

Lewis, Bonhoeffer and Dallas, Texas

My own story, as it relates to the larger events, begins in the spring of 1967. Raised in a home where both my parents were members of the Churches of Christ (one of the three major groups to come out of the American Restoration Movement), I was baptized and became a church member as I entered my teens. I can remember that my peers in the church seemed to be baptized in clumps, and I wanted to be sure that I was doing it because of my own decision for Christ and not peer pressure. I picked a Sunday night when no one else was being baptized and let the minister know I was ready.

I have a memory of being on the stairwell at school the next day and telling one of my friends what I had done. As we look back on baptism, we can always say there was so much more that it would have been good to understand. Whatever happened there, it was an act of adolescent faith and obedience, but faith and obedience, nonetheless. (I will return to this experience much later in the book.)

At first I was quite zealously involved in activities the church offered for my age group. Later in high school, all that fervor would be gone as my life revolved around academics, sports, cars and an interest in girls, though the latter was seldom acted on. I was regarded as a good kid, but was hardly a model of spiritual commitment even by the standards of our very average church.

However, as I neared the end of my sophomore year at what is now the University of North Alabama, I had a thirst for something more than my self-centered lifestyle. That need led me to finally respond to several invitations to the meetings of a campus ministry group sponsored by the Churches of Christ. Though the "The Total Commitment Movement" as it would be called by critics, had yet to develop, in campus ministry devotionals I heard a call to serious commitment. In my own Bible reading and in the writings of C.S. Lewis (*Mere Christianity*[1]) and Dietrich Bonhoeffer (*The Cost of Discipleship*[2]), discovered browsing in a little book store near campus, I would hear that call

---

1. C.S. Lewis, *Mere Christianity* (New York: Macmillan Publishing, 1943, 1945, 1952).
2. Dietrich Bonhoeffer, *The Cost of Discipleship* (New York: Macmillan Publishing, 1949).

more clearly. Only much later would the irony strike me of a guy from the Churches of Christ in the Deep South in the 1960s finding a fresh view of Jesus from an English Anglican and a German Lutheran. Other works by these two authors would influence me for many years.

By the end of the summer of that year I had wrestled with Jesus' message—particularly the call to deny self and take up the cross (Luke 9:23 and other places); talked through my struggles, questions and doubts with friends; and made a commitment to Jesus that was in my mind a full one. I have a reel-to-reel tape made just a little later in which I am speaking to a congregation on the topic: "Total Commitment to Christ." This was certainly one of the defining times in my life. I was seriously turning away from a life focused on myself, my pleasures and my accomplishments, and having a heart-felt desire to take up the cross and follow Jesus.

I never remember formally expressing that I was repenting, but this is exactly what I was doing. Feeling like a new person, I was motivated each day by thoughts of my relationship to Christ. While I was determined not to be a slacker in my college classes, I found much more fulfillment in studying those things that took me deeper into the life of Jesus and in sharing my faith with others.

A year later in the fall of 1968 I was chosen the president of the Christian Student Fellowship, and as such, I received an impressive brochure in the mail describing an event billed as the International Campus Evangelism Seminar to be held at the Hilton Inn in Dallas in December of that year. I can still remember how I read that cutting-edge brochure (sharp even by today's standards) with wide-eyed expectation. I can still see in my mind the picture of the Hilton Inn and remember the excitement that was generated as I thought about 1,000 Christians from many states in one hotel for four days.

The only church events with that kind of attendance that I had heard of were on the campuses of Christian colleges. For Christians to be in a hotel signaled the beginning of something new, but none of us, of course, could have realized that we were witnessing what would seem later to me to be the birth of a movement.[3] (By the way, I recently found that brochure and showed my family that the cost of the hotel was $5 per night, per person, with four to a room, and this was in a Hilton!)

This event was being sponsored by Campus Evangelism (CE), a program of the Broadway Church of Christ in Lubbock, Texas. The leaders of CE were Jim Bevis (a native of my own part of Alabama), Charles Shelton and Rex

---

3. As you keep reading you may see why for some like me "the movement" began in Dallas in 1968, for others it began even earlier in the campus ministry in Gainesville, Florida, in 1966, and for others it didn't really start until 1979 in a Concord, Massachusetts, living room.

Vermillion. Their ministry at Texas Tech in Lubbock was called Campus Advance. The brochure mentioned that this was actually the second CE *international* seminar, the first having been held in 1966. As a member of the Churches of Christ and one convinced of the failings of denominational teaching on salvation, I was rather amazed to see that Bill Bright of Campus Crusade for Christ had been a speaker at that first seminar. Churches of Christ were known for having no contact with speakers outside their own fellowship unless the format was a well-advertised debate.

I would later learn the leaders of CE had brought Bright in to give those in the Churches of Christ a vision of what could be done, and that they had adapted Campus Crusades' "Four Spiritual Laws," producing their own attractive evangelistic booklet titled "Guideposts to Life on a New Plane."

The new booklet described the importance of baptism into Christ, something that was missing in the Campus Crusade material. They quoted Romans 6:4 from the J.B. Phillips translation and took the booklet's title from that same passage:

> We were dead and buried with him in baptism, so that just as he was raised from the dead by that splendid revelation of the Father's power so we too might rise to life on a new plane altogether.

Poster for CE Seminar 1968

I am still not sure how it all happened, but in that bastion of theological conservatism in the church culture we were in, I somehow received permission to organize a group to attend the Dallas event. In retrospect, I imagine that this CE movement, full of suspect innovations, just had not hit the radar screens of the conservative church leaders in the Southeast. That would soon change.

Right after Christmas 1968 a group of thirty of us (including my wife to be, whom I would propose to two months later) boarded a bus and traveled to Dallas, Texas. The theme of the event was "Say So!" based on Psalm 107:2 in the KJV:

> Let the redeemed of the LORD say so, whom he hath redeemed from the hand of the enemy.

As anticipated, there were about 1,000 people in attendance, primarily college students from across the Bible Belt, Florida and California. The song leader for the seminar was someone named Chuck Lucas. He was introduced by the seminar leaders as the director of a CE "pilot project" in campus min-

istry at the University of Florida. He would be supported by CE but would be leading a Campus Advance effort in connection with the Fourteenth Street Church of Christ in Gainesville. He had with him a student leader that Sheila and I met; his name was J.P. Tynes.

Twenty years later we would be in a group led by J.P. in the Boston Church of Christ. I would learn just recently from my friend Sam Laing that he was also in Dallas for this event and that the ministry in Gainesville had been started two years before the seminar.

Chuck Lucas leading singing at the '68 CE Seminar
Photo by Mike Haynes

The seminar put great emphasis on sharing the gospel with others. At the time most campus ministries in the Churches of Christ were focused primarily on holding on to what were called "preference students" (i.e. those who said they preferred the Churches of Christ when they registered for classes at their college or university). The goal of campus ministry was often to try to keep students from losing their faith, since they were not attending Christian colleges. On those campuses where the church had established a "chair of Bible," credit courses in the biblical studies were taught as sort of "satellite" classes connected with a Christian college, but on most campuses there was little emphasis on evangelism. CE hoped to change that. They had printed up thousands of the aforementioned booklets, "Guideposts to Life on a New Plane." We were encouraged to begin to use this tool in cold-contact evangelism even while we were at the hotel.

At some point during the seminar I met a young woman from Kansas who had come to the event with some friends but had little knowledge of the Bible. Using the new tool and adding to it other scriptures I knew, I shared with her what I understood about how to become a Christian. I can still remember getting up very early on Saturday morning to drive across Dallas where a minister opened his church building so she could be baptized into Christ. For several years after the seminar I corresponded with her, before eventually losing contact.

In the church I had grown up in there had been some emphasis on evangelism. While we were slow to get grace, we were better at getting commands, and Matthew 28:19–20 (KJV) was pretty clear to us:

> "Go ye therefore, and teach all nations, baptizing them in the name of the Father, and of the Son, and of the Holy Ghost: Teaching them to observe all things whatsoever I have commanded you: and, lo, I am with you alway [sic], even unto the end of the world."

Shortly after I got involved in the campus ministry, I had attended at my local church a series titled "Journey to Eternity" taught by Mid McKnight, who spoke around the country in an effort to wake up the church regarding its mission. His messages had convinced me that it was thoroughly biblical for every Christian to be concerned about helping others find salvation, but seeing so many gathered in Dallas from other campuses inspired me to put that conviction into action and to make the focus of evangelism more Christ than the church.

If the seminar was organized to put neglected emphasis on evangelism, it also seemed to be designed to critique much that was wrong in the Churches of Christ. Seminar speakers emphasized the importance of grace, the sin of racial discrimination (a huge issue in 1968), the power of the Holy Spirit, the real meaning of fellowship, and the need for worship that was transforming not just routine. It would be prophetic preaching on these subjects that would shortly raise the ire of other church leaders.

For me, the event was life changing. I would never think about much of anything in the same way again. For several years I replayed the tapes from the event over and over on my big Sony reel-to-reel tape recorder. Thirty-nine years later, I can still remember most of the speakers including Wesley Reagan, Jim Reynolds, John Allen Chalk, Roy Osborne and Andrew Hairston, as well as key lines from all of their messages. The Jesus I had become convinced of while reading the Scriptures and the writings of C.S. Lewis and Dietrich Bonhoeffer, was now more alive than ever for me. Over the next four decades I would see and experience some great moments and some low ones, but it would be this Jesus and his grace that would keep me on the road.

Some time ago I decided to start every time with God in the morning by repeating the confession I made when I was baptized. When I repeat those words, "Jesus is Lord," it immediately gets me focused, clarifies my thinking and gives me fresh direction for a new day. It brings me back to the crucial issue.

–From *Letters to New Disciples*, Chapter Three, "Jesus Is Lord"

2

Trouble in Tennessee

In 1969 the United States would put a man on the moon, but there was, of course, no Internet, and news within the Churches of Christ traveled fairly slowly. Our student group had returned from Dallas with renewed zeal. We had been given a vision of an exciting form of Christianity, quite in contrast with the somewhat stale routine form of religion we were accustomed to in our churches. As we reported about our trip to Texas, we were generally met with pats on the back by those happy to see their young people not buying into the radical rebellions of the '60s, but finding things in "the Lord's church" that they were excited about. Few questions were asked.

About five weeks after we returned from Dallas, all that changed. Ellis Coats, one of the two campus ministers at our Christian Student Center, returned on Tuesday afternoon from a trip to Henderson, Tennessee, where he had traveled that day to attend the Annual Bible Lectureship at Freed-Hardeman College (a center of doctrinal conservatism in the Churches of Christ). He came back with the word that it had been announced that the Open Forum to be held on Thursday would be devoted to grave concerns about the CE seminar recently held in Dallas. The phone lines had apparently been burning. Calls had poured into lectureship leaders that something very "unsound" had gone on in that Dallas hotel.

On a Tuesday, in one of the general sessions of the lectureship, the long-time moderator of the Open Forum had announced that brethren everywhere were concerned about this Dallas meeting and that there would be thorough discussion of those concerns on Thursday.

Ellis, himself a Freed-Hardeman graduate, talked with me about what should be done. He decided to call the leaders of the CE program in Lubbock and tell them about this development. Ellis knew Jim Bevis personally, and he urged them to come to Tennessee. Eager to stop a potential fire storm, they all three decided to fly to Memphis, rent a car and meet us in Henderson on Thursday, where they would ask to present their case in response to the many rumors that were flying.

We were expecting Jim Bevis, Charles Sheldon and Rex Vermillion. When we met at a restaurant for lunch prior to the Open Forum, they had with them another man, Dudley Lynch, the editor of the *Christian Chronicle* (which I knew was considered by many to be a "liberal," and therefore very suspect, paper in the Churches of Christ). Though I was a twenty-one-year-old student and quite uninitiated in church politics, I still sensed that this meeting was not going to go well. However, I knew how transforming the events in Dallas had been for me, and I knew which side I was on.

I had grown up in the Churches of Christ and was well aware of reports of preachers that were harsh and adversarial in church controversies. I had heard a few stories about the Open Forum, but nothing really prepared me for the experience. Having returned a few weeks earlier from the electric and joyful atmosphere of the Dallas Seminar, I felt something totally different when I walked in and took my seat in the college auditorium.

I know it will be hard for some readers who were never in the culture of the mainline Churches of Christ in the '60s and '70s to imagine just how legalistic, self-righteous and downright vicious some prominent and respected leaders were at the time. But to understand the reactions to the movement I will describe, you must try to appreciate this reality. Historian Richard Hughes has documented how "the fighting style" had developed in the Churches of Christ in the late nineteenth century.[1] It was still alive and well in the 1970s, and we would see it often in that decade as those in positions of influence and power reacted to a growing reform movement in a church culture that desperately needed it.

The moderator (there is irony in that term, for he was anything but moderate) ran this event with an iron hand. The crowd was completely under his control. He described the great danger that exists when so many young people meet in an environment like we had in Dallas, and he let everyone know that it was his duty to devote the forum to a discussion of the various reports of what had been done and taught there. He was particularly concerned about the things that might have been taught about the Holy Spirit (as he was the chief spokesman in the Churches of Christ of the view that says the Holy Spirit lives in a Christian "through the Word only," a remarkable deistic doctrine that can still be found in some quarters of that fellowship today).

Charles Shelton was eventually allowed to speak and represent the group from Lubbock. The crowd had been thoroughly prepared by the moderator to reject any attempt that Shelton might make to explain the Campus Evangelism program. Charles started with a joke. Before I share what he said, let me give you a little background: After the Dallas Seminar many rumors had spread

---

1. Richard T. Hughes, *Reviving the Ancient Faith* (Grand Rapids: Wm. B. Eerdmans, 1996), 176-185.

about what went on there. The most widely told story was that the leaders claimed they raised a cat from the dead. Yes, that was seriously passed from preacher to preacher. Knowing that most likely everyone in the auditorium had heard that story, Charles Shelton said, "Brethren we flew into Memphis today and rented a car to drive here to Henderson. On the way, we hit a cat. We got out of the car and tried our best to raise him from the dead. But we couldn't do a thing for him!"[2]

His attempt at humor was met with absolute silence. I could feel the hostility from the older woman who sat beside me and from a host of others around us. When Shelton sat down, the moderator sarcastically responded to everything that was shared and effectively criticized a few more moderate preachers who stood to say that it would be a mistake to rush to judgment.

One interchange was particularly memorable. A preacher I would later have to admire for his courage stood and addressed the moderator as his friend and said, "Why even you and I sometimes disagree with one another."

In response, the moderator leaned threateningly over the lectern, and said, "Yes, and when we do, I am right and you are wrong." There was no hint that he was joking.

At this the crowd uttered a collective, "Oooooo." (Later, wondering if I could possibly have misunderstood, I would replay the tape, again on my trusty reel-to-reel, and confirm that this in fact was the statement made without a hint of humor.) Almost a decade later when charges of "cultism" would be made against a more developed campus ministry movement, I would think back to this experience and conclude that I had never been in anything that felt more like a cult than on that day at this assembly at a respected Christian college.

Sheila and I recently (2007) have been back in touch with Rex Vermillion. This is his recollection of the happenings that day:

> The atmosphere at the Freed-Hardeman College Lectureship Forum was as hostile a situation as I've ever been in. Of course, I haven't been in military combat, but the place had the feeling of a lynching mob. There was a dreadful absence of the sentiment so often seen on signs at the edge of towns advertising Churches of Christ: "Come, let us reason together."

The Campus Evangelism effort would be a shooting star in the Churches of Christ. That cool February Thursday in western Tennessee was the begin-

---

2. At a lunch meeting with Jim and Anne Bevis in 2007 my wife asked Jim if he had any idea how the dead cat story got started. Amazingly, Jim told us how at the Dallas Seminar one of the class teachers was a pretty hip fellow with connections to the Jesus People of the late '60s. As he taught his class, he described Jesus raising this cat (as in "cool cat") from the dead (apparently referring to Lazarus). And the rest is history. Such is the stuff of urban legends.

ning of the end for something that seemed to have such promise. Dudley Lynch would defend the young leaders on the pages of his paper, but that probably did more harm than good. More importantly, the moderator and his supporters had labeled CE a dangerous movement and that was enough for a fellowship of churches that prized "sound doctrine," lived in fear of apostasy, and understood the need to stay in the right camp. Within days churches throughout the country knew to stay clear of this fledgling movement.[3]

However, looking backward, one might say that God started a fire in Dallas and had other plans to spread it.

The crucial issue in this world is Jesus. Everything connected to him will endure. Everything without a connection to him will spoil, fade and perish. Things that seemed glorious and received the headlines and television coverage will not matter. Only those things tied to Jesus are destined for immortality (2 Timothy 1:10).

–From *Letters to New Disciples*, Chapter Four, "Life with a Purpose"

---

3. For more information on the culture of the Churches of Christ, see Appendix Fourteen, "A Brief Primer on the Restoration Movement." You may be helped by reading this before you go further in the book.

3

Unaware of a Quiet Revolution

Though the Freed-Hardeman College Open Forum would have a chilling effect on the CE movement, the seeds planted in me at the Dallas Seminar still longed to grow. Finishing my undergraduate degree with two majors not related to biblical or theological studies, I nevertheless was able to enroll at Harding Graduate School of Religion in Memphis.

At the end of August 1969 I was married to a very special woman who would become my most precious companion on the journey. After a honeymoon in the Smoky Mountains, Sheila and I moved to our new home, an apartment in the Christian Student Center in Memphis. Prior to our marriage, we had gone there to interview with the campus minister, Terry Smith. The interview went well, and Terry offered me a part-time job as associate campus minister while I attended graduate school. For the first time, I had a ministry title, but few knew that my job included cleaning the toilets in the building's four bathrooms every night after all the students left and the doors were locked. It was good training in servant leadership.

Out of sight and out of mind was the campus ministry in Gainesville, Florida, that had been mentioned at the seminar in Dallas. Eighteen months later, I would learn that the Fourteenth Street Church was beginning to have an evangelistic impact on the University of Florida campus that was unprecedented in Churches of Christ.

The ministry at Memphis State did include the teaching of credit Bible courses (I remember sitting in on Terry's class on Romans), but there was also a fairly significant outreach to students who did not come from a background in Churches of Christ. Terry was probably the first person I walked with who had a passion for his relationship with Christ, and though we did not use the terminology in that day, he "discipled" me in many ways.[1] Under his leadership, we held the first of a series of annual seminars (or conferences) that would bring together students from around the Southeast. I still remember the themes of the first two: "Why Jesus in the '70s?" and "How Tremendous Is the Power."

My earlier Bible study while still an undergraduate had convinced me that Jesus was far more radical than the man I had heard portrayed in sermons. I

1. The term here refers to having someone consistently in your life who serves as a mentor, modeling behavior and heart, and one who gives encouragement, feedback and correction.

had seen clearly that he called for nothing less than a total commitment. During these years in Memphis my study led to another conviction that has affected nearly every day of my life for the last thirty-eight years. As I worked on my master's degree, I took the required Greek courses. Armed with a little knowledge of that language and having become what Professor Jack Lewis would call a ping-pong Greek scholar,[2] I remember that the first word I ever studied carefully (using the famous *Kittle's Theological Dictionary*) was the word *koinonia*.

For as long as I could remember I had heard the King James Version rendering of Acts 2:42: "And they continued stedfastly [sic] in the apostles' doctrine and fellowship, and in breaking of bread, and in prayers." In the Churches of Christ, the emphasis here always fell on "the apostles' doctrine." I had never heard an explanation of "fellowship." This, of course, is the first occurrence in the New Testament of *koinonia*. I discovered it was the richest of words, deriving from the word *koinos* which means common (as in two verses later: "All the believers were together and had everything in common."). I found that the New English Bible, published a few years earlier, had maybe the best translation: "They devoted themselves…to sharing together in the common life."

As I found that the word was often used outside the New Testament to refer to marriage, I realized that this word, used nineteen times in the NT, was saying that life as a follower of Jesus meant an intimate and deep involvement with other people who shared a common faith.

It would be several years before I would do the ping-pong scholar exercise with the word *allelon* and understand all the ways God wanted us involved in the lives of "one another," but *koinonia* was enough to convince me that "fellowship" was far more than having punch and cookies in a hall with that name.

A few years later in 1973 it would be the study of *koinonia* that would lead to my first published work— a little eighteen-page booklet titled *New Life in Groups*. Starting with a chapter on this Greek word, the key idea was that in small LIFE groups (it stood for "Love in Fellowship Extended," but was not original with me), Christians could begin to experience much more of what the New Testament meant by "fellowship."

---

2. By this he meant one who went back and forth from the interlinear Greek Bible to the Greek lexicon like a ping pong ball going back and forth across the table.

My tenure as Terry's associate was cut short due to an incident that was a reflection of the American scene in the 1970s. From time to time the students in our campus ministry would be given the opportunity to lead the evening worship service for the Highland Street Church that served as the overseeing congregation for the campus ministry. On one of these occasions, Terry asked me to make the arrangements for the service.

As I put together a plan for the evening, I quite naturally included an outstanding law student whom I had grown quite close to. Three days before the service, one of the elders spotted the order of worship and informed me that a change would have to be made. The law student was black, and I was told that no one of his race had ever stood in the pulpit, and it could not happen.

I was incredulous. Though I had grown up in the South and knew the history of racial relations all too well, and though Martin Luther King, Jr. had been killed at the Lorraine Motel only a few miles from our campus less than two years before, I had naively believed that we in the church were much further down the road than we were. I had two lengthy meetings with all nine or ten elders—a rather intimidating experience for a twenty-two-year-old—but they would not budge from their original decision. My numerous appeals to various Scriptures and biblical concepts were of no avail. Though I was not terminated immediately, at the end of the semester, I was told that the elders did not think it best that I remain with the ministry.

Sheila and I moved out of the student center apartment. She began a new job teaching school in the poverty of the Mississippi Delta, and I devoted myself to my studies. The year after my dismissal, there seemed to be a softening among some of the elders, and several eventually told me that the stance they had taken some months before had been the wrong one. As the seminar for that year was planned, Terry wanted to invite me to give the opening message, and surprisingly, all the elders agreed. Little did I know how that invitation would change my life.

HOW TREMENDOUS
THE POWER
FOURTH ANNUAL SPRING SEMINAR
UNIVERSITY CENTER, M.S.U.
FEBRUARY 5-7

In February 1971 I gave the theme speech, "How Tremendous Is the Power." Present in the audience was Chuck Lucas, the leader of the campus ministry in Gainesville, Florida. He had flown to Memphis with a recent convert, a student named Tom Brown. They had come on a mission to look for candidates for a "women's counselor" position in their ministry that was soon to become open. It can hardly be overemphasized what a huge change this represented when the Gainesville church had initially hired Martha Bell to fill this role. To my knowledge this was the first congregation within the Churches of Christ to hire a woman for anything other than secretarial work.

After my speech, Tom approached me about having lunch, and we arranged for time together. As he told me the story of his conversion on the campus at the University of Florida and then of the others he was able to bring to Christ, my heart leapt. This was the beginning of a relationship that would have great impact on my life (and a relationship that is still special to me today).

At that lunch meeting with Tom, I began to get an idea of a quiet revolution that was taking place at the University of Florida. Since the Dallas meeting, I had heard very little about it, but it was evident to me that they were moving into new territory and that the spirit of commitment and evangelism I had seen at that seminar in 1968 was not dead. As a graduate student trying to focus on the completion of my degree, I felt I could only file this information away and come back to it later.

In the fall of 1971, having received my master's from Harding Graduate School, we moved to Springfield, Missouri, where I would do an internship in campus ministry under Dr. John Wilson. In January 1972 our first daughter, Amy, was born, and at the end of my internship I was asked to remain on the staff of the South National Church in Springfield as a teen minister. We would remain in Springfield for nine years where our three daughters were born.

During one period in this mid-sized city, we had quite a remarkable group working in different ways on the campus of what is now Missouri State University. John Wilson, professor of New Testament and advisor to the campus ministry, would go on to be dean at Pepperdine University. Richard Hughes, professor of church history, would become one of the more important church historians in the Churches of Christ and write some groundbreaking books. Royce Money, who ministered in a local congregation and taught in the department of religious studies, would become the president of Abilene Christian University, where he still serves today. Prentice Meador, the "pulpit" minister at South National, held a Ph.D. in speech and was already a well-known speaker in Churches of Christ. He remained in Springfield for some years after we left and later became the minister for one of the largest churches in Dallas. Kathy Pulley, who was a student in our ministry in the earliest days, would get her doctorate at Boston University and now teaches in the department of religious studies at Missouri State University.

Just after beginning my teen ministry work, I surprisingly received a call from Chuck Lucas. I probably had met Chuck when he came to the seminar in Memphis the year before, but we had spent little time together. He had thought well of the speech I gave at that event and invited me to do two speeches at the Florida Evangelism Seminar in August '72. Only twenty-four, and just getting my feet wet in a new position, I wasn't sure I was the right person, but I accepted.

I suspect that you, as I, can look back and see most interesting and sometimes improbable ways God works. Had I not been asked, most unexpectedly, to give that speech in Memphis, my connection with the Gainesville/Crossroad ministry might never have come about. It was only because of that speech that Chuck Lucas would invite me to Gainesville and that my friendship with Tom Brown would begin. Surely in all our lives, there are dozens of such things that probably go unnoticed, where God is putting someone in our life or is putting us at a certain place at a certain time to fulfill some larger purpose that he has for us. Amazingly, I had not thought of these connections until I began to write down my memories for this book.

That summer the National Campus Ministers Seminar (NCMS) for the Churches of Christ was held in Memphis the first week in August. I would learn that this was the sixteenth such event (having begun in 1959 as the National Bible Chair Lectureship). I would be involved in this annual meeting for the next fifteen years and will refer to it quite often in the coming pages. For a decade and a half it was the key ministry event in my life each year.

After attending the first half of that seminar, I left Memphis to fly on to Florida to speak at the Florida Evangelism Seminar. While in Memphis I heard from various campus ministers that they would like for me to make an appeal to Chuck Lucas to change the annual date of the Florida meeting so that the two events would not conflict. The Gainesville church had held their seminar for at least three years also during the first week in August. The brothers meeting in Memphis were hearing more and more about the Florida work and were eager to have those from Florida be more connected to the other ministries.

After my first-ever plane ride, I arrived in Gainesville, checked into my room, only to discover that the legendary evangelist and editor, Reuel Lemmons, was to be my roommate. I had read and appreciated his provocative editorials in the *Firm Foundation* and felt blessed to have this privilege.[3] He addressed me warmly with his Texas drawl and treated me like I was a veteran of many spiritual wars.

At the seminar I enjoyed a reunion with Tom Brown and was inspired by the preaching of Roy Osborne (who had spoken in Dallas), Reuel Lemmons, Chuck and others. Having just come from the meeting in Memphis, the contrast in emphasis between the more traditional ministries and the ministry in

---

3. See Appendix Seventeen for examples of Reuel Lemmons's writings.

Gainesville was not lost on me. Unlike other campus efforts mentioned earlier, the ministry in Gainesville (like the CE movement) had a decidedly outward focus. This was just one of a number of differences that would bring tension as those from the two different perspectives began efforts to come together.

At one point in the seminar all the students who had been baptized in the previous year were asked to stand. I was astonished at the number that stood, and I believed immediately that we had much to learn from those leading this ministry. Since my senior year in college I had been speaking in churches about the great opportunities for the gospel on the college campus, but I had never seen anything like what was happening there at the University of Florida. It seemed to me that there were three keys to their success: (1) a message that called every student to make Jesus Lord of his or her life, (2) their use of small evangelistic group Bible studies called "soul talks" and (3) the encouragement for every Christian to have a prayer partner with whom they met weekly and with whom they kept in close touch.[4]

During the week I was able to speak with Chuck about changing the date of their seminar for the next year in order for him and some of his associates to attend the NCMS. It was eventually announced that this change would be made, and Chuck did join us in New Mexico the following year. The revolution was continuing. The quiet part was just about over.

You do not read very far in the Bible before you see that this God who is talked about wants relationships. He values them. The Bible makes it clear that there is even relationship within God (between the Father, the Son and the Holy Spirit). From the earliest part of Genesis we see that God wanted a relationship with the man and the woman. This has always been what it is all about.

–From *Letters to New Disciples*, Chapter Two, "Walking with God"

---

4. I have read various claims on the Internet, including those in Wikipedia, that the Crossroads Movement took much of its teaching from popular Charismatic Movement teachers of the 1970s, including Bob Mumford and Derek Prince, who started something often called "The Shepherding Movement." However, I never saw any evidence of this and never heard anyone who thought there was a connection until some thirty years later. It was also widely believed that they were much influenced in their philosophy and methodology by Robert Coleman's book *The Master Plan of Evangelism*, which seemed to me to represent sound biblical thinking. However, in recent communication with Chuck Lucas, I learned that he did not read that book until 1975. According to Chuck, they had been more influenced in the early days by *Mandate to Witness* by Leander Keck.

4

Albuquerque

In the early summer of 1973 I left my short-lived work with the teen ministry to return to the work I most desired—campus ministry. John Wilson, who had a doctorate in New Testament studies, had decided to accept a position on the faculty at Southwest Missouri State (now Missouri State University), and I assumed the role he had held for some years—director of the Christian Student Center. Primarily because of John, I was also able to continue as a supply instructor in the department of religious studies and was able to move from being his assistant in a course titled "Religion and Human Culture" to having my own classes.

For seven years I taught "Introduction to the New Testament" each semester. While I enjoyed teaching, particularly going completely through the New Testament twice a year, my primary interests were more in the ministry, and I attempted to incorporate some of what I had seen in my time in Florida into our work, with modest evangelistic results.

To prepare for the '73–'74 school year, John and Claudette Wilson, Sheila and I and another couple traveled in John's wide-body Chevy Impala from Springfield to Albuquerque, New Mexico, for the NCMS. That week was unforgettable for several reasons and historically important for at least one.

These were the days of the hippy-styled "Jesus Movement" (check out the movie *Godspell*), and on any campus one could usually find one or more "Jesus papers" which were printed on cheap newsprint and touted the reasons one should accept and follow Christ. John had the idea of producing our own Jesus paper ("The Root of Jesse"—Romans 15:12) with a cool look but a much stronger New Testament message. We printed 100,000 copies.

By the time of the Albuquerque seminar, we still had a number of boxes on hand. Some of the campus ministries had indicated that they would buy them if we could bring them to Albuquerque. John found an old trailer, on its last leg (or maybe its last axle), and we pulled several hundred pounds of newspapers across the desert getting about six miles to the gallon and only able to go about forty-five mph up steep hills. Having fulfilled its purpose, the trailer was put out of its misery when we arrived.

At the Albuquerque seminar one of the speakers was Dr. Tom Olbricht, a professor of biblical theology at Abilene Christian College. It was my first time to meet him, and that event will always be memorable for me because of his messages on the lifestyle of Jesus in the Gospel of Mark. They influence my thinking to this very day. He would later do an excellent book on the subject, *The Power to Be*, which was just recently reprinted.[1] Thirty-one years later the Lord would give Tom and me an unusual opportunity to have a very special relationship.

When it comes to the history of what would eventually be called the Crossroads/Boston Movement and its relationship with the Churches of Christ, this seminar in New Mexico was most notable for another reason. Chuck Lucas attended for the first time and was asked to be on a panel about evangelism. He was accompanied by one of the University of Florida students who was training for the ministry—Bruce Williams, who now serves as the lead evangelist in the Los Angeles Church of Christ.

These campus ministry seminars had an air of informality. Almost no one wore a coat and tie, and messages were delivered in a fairly low-key style, more like what you would get in an academic environment. Most of these men, after all, were primarily Bible teachers, not evangelists.

On what I believe was the second day of the seminar, after a morning lecture from Dr. Olbricht and some morning classes, a table for the panel was set up after lunch in front of the participants, a group I would estimate to be less than a hundred. Chairs were provided behind the table for the four panelists. Chuck was the last to speak. The other three men had spoken casually while seated in their chairs. Chuck was dressed in a coat and tie, and when his turn came, he placed a lectern on the table, and delivered a forceful message on the need for evangelism and how many ministries were failing.

I don't remember much of what he said. If I were to play the tape today, I imagine I would hear things that needed to be said. Chuck's messages were always thoroughly grounded in Scripture. What I do know is that these fellows, some of whom had been at these meeting for years, felt thoroughly rebuked by someone attending his first. They felt that the work they had been doing, sometimes with great resistance in very tradition-bound churches, was being completely devalued. Many who had lobbied me in Memphis to have Chuck come to this meeting, were in something of a state of shock.

I am sure that Chuck saw himself as a reformer on a mission from God to get campus ministries everywhere to wake up. What he probably didn't realize is that these men (and some women) also considered themselves as reformers

---

1. Thomas H. Olbricht, *The Power to Be* (Abilene, Texas: Hillcrest Publications, 2003).

and not part of the establishment. Years later, Chuck and others from Gainesville would feel similarly devalued by another young and bold man wearing the mantle of a "prophet."

As the only one there who had been to Gainesville, had been well-received there, had seen the fruit of their ministry in people like Tom Brown, and had been impressed with the changed lives I had observed at the Florida seminar the year before, I made what efforts I could to keep people listening, but it was a tough sell. As years went by, I suspected that some of those campus ministers could never quite get over what they felt that day.

Two years later, after more time to develop a relationship, I would talk with Chuck about ways he was communicating and what effect it was having, but at this event I said nothing to him. He may have very well felt that he was like Jesus cleansing the temple or delivering his blistering message to the Pharisees in Matthew 23. However, some years later in a *Campus Journal* editorial, a national publication I will describe shortly, I would write that Chuck had told me that if he had it to do over again, he would have taken a different approach.

The significance of that event in Albuquerque is that it was the beginning of nearly fifteen years of tension among campus ministers in Churches of Christ—a tension that would begin to spill over into the larger body. By saying this, I don't mean to place the blame on Chuck or those he trained. There were major issues in campus ministry that needed to be challenged. There were things in my life that needed to be challenged, and I thank God that they were. But the fact remains that from August 1973 there were two camps—two very different ways of doing campus ministry that became increasingly defined. There were a diminishing few of us who felt there was wisdom in trying not to take sides but to keep the two groups talking to each other. In my endeavors on this behalf, I felt as though I was living on what a Web site now calls itself: Lonely Planet.

To give some idea of the personal effect of this on me, I can remember that every June I would begin to feel something in the pit of my stomach, anticipating the conflict that would be coming when we gathered for the seminar a few weeks later in August. On at least five occasions I was asked to do one of the main messages, and on another occasion I was asked to co-direct the seminar. My concern each time was to speak to each side of the divide.

There is no question that there was far more about the Gainesville approach that I wanted to imitate and support, but I also had an appreciation for the hearts of others who were not of that persuasion. My hope was that if we could keep talking, the latter group would see the way the Florida ministry was implementing important biblical concepts and that the Florida brothers would see that the others had important gifts to bring to the table. I wanted to believe that we could have unity even if we had diversity.

In some ways it is remarkable to me that this group continued to meet together for as long as it did (at least through 1985). When the Boston Movement severed ties with the mainline Churches of Christ, I understand from talking with others today, that it took many years for the campus ministers who did not align with Boston to recover from their pain and confusion and regain any momentum.

Only God knows where all the fault lies for what happened. All those involved will have their opinions. In hindsight, we can say that there were a great many things that could and should have been done differently. Isn't that usually the case? All of us who were involved should examine ourselves and ask God to give us grace and to guard us from self-righteousness. I am encouraged today that God is giving us an opportunity to confess, forgive and resume conversations.

Having met J.P. Tynes, Tom Brown and Bruce Williams, all Crossroads trainees, I would soon meet another man from Gainesville with whom I, much later, would work closely for many years.

Here is the man who knows more about how to live than anyone, and he says the one who is great is the one who is the servant—even the slave—of all. He was the divine Son of Man, but he says "even I did not come to be served but to serve." Indeed, following this Jesus means a radical realignment of your thinking.

–From *Letters to New Disciples*, Chapter Twenty-Two,
"The Power and Satisfaction of Serving"

5

Abilene, Abilene

In the summer of 1974 the chairman of the department of missions at Abilene Christian College invited John Wilson to come to Abilene and teach a course in campus ministry as a part of their summer seminar in missions. This was an intensive three-week course for three credit hours and could be taken either at an undergraduate or graduate level. I took the course on the graduate level and helped John in developing some of the materials.

Our daughter Amy was two, and she and Sheila came with me and spent the three weeks in Abilene, often in a small apartment (out of the withering Texas heat), while I was in class. We thought very differently in those days about the women's role, and it would only be later we would see the need for the women to get training similar to that of the men. We have the ministry in Gainesville to thank for that shift. Ann Lucas and Geri Laing served as role models, showing women that they could take care of their homes and families and still have an effective ministry as they reached out to their friends and neighbors.

Two men and one woman came from the Florida ministry. I can remember that John had a strong suspicion that they came as much to teach as to learn. I do know that they had no shortage of contributions—many which I found to be helpful and some I found to be naive.

I enjoyed playing tennis with one of the men who came from Florida. Don Burroughs later served in the ministry in Atlanta and was an elder there with one of the churches associated with the ICOC.

The other man and I clashed a bit over the issue of whether there needed to be more emphasis on grace or more emphasis on change. I was troubled by a very legalistic background I had in the Churches of Christ and felt that we had missed the grace of God. He had been baptized in Gainesville after growing up in a "faith only" environment where there was much emphasis on grace but little emphasis on putting faith in action. We eventually talked our different perspectives through and would connect many more times through the years particularly at campus ministry seminars.

When I wrote the first draft of this chapter, I was in Boston where he and I worked closely together for eighteen years, serving as fellow elders for ten years. His name: Wyndham Shaw. Today he and his wife, Jeanie, are among our most-trusted friends, and we are all thankful for a friendship that spans nearly thirty-five years.

That seminar in missions at Abilene would also become important to me because of another relationship that was built during those three weeks, and that was with George and Irene Gurganus. Dr. Gurganus was the chairman of the missions department, after having served the church for many years in Japan after World War II. He was most interested in the role campus ministry could play in world missions. Our paths would cross again, and God would use him and Irene to make a world of difference in the life of my entire family.

Being around those from the Gainesville ministry was always inspiring to me even when I might be troubled by some of their attitudes or theology. I had never been with people this excited about reaching out to the lost, or with those who were so purposely involved in each other's lives.

We returned from Abilene only to load up the car a few weeks later and drive to the University of Texas in Austin for the 1974 NCMS. I have few memories of that event, except that on the drive back to Missouri, Sheila and I were listening to the car radio when Richard Nixon read his resignation and the new president, Gerald Ford, said, "Our long national nightmare is over." The Watergate generation was disillusioned, but we looked forward to proclaiming Jesus, whose integrity could not be doubted.

While differing opinions often start conflicts, most conflicts eventually involve some sin that must be dealt with in a biblical way. This is where we have such an advantage over the world. We call sin by its right name, and we deal with it in a godly way. This healthy, biblical approach to dealing with sin enables us to resolve conflicts that in the typical family, workplace or neighborhood may go on for years.

–From *Letters to New Disciples*, Chapter Nine, "Resolving Conflicts"

6

Gainesville—Joy and Pain

After the time in Abilene, I was invigorated and ready to embrace a new year in the ministry. Following the Gainesville model, we had hired our first women's counselor in the fall of 1973. She had left us after a year, and we hired Rita Albertson in the summer of 1974. She would remain in our ministry several years. Our staff was composed then of me, Rita and an intern, Cloyd Taylor, who was there to serve for nine months and went on to get his doctorate in counseling. That year we saw more students baptized into Christ than at any time in the history of the SMSU campus ministry, and there was no doubt that things we were learning from Gainesville both about methods and attitudes were making a big difference.

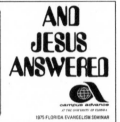

Brochure for the 1975 Florida Evangelism Seminar

SPEAKERS

ROGERS BARTLEY, Elder, Crossroads Church of Christ, Gainesville, Florida
JACK EVANS, President, Southwestern Christian College, Terrell, Texas
BOB HENDREN, Minister, Donelson Church of Christ, Donelson, Tennessee
TOM JONES, Director, Christian Student Center, Southwest Missouri State University, Springfield, Missouri
SAMMY LAING, Campus Minister, Crossroads Church of Christ, Gainesville, Florida
CHUCK LUCAS, Minister, Crossroads Church of Christ and Director of Campus Advance, University of Florida, Gainesville, Florida
E. W. McMILLAN, Professor of Bible, Columbia Christian College, Portland, Oregon. Founder and Former President of Southwestern Christian College and Ibaraki Christian College (Japan) and Former Head of the Bible Department at Abilene Christian College. Preacher for 65 years.
K. C. MOSER, Preacher, Author, Retired from the Bible Department Lubbock Christian College, Lubbock, Texas. Writer of numerous books including: THE GIST OF ROMANS, ATTRIBUTES OF GOD, and THE WAY OF SALVATION
JOE SCHUBERT, Minister, Bammel Road Church of Christ, Houston, Texas, Former Dean of Oklahoma Christian College
RICHARD WHITEHEAD, Elder, Crossroads Church of Christ, Dean of Admissions and Registrar, University of Florida, Gainesville, Florida

Speakers for the 1975 Florida Evangelism Seminar

As a result, in the summer of '75, I welcomed a second invitation to come to Gainesville and speak again at the Florida Evangelism Seminar where the theme was "And Jesus Answered." My message was to be titled "Who Do Men Say That the Son of Man Is?" First came a trip to Boise, Idaho, for the NCMS and then as soon as I was back to Missouri, I boarded a plane for Florida.

My second visit there was even more inspiring than the first. Once again I found that I was the roommate of a legendary leader. This time it was E.W. McMillan—

who was in his eighties, but still vigorous in his work at Columbia Christian College. Also speaking at that seminar was another spiritual giant—K.C. Moser— who was known as one of the few champions of the message of grace in the Churches of Christ. I enjoyed lunch with K.C. and his wife and felt greatly humbled to be on the program with them. I always appreciated that the Gainesville leadership saw to it that the message of grace was held high even as the call for "total commitment" was made.

The whole experience with what was now called the Crossroads Church— their commitment, their relationships, their evangelism, their amazing racial diversity—fueled my vision of what could be accomplished on our campuses. I was excited about the new intern we had selected and returned from Florida eager to go after our best year ever.

The internship concept as it had been initially developed by John Wilson was seen as something like a medical residency. Once a person completed it, the expectation was that he would be ready to assume a full-time position in campus ministry. The disciple of Jesus who came to us in 1975 was Mike Fontenot, a graduate of LSU and Fuller Theological Seminary. During the year Mike and his wife, Terrie, were with us, God blessed us again with a number of conversions that surpassed all previous marks.

After his nine-month stint with us, Mike (and Terrie) accepted the leadership of the campus ministry at LSU in Baton Rouge, Louisiana. They would eventually plant a church in Sydney, Australia, unite with the Boston Movement, go on to serve in various leadership roles in the ICOC, and they now lead a thriving church in the Hampton Roads, Virginia, area.

It was sometime in 1974 or 1975 that I decided something was needed to ground young Christians in their new walk with Christ. I wrote and published another booklet that was approximately thirty pages and titled *Your First Forty Days*. It had the following chapters:

Week One – Dead to Self – Alive to Christ
Week Two – No Life Outside the Body
Week Three – Go, Make Disciples
Week Four – The Father, Son and Holy Spirit
Week Five – Submit to Every Authority
Week Six – Fight the Good Fight

Being naive and thinking it would be generous to not copyright the booklet and give permission to anyone to reprint it, I saw many ministries do just that. I learned a lesson when someone several years later brought me a copy of a version of the material done by a ministry in Iowa. They had used the

same title but had removed every reference to
dying to self. (Somebody had bought into late
1970s pop psychology.) I have reserved all rights
on published material from that day forward.

With full permission, a student from Hong
Kong baptized in our ministry would later trans-
late it into Chinese and distribute it in his native
city where they would be taught to die to self in
Cantonese! (He and I still exchange emails.) The
material in this booklet was eventually expanded
into a larger book titled *Foundations for a New Life*
which would later morph into *Deep Convictions*,
with the latter having been used by over 100,000
new believers.[1]

Your First Forty Days in Chinese

There seems to be no good place to inject this, but it will be significant
later on. So I will just mention it here. After my trip to Boise and the following trip to Gainesville, both by plane, I experienced severe vertigo that lasted
for several weeks. Doctors were not able to determine the cause, and so after
waiting almost a year, I tried to travel by plane again, this time to Texas to
speak at an event in Lubbock. On my return flight the vertigo returned. I fre-
quented the tennis court in those days, but for several weeks I was unable to
do much of anything athletic because of the vertigo. I often had trouble walking or standing.

More tests were unsuccessful in determining a cause with one doctor saying that I should probably minimize flying because I appeared to have an over-
active inner ear. Whether or not this was related to MS with which I would
later be diagnosed, we don't know. But from 1976 to 1987, I did the "John
Madden thing"[2] (except that I had no private bus!). I stayed off planes, either
driving or taking the train for all trips—some of them very long ones.

While things in Missouri were quite encouraging, in Florida it must have
been a different story. The Crossroads Church was increasingly being accused
of various abuses and doctrinal errors by preachers in other Churches of
Christ. As was common in the culture of the Churches of Christ, the printing
presses were cranking as various brotherhood writers were labeling
Crossroads as dangerous and were warning the churches to avoid them. (As
early as 1909, someone had observed that churches in the Restoration tradition did not have bishops; they had editors.)

---

1. *Deep Convictions* is still available from DPI.

2. The well-known American football commentator refuses to fly, taking his bus back and
forth across the country to be a part of a weekly broadcast.

I had little knowledge of it until after the fact, but on November 10 and 11, 1975, a major meeting was arranged between Chuck and the Crossroads elders with some high-profile leaders in the Churches of Christ from across the nation and even beyond.

The meeting was worked out by a missionary to Thailand named Parker Henderson who had his own roots in the Gainesville community. Also present were J.D. Bales, a professor at Harding College; Richard Rogers, a teacher at the Sunset School of Preaching in Lubbock, Texas (who was not a critic but more of a neutral party); several other lesser known men, and Ira Y. Rice, Jr. Rice was famous or infamous depending on your perspective. He had been a missionary to Asia and had written a series of volumes titled *Ax on the Root* and had edited a periodical titled *Contending for the Faith* in which he had reckless-ly accused a wide variety of people of all kinds of heresies, seeing himself as the guardian of the church and orthodoxy. When I saw his name on the list of people who attended the meeting, I was quite shocked that Chuck had agreed to a meeting where he was present.

However, in the December 2, 1975, issue of the *Christian Chronicle*, by this time under more conservative ownership, Parker Henderson wrote an article titled "The Brotherhood's Finest Hour—Gainesville Difficulties Corrected" in which he stated that the issues that had concerned all these men had been resolved. A bulletin from the Crossroads Church dated November 16 made it clear what the issues were and how they were resolved. Seven charges were presented, and to each of them the Crossroads leaders gave an answer that pleased their critics. For a copy of that bulletin insert, see Appendix One. If anyone has any doubt that the Crossroads leaders bent over backward to work with their critics, this would be exhibit A to prove their efforts for unity. What I'm sure I didn't appreciate was the wear and tear this was on Chuck.

The NCMS for 1976 was scheduled to be held at the new building of the Crossroads Church in Gainesville, and Sheila and I drove there with our two daughters (Bethany having been born in March). I still find it quite remark-able and even important that this seminar was in Gainesville at all. The loca-tion of the meeting for the upcoming year was always determined, by secret ballot, in a business meeting at the close of the three-day event, after interest-ed ministries had presented their invitations.

At the 1975 meeting in Boise, the overwhelming number of people present not only had no connections with Gainesville, but were still feeling the sting of things said in Albuquerque. Yet, in spite of that, the group voted to accept the invitation of Crossroads to host the seminar. I have respect for those brothers, who though they were feeling unappreciated by the Crossroads leaders, nevertheless, thought there was something important enough about the Gainesville work that we should go there. Had they known the plan that would emerge for the seminar, I expect the vote might have been different.

When the program for the seminar came out, it seemed that seventy-five to eighty percent of the speakers and teachers were from Crossroads. I was asked to give the opening address, and I remember that John Wilson led a morning devotional. Alonzo Welch, a long-time mentor of Chuck Lucas, did at least one main speech and maybe more. I am sure there were some other non-Crossroads people, especially in a few of the classes, but the bulk of the program was composed of men and women from Gainesville.

This was unprecedented for a meeting which always represented a wide variety of ministries. You don't have to guess about the attitudes some struggled with as they drove across the country to Florida (and most did drive). Personally, I was eager to hear from the Crossroads leaders because it was their practices and emphasis I was most interested in. However, I knew how the program must have looked to some of the others and how they must have felt after selecting Crossroads to host the event.

Fall 1975 *Campus Journal*

Though I was constantly learning and bene-fiting from the ministry in Gainesville, I had begun to hear some things that concerned me, and had actually begun to address those concerns in writing prior to the seminar. In the fall of 1975 I had accepted the position as editor of the *Campus Journal*. This quarterly publication was originally started as the *Bible Chair Journal*, and was by this time the main publication for all campus ministries in the Churches of Christ. John Wilson had served as the editor for many years, but as he moved on to a role in academia, he felt it was better for an active campus minister to serve as editor.

Article in Fall 1975 *Campus Journal* by Bruce Williams, Tallahassee, Florida

So the board of the *Journal*, upon John's recommendation, asked me to accept the work. Each issue featured a short editorial usually written by the editor. Occasionally, we would feature a guest editorial. Looking at back issues of the *Journal*, one can see that I began with a desire to encourage others to catch the spirit that I was seeing in the Gainesville ministry. However, by the summer prior to the Crossroads-hosted NCMS, one can see that I was raising some flags of caution of my own, as I saw an attitude that basically said, "Our way is the only way that works."

In the Summer 1976 issue, which would have been released just before the seminar, I wrote:

> If we are to provide any leadership in a movement toward New Testament life and faith on the campuses, we must…avoid sectarian ways of using Biblical terms. We must never bind something on another person when the Scriptures have not made that a clear command or responsibility.

In concluding, I attempted to address two extremes that I could see developing. I expect the first part of what I said was not taken particularly well by the leadership at Crossroads. I wrote:

> Students will listen to our message if we are examples both of conviction and openness. Some opt only for conviction and their conviction turns to snobbery, bigotry and exclusiveness. Some opt for openness and their openness turns to free-wheeling "believe what you want to."

As I read those words, I am reminded of how much advice a twenty-nine-year-old editor needed and how far I had to go in developing healthy relationships with those I was concerned about. But suffice it to say, I traveled to Gainesville both troubled by the tension I knew would be there, especially because of the program, and by some tendencies I was seeing in their ministry. The notes from the speech I gave to open the seminar have long since disappeared. I cannot even remember the topic I spoke on. I know I used a text from Isaiah and attempted to address the attitudes I saw "on both sides of the room." It is funny how one's memory works. I can remember only two responses to the message. One came from Stephen Eckstein, one of the veteran campus ministers who may very well have been present in 1959 at the first Bible chair lectureship. He was concerned that I had not looked at the Isaiah passage in the historical context (and he was probably right). The other came from an enthusiastic Crossroads-trained leader, Kip McKean (recently of Charleston, Illinois, and Eastern Illinois University), who wanted to set up lunch with me.

During the classes which were taught mostly by young Crossroads minister trainees or ministers just recently sent out, I heard things that confirmed some of my concerns, and so I spoke with Chuck and told him I would like to sit down and talk with him and the two Crossroads elders before I left. I mentioned that I would like for John Wilson to join us. At that point I still felt very supportive of their ministry and saw myself as one benefiting from it. Instead of just taking a shot at Crossroads through the *Campus Journal*, I wanted the time to talk through some of my questions, and wanted to be able to assure some of the older brothers that Chuck was willing to listen. Chuck was only willing to meet with me and John Wilson along with Sam Laing, his associate. He did not want the elders to be included.

In that meeting, I presented my concerns to Chuck. I discussed several things. First, it seemed that they had certain rules in their ministry (an example was rules for dating) and that if other ministries didn't practice those, they were treated as if they were not spiritual. Related to this, there was the not-so-subtle message that there was only one right way to do campus ministry and that was their way.

Another concern I remember is that it seemed there was one way of being a leader and everyone needed to conform to that image, from the way they spoke, to the way they dressed. I did not feel my concerns were heard. As we say, "The meeting did not go well." Chuck felt that I was becoming just another one of the critics. Given the year he had just gone through, in hindsight I can see why he would have had that feeling.

Chuck routinely took his leaders and those who had already gone out from his ministry to a retreat after the Florida Evangelism Seminar every year. I would learn years later from people in that group that Chuck did bring up some of my concerns to them after I spoke to him, but he did not give me any indication at the time that he thought what I was saying had validity.

I valued what I had learned from the Gainesville leaders. The feeling that we might be losing the connection we had enjoyed was painful. Thinking about what it all might mean for the campus ministry movement was even more painful.

After the seminar we took our two daughters to Disney World, but I felt no "Zippity Do Da" on the 1,000-mile drive back to Springfield. It would be two years and some challenging times before I would have some crucial things revealed to me that would put the joy back in my heart.

Being devoted to Christ means being devoted to that to which he is devoted. Being a disciple of his means following in his steps and laying your life down for that for which he laid down his life… Jesus loved the church and he still loves the church. He gave himself up for her to make her great. As his disciple, one of your deepest convictions must be to love his church, to sacrifice for his church, to build up his church. Selfish decision-making must die. Truly, in losing your life for his sake, you find it.

—From *Letters to New Disciples*, Chapter Seven, "Commitment to the Body"

7

'Don't Harden Your Heart'

The school year 1976–77 was not a good one in our ministry. The Fontenots had moved on to Baton Rouge, and we had two interns that year, both graduates of Pepperdine University, both California-style guys who cared for others. Each of them was talented but each was working through various issues of his own, as was the guy who was training them.

As in all my years in Springfield, I was teaching in the department of religious studies, and some of my study was creating some new intellectual questions for me. My natural man is a doubter. More troubling to me was the strained relationship with Crossroads, but I felt fairly helpless to do anything about it. My one attempt to talk things through had, in my view, been rebuffed, and I did not know what else to do.

In the summer issue of the *Campus Journal* I wrote an editorial titled "Practical Wisdom or Biblical Truth." Rereading that piece today, it is obvious to me that I was saying we need to be grateful for some of the things being learned in our campus ministries about bringing people to Christ and maturing them in him. Those were things, of course, being learned particularly from the Crossroads ministry. But I added this word of caution:

> As we collect our practical wisdom, we must not "absolutize" it or elevate it to the level of eternal truth.

I went on to say,

> If something has been omitted from the Scripture, we can be sure there is a good reason for its absence. Perhaps it just isn't true, or more likely, it just isn't true for every situation.

I ended this piece with an attempt at conciliation:

> We are thankful for all those who have shared their wisdom from their experiences with others, and it is our prayer that more and more of us will be open to the good things that others are learning. But let us keep all of that on one level and maintain the unity of the Spirit and the bond of peace on a much higher level.

From what happened next, it would be obvious we were not ready to accept such a calling.

The NCMS in the summer of 1977 was held in Lubbock, Texas, and I remember it as a painful experience almost from beginning to end. Under the direction of the Broadway Church (ironically, the original sponsors of the CE ministry of the '60s), the program featured plenty of diversity, but the tension between the Crossroads ministers, who surprisingly were there in large numbers, and the other campus ministers was thicker than a West Texas sand storm.

There was the feeling among the non-Crossroads folks that the Crossroads men and women all dressed just alike and did their hair alike and wanted to make everyone in their ministries be just like them. It may have been at this meeting that I heard the word "clones" used for the first time to describe what some thought the Crossroads-trained ministers wanted to produce.

The theme messages for the week came primarily from the book of Joshua, but what we all needed was a strong dose of the message of the cross. In my judgment, the annual campus ministers' seminar never resembled the church at Corinth more than it did at this meeting. No, there was no immorality or drunkenness, but the divisions in the group were evident to all. Panel discussions were quite confrontational, and few people seemed to be trying to listen to anyone who disagreed with them. It seemed most everyone had an ax and was eager to grind it.

It must have been a discouraging experience for the campus ministry staff of the Broadway Church, including Charles Mickey and Milton Jones. They had worked hard to plan a spiritual program, but there were forces at work beyond their control.

Those who had been around for many years were nursing hurts from Albuquerque four years earlier and Gainesville the year before, but the art of spiritual conversation and conflict resolution seemed nowhere to be found. Alonzo Welch had spoken the year before on the theme of "Action or Reaction?" He had pointed out that the gospel is a many-sided truth and that we must avoid extremism. I am not sure we heard him.

The theme of the '77 seminar was "The Lord with Us," and though there were some great messages from Tony Ash, Landon Saunders and others, it was not a time when I felt that a "sweet, sweet Spirit" was in that place.

I certainly cannot hold myself up as any kind of example at this meeting. I was weary of the conflict, licking my own wounds, and making no courageous efforts for us to restore righteousness in our relationships. I was nearing a personal low point. In the words of the writer of Hebrews, I was drifting and my heart was growing hard. Within three months I would see this ever so clearly.

Looking back it is quite surprising that the whole group, now with large numbers of Crossroads-trained people voting, chose to have the seminar the next year in Searcy, Arkansas, the home of Harding College, a Christian school. Terry Smith, whom I had worked with at Memphis State, had moved to Searcy to begin a campus ministry there—obviously with a focus more on students who were already in the church. Terry was convinced that most of these students knew little of the real Jesus. Whatever case Terry presented for having the meeting there, it must have been persuasive to enough people. It is entirely possible that the Crossroads-trained people just didn't have the numbers yet to select one of their locations and that the other guys preferred Searcy over a Crossroads-oriented location.

It is hard to overemphasize how important the difficult event in Lubbock was for me. The outcome of this annual seminar—for good or for bad—had a great deal to do with how I started the new school year. Those of us in campus ministry often felt somewhat lonely in the churches where we were. We had some of the classic "town and gown" issues to deal with in the local church.[1] Our closest relationships were often with students. The fellowship provided by the campus ministers' seminars often met some large needs, and when that meeting ceased for many of us to be a place where those needs were met, we felt it. I am sure the impact on the Crossroads-trained people was entirely different because they still had their close-knit fellowship that grew not only out of common philosophy but an actual shared life, past or present, at the University of Florida.

As the new school year began, I wrote an editorial titled "Religious Freedom and Biblical Authority." In non-specific terms I described what I believed was a growing tendency among us to bind things that God had not bound. I actually was thinking also about some things from some other ministries besides Crossroads, but there is no doubt their ministry was the one I primarily had in mind.

Chuck was on the board for the *Campus Journal* and the Crossroads Church took three hundred copies of each issue—by far the largest of any ministry. After the issue came out, I received a phone call from one of the Crossroads leaders telling me that Gainesville was canceling their subscription entirely. This was the third editorial I had written over a span of eight CJ issues with my concern for the Gainesville tendencies in mind. In each one I had tried to challenge other opposite dangers as well, but I suppose Chuck felt enough was enough.

In hindsight I see that the Crossroads ministry was a target of almost everyone. One "liberal" publication accused them of "Out Church of Christing

---

1. "Town and gown" is a term used to describe the two communities of a university town; "town" being the non-academic population and "gown" the university community.

the Church of Christ." The conservative critics had a litany of charges that they ran in article after article. Pressure was put on those who came to speak at Crossroads to no longer go. Of course, the world was against them, but when those on both the left and the right in the church are against you, that can get to you. There were probably times when they handled that remarkably well and other times not so well. I later learned they felt that when the very publication they were buying for their students was undermining student morale, they had no choice but to stop taking it.

I wish I could remember more of what happened next. I know how I felt about a board member canceling a large subscription without talking it over with me, but apparently I made no effort to reach Chuck (a serious error on my part). I remember that the message I had received was terse and delivered with finality. After several years of trying to be an agent of reconciliation, it seemed as though I was going to have to align myself with one group and be cut off from another. It was a place I had hoped never to be in.

So, I did not begin the '77–'78 school year in good shape. Much like Psalm 88, it started bad and got worse. For the first time that I can remember (but not the last) I would deal with depression. I went out for a drive one September morning just trying to get in touch with what was going on with me. I felt conflicted in a host of ways. The issues that tumbled in my mind included the intellectual, the theological, the relational, and the question of how to show integrity in all these areas. Someone who knew me at the time would much later write on an Internet bulletin board that during that time I seemed to be chased by demons. He probably never suspected that I would see his post, but what he wrote is not far from wrong.

In those days by my phone in a simple little frame I had the words of Dietrich Bonhoeffer: "I believe God will give us all the strength we need to resist in all times of distress, but he never gives it in advance, lest we should rely on ourselves and not on Him alone..."[2] I had always found that line, written in a Nazi prison, to be good for my soul. However, in November 1977 I was straining to hold on to such faith.

Though I was struggling, I still accepted an invitation to go to Baton Rouge, Louisiana, and speak for a seminar at LSU being planned by Mike Fontenot. Also on the program was Tom Brown, who was now the campus minister at the University of Colorado in Boulder. I don't recall having any conversations with Tom during that year of strained relations with Crossroads, but all my experiences with Tom had been good, and I looked forward to seeing him.

---

2. Dietrich Bonhoeffer, *Letters and Papers from Prison* (London: SCM Press, 2001), 11.

As I recall both of us spoke at the Friday night session, with me speaking on "one another" relationships, and then we found a room in the LSU student union where we could talk. We continued our conversation, sitting in hard chairs in that inhospitable function room until 3:00 in the morning. Our time was focused on the various concerns I had about the Crossroads-oriented ministries, the difficulties I was having communicating with the leadership there, and other related issues.

Now twenty-nine years later, I can remember almost nothing of the specifics we discussed. What impressed me then, however, and what I still remember today, is that when I talked with Tom and as I heard his messages at the seminar, I was impressed with his heart. As God would have it, Tom spoke in at least one of his messages about the three passages in Hebrews that say, "Today if you hear his voice, do not harden your heart" and elaborated on that statement and helped us apply it.

As I listened to Tom and spoke with him until that early hour on a Saturday morning, the thing I remember clearly is that I knew my heart was not where Tom's was. I kept comparing my seminar presentations to Tom's. Technically, I think I did a good job. The organization was good. There was plenty of biblical basis for what I said, but when I listened to me and listened to Tom, I heard a different heart. His was more open, more eager for input, more surrendered, more trusting, more calm and more secure.

Sure, in their ministries there were tendencies that needed to be checked, and there were things that needed to be addressed, but I had allowed my heart to get to a very bad place. I had become critical, cynical, negative and joyless. At that seminar I got in touch with the fact that my first priority was to deal with my own heart. I began to realize something that would later be important in all kinds of arenas: we can be right about the issues, but very wrong in the attitudes of our heart.

The writer of Hebrews also says,

> See to it, brothers, that none of you has a sinful, unbelieving heart that turns away from the living God. But encourage one another daily, as long as it is called Today, so that none of you may be hardened by sin's deceitfulness. (Hebrews 3:12–13)

Because I was still not flying, Sheila and I had a twelve-hour drive back to Missouri after the seminar, giving me much time to quietly reflect and to talk things out. My conclusion was that though I was a respected minister and had a pretty strong spiritual resume, I had developed a sinful, unbelieving heart. I had stopped trusting God, and I had moved into a negative mode where I was not soft and open to what he wanted to do in my life. Suddenly the issue was not so much the attitude of the Crossroads leadership, but my heart, and my need for repentance.

Jesus' words from Matthew 6 came to my mind:

> "The eye is the lamp of the body. If your eyes are good, your whole body will be full of light. But if your eyes are bad, your whole body will be full of darkness. If then the light within you is darkness, how great is that darkness!" (Matthew 6:22–23)

In Scripture the eyes are sometimes connected to the heart (Ephesians 1:18). When the heart is bad, the eyes will be bad. When the eyes are bad, we will not see clearly. My conclusion was that I had been trying to see and analyze a variety of things, looking through some bad lenses that came from a heart that was not submissive, trusting and pliable. My conclusion was that what I needed to do was to suspend my judgments about all these things I was trying to evaluate, and focus instead on having a humble, trusting heart. In due time, I believed I would see more clearly to make right judgments.

We arrived back in Springfield on Sunday night in time for the evening service. In those days there was always an "invitation" at the end of every sermon, and I had already decided well before we got back to Missouri that I was going to respond, go before the congregation and acknowledge my sin and desire to change my heart. After the message, I did just that.

Since I was on the staff of the church, I asked if I could make my own statement, instead of following custom and having something read one for me. I tried to make it clear to the congregation that not only had I been convicted about some dark things deep within me that I had not dealt with before, but that this whole experience of getting in touch with the need for repentance was resulting in me feeling liberated and thankful.

The response of the membership took me by surprise, but was a foreshadowing of things to come. Very few expressed gratitude for what I had shared. The prevailing comment was more along the lines of, "We think you are a wonderful person;" "Don't be so hard on yourself;" "I don't really think you needed to do that."

Later on as I continued to talk about my experience and processed the responses of people, I would conclude that my brokenness and vulnerability was somehow threatening to people. It seemed to me that there were things in their own hearts that they weren't ready to deal with, and having one of their spiritual leaders talk so openly about such things, made them very uncomfortable.

I am aware that not everyone who was on the scene at the time would agree with that assessment, but a continuing string of reactions convinced me it was valid.

Not long ago I was in a meeting where we each were asked to share about our conversion. When it came my turn, I stated that in my life there had been several. I personally believe that we may have a number of defining moments that are so significant and result in such a dramatic change of perspective that they can be described as conversion.

This experience in November 1977 was a major conversion experience for me. I was "a good boy" who had grown up in the church, had started preaching at age twenty, had found myself in various positions of spiritual leadership before I was thirty, but this was probably the first time I had been convicted about the sinfulness of my own heart, and at the same time the marvelous grace of God that can deal with it. I had been an advocate of more preaching on grace, but now it was as if all the passages on the grace of God exploded to life.

Some will certainly say, "But you didn't get all your questions answered about the Crossroads ministry" or "There were still things about the Crossroads ministry that needed be addressed." Yes, that is true, and, honestly I would later learn there was even more than I knew. However, when one has an experience much like Isaiah describes in chapter six of his book, when one sees the holiness and righteousness of God, sees his own unclean lips and unclean heart, and then hears the pronouncement of grace and forgiveness, he finds himself in a joyful and grateful mode which overwhelms other issues.

Our heritage in the Restoration (Stone-Campbell) Movement with its roots in the logic of Bacon and Locke has always made us uncomfortable with an encounter with God that cannot be reduced to a formula, but what happened to me in that year was an encounter of seismic proportions that affects me to this very day.

Some may question my reasoning, but my conclusion was that a ministry that had matured a Tom Brown, and a ministry that was helping me get in touch with myself, my need for repentance and my need for God's grace, was doing something right. I hope no readers will misunderstand. I never thought Tom was perfect, but he had a heart I needed.

I don't think I suspended my ability to think or question. I believe my actions in the next few years show the opposite (though one is certainly free to disagree), but I was looking at the issues in the church in a whole new light. I would submit that anyone who is looking through eyes of gratitude and evaluating with a heart that is humble, soft and trusting is seeing more clearly than one who is cynical, hardened and skeptical. There are certainly dangers in naiveté, and there is a place for healthy skepticism, but I would emphasize the word "healthy." That is precisely what mine was not and could not be until my heart changed.

How important was this experience in my life? God only knows the full answer to that. As for me, I believe it was a "saving" experience. Given the trajectory my life was taking for the fifteen months leading up to it, I believe it is entirely possible that I was on my way to leaving God. I would not have ever said I was on my way out, and maybe I would not have thought it, but the seriousness of a hardening heart cannot be overemphasized. I am convinced that is just what was happening to mine, which means it was also becoming increasingly sinful (bitter, competitive, resentful) and increasingly unbelieving.

I am now convinced that there is a definite connection between a heart that is not pure and a head that has doubts, with the former leading to the latter. It is amazing how quickly those intellectual questions became minor issues when my heart changed. I believe the conversations with Tom Brown and the exposure to his heart helped me see the darkness in my own life and brought me to a point of godly sorrow that led to repentance, and that repentance, as I sought to carry it out, left no regret.

I know there are those who have trouble understanding the relationships I went on to develop with Crossroads-oriented ministries. I would just hope they can see that in a very real way, I found liberation through the help, example and inspiration of one of their ministers. Might I have had a different experience with someone else with Crossroads training? I am sure that is true, but the God who works in all things, didn't bring me together at this crucial point in my life with someone else. He brought me together with the man who could most touch my heart. I was deeply grateful then. I still am.

I know not everyone had this experience with Crossroads-trained leaders. I just know what God was doing to bring me to life again. I would later have my own painful moments with this movement, though it would seem from various reports that my experiences were more limited than those of others. Who can figure out all the ways God works in our lives and why he allows some of us to have one experience and some of us another? Like Peter, in John 21, who questioned why his lot would be tougher than that of another disciple, it would seem we need to focus more on what God is doing with us and not what is happening with the other guy.

If my old friend who commented about the demons was right, I would want him to know that they must have fled at this point. I didn't see any drowning pigs, but I certainly felt that I was once again "in my right mind" (Luke 8:32–35). Some challenging, but some of the best, years were just beginning.

Hate sin. It wrecks lives, homes, marriages and relationships. Plan. Pray. Get all the help others can give you so that you will not sin. If one plan does not seem to be working, get help and get a new plan. However, if you do sin, do not give up. Give it back to God. Come humbly before him. Be broken over it (Psalm 51:17). Have "godly sorrow" about it (2 Corinthians 7:10–11). After all this, however, accept God's forgiveness. Rejoice in his grace. Marvel at his grace. Stand amazed at his grace. Then get up and go after righteousness again with a grateful and determined heart.

  –From *Letters to New Disciples*, Chapter Six, "Dealing with Sin"

8

New Heart, New Power

I said earlier that I have had several conversion experiences in my life, but none was more powerful for me than the one I just described. This encounter with God fit so well with the Scriptures, and the fruit it produced was that promised by the Scriptures. The difference in me from September 1976 to the late fall 1977 was like night and day. I was energized. I was spiritually alive. The man who had struggled for over a year with having anything to say, was now eager to preach and teach. Bible study once again became for me an adventure.

With the eyes of my heart now open wider, I was seeing things I had never seen before. As never before, the message of the cross became for me the wisdom and power of God. I developed deep convictions about the contrast between the world's wisdom and God's wisdom and developed a series of evangelistic Bible studies on that theme that I still use to this day. I had preached and taught the cross, but never out of a conviction that I now had.

It was also during this period when the Beatitudes (Matthew 5:1–12) would come alive to me, and I would see them as the key to the heart change needed to live the life of a disciple. Over the next few years I would present my series of nine lessons based on those statements in several churches. Today I probably get more positive feedback on my chapter on the Beatitudes than any other in my book, *No One Like Him*. On so many fronts conviction burned in my heart. I could say, to paraphrase Paul, "I pray all men will become as I am" (Acts 26:29). That feeling was as real as it was new.

Some of the students in our ministry were excited about the changes they saw in me and began to seriously take inventory of their own lives. Others were kind but skeptical, with one honestly telling me he was just going to have to watch my life for a while to see if this was real. I told him I would honor and support his approach. Some months later, he said he "believed."

To digress for a moment, I have heard several programs on TV and radio recently describing how bad the economy was in 1978–79 with the country in a condition known as *stagflation*. That is when the economy is stagnant and wages are not growing, but inflation is high at the same time (it was 13% in 1979). To add to the woes, interest rates on home mortgages went as high as

17%. Most today cannot imagine such an economic disaster. It was during this period that one economist developed a formula including all these things which he titled "the misery index." But here is the odd thing: Until I heard these stories, I could not have told you that times were that bad. I look back at 1978–79 as the best years of my life.

When we are getting our hearts to the right places—meaning soft, yielded, submissive and trusting—and consequently are connecting with God and his Spirit, things the world finds so important don't have that much impact on us. That is a lesson we all need to learn and that I need to hold on to. I would later understand how important this truth is when we face a radical change in our health or other circumstances.

Some of the adults, including some leaders, in our congregation were not pleased with what they saw in me, and I am sure that just as new Christians, in their zeal, often blow family or friends away, that I, too, as one who almost felt like a new convert, did not handle every situation in the right way or communicate my convictions with the best judgment.

Even now after all the years, I still pray that I might understand how I may have hurt someone. We did have a clinical psychologist in the church who felt the things I was saying about the heart, dealing with sin and going to the cross were going to damage people's self-esteem and hurt them emotionally. Though I expect he and I would still disagree on some fundamental issues today, I now believe that I did not give careful enough consideration to people's backgrounds and the way they processed the message they heard. For that I am sorry.

With gratitude in my heart for the impact of Tom Brown's life, I reached out and began to have increased contact with him. In the summer of 1978 my family vacationed in Colorado, and we spent a week with the Browns and with the ministry in Boulder. During that visit we met a number of students that we would later know as leaders in other ministry settings including Tom Marks, Tom Snyder, Gregg Marutzky and Tom Turnbull. I had learned earlier much about the use of "soul talks" and "prayer partners," but this time, I was not so concerned about methodology; rather, I was eager to see how the leaders connected with people's hearts. I was not disappointed.

The NCMS was held in August 1978 in Searcy, Arkansas, and I was asked by Terry Smith to speak to

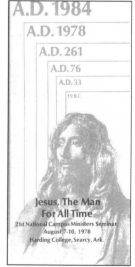

Brochure for the 1978 National Campus Ministers Seminar

the whole group about bringing the message of the cross into our marriages. The changes I was making were definitely being felt at home. My new perspective had helped me see how I had been dragging Sheila down with my negative, complaining and bitter heart. I now found it a joy to go to the cross in my marriage and die to that defiling stuff. We found in a fresh way that he who loses his life (in marriage and everywhere else) really finds it. With conviction and gratitude, I made that speech.

At that seminar, I sought out Chuck Lucas to share with him personally about my time with Tom and the changes that had subsequently come to my heart. I am sure he had already heard from Tom and others about these things, but I wanted him to know personally of my gratitude for the ministry in Gainesville. It may seem odd, but I do not remember if I or Chuck brought up the incidents that had happened almost two years before. I don't remember any apology from Chuck, but then, I wasn't really looking for one. My perspective was so different that I was not concerned about revisiting those issues.

As for the concerns about their ministries, the time Sheila and I spent in Colorado had quelled many of our fears. We not only had been in Boulder but had gone to Ft. Collins where Andy and Pat VanBuren (another Crossroads-trained couple) were serving the campus ministry. In neither place did we see things that troubled us. I am sure part of this difference is that I was now looking with the eyes of a different heart. In both places they seemed as open to my thoughts as I was to theirs. I remember giving Tom some input about the leadership of one young brother and he eagerly received it.

After our times with the Browns and VanBurens, Sheila and I had laughed about the idea that the Gainesville people were just "clones." They were all so obviously very unique and individual personalities.

At the close of the Searcy seminar, the site selected for the next meeting was Boulder, where Tom would be the host. I don't remember who offered another option, but it is likely that the Crossroads ministries now had enough votes to carry the day.

From this point on, I would develop growing relationships with those in the Crossroads and eventually the Boston Movement, years later becoming an elder in Boston. At various times there would be other concerns and questions and some quite confrontational talks, but there would never be another time when I would feel the kind of estrangement from people in those ministries that I had felt before. I am sorry that this was not the experience of everyone.

For years I have been coming to the cross, and yet, its power is undiminished. Each time I come, I am affected as though it were the first time. I find this remarkable. It is amazing that something God did on such a hated tree so long ago has the ability to put *everything* in proper perspective. It is incredible how it speaks to us whatever condition we are in—comforting, challenging, convicting—giving us just what we need the most. No wonder Paul would write: "For I resolved to know nothing while I was with you except Jesus Christ and him crucified" (1 Corinthians 2:2).

–From *Letters to New Disciples*, Chapter Twenty-Three,
"At the Foot of the Cross"

9

Convictions, Conversions and Controversy

In the fall of 1978 we added to our campus ministry staff two interns who had both been baptized and raised up in our ministry—Greg Jackson (now an elder in Denver) and Larry Sharp (now an evangelist in Normal, Illinois). Today hiring interns from our own ministry would seem an expected development, but then in our ministry, it was a first, and I should add there was considerable doubt among the elders and other leaders about the wisdom of this. I am convinced that the primary worry was that these two brothers had been very close to me, had been very encouraged about the changes I was making, and had been excited about our growing relationship with Tom Brown and others like him.

The elders and other senior leaders were becoming concerned about getting too closely linked with the Crossroads ministry, and I think there was a feeling that it would be good to have interns (probably from Christian colleges) who had no connection with all this.

Be that as it may, approval for Greg and Larry was eventually given for the school year 1978–79. They joined a staff composed of Dennis Files, who had completed an internship the year before, and Lynda Caine, our women's counselor, and me. That year we saw the most effective outreach to the campus in my nine years in Springfield. More than fifty students were baptized into Christ, and the spirit of the group had never been better. Many of those who came to the Lord that year are now faithfully serving in various congregations, many as leaders, particularly in the Midwest.

Ironically, the February 15, 1979, issue of the Gospel Advocate—a widely circulated publication in Churches of Christ—featured an unusually long article on the dynamic growth of our congregation and praised our campus ministry for its evangelistic effectiveness—an accolade I don't remember them often giving. Why ironic? Because in the following issue, February 22, an article in that same paper that would reverberate for years appeared with the title "Cultism in the Church." This followed an earlier article titled "The Total Commitment Movement." Both were highly critical of the Crossroads-oriented ministries. Together they set off alarms throughout the Churches of Christ. A long letter I wrote to Advocate editor Ira North received a polite but non-committal reply.

Chuck Lucas published a lengthy response to the criticism, but the fire was out of control.

Just three months earlier, in November 1978 the world had been shocked by the suicide deaths of the members of the People's Temple at Jonestown, Guyana. Few words aroused more fear than the word "cult." Now it was being used, not just by outsiders, but by those in the church to describe many of the campus ministries. In the South National Church in Springfield those of us working with students felt increasingly under scrutiny from the church leaders and university administrators. New tensions developed.

I could understand why the elders would be concerned. They had seen me at one time quite troubled with the Crossroads approach. Then they saw a major shift in my views, and at the same time they were hearing increasingly loud voices from the brotherhood using frightening language. Was Tom getting swept up in something dangerous? How can we keep this thing under control? The elders had much affection for me, but things were happening that seemed troubling to them, and we had a number of meetings that were uncomfortable for us all. Gradually, and not so gradually at times, trust was eroding. Fear was growing.

I well remember conversations I had with the elders who were concerned that our students were too involved in each other's lives and decisions. They felt some were relying too much on the advice of those older than they were. They wanted to know if I felt relationships could be abused.

I certainly agreed that there could be abuse, but shared that any biblical teaching can be abused. Examples include everything from grace to obedience to baptism. But I asked them if neglect of others wasn't also just as damaging. I shared that when people are not involved in each other's lives, are not helping each other to overcome sin (Galatians 6:1–2), and are not admonishing and teaching one another (Colossians 3:16), great damage is done to the church, though it doesn't make headlines. How can we guard each other against the deceitfulness of sin and hardness of heart (Hebrews 3:13) if we are not deeply involved in each other's lives?

I took paper and pen and drew a line representing a continuum. It looked something like this:

No Involvement ————————————— Unhealthy Control

I told them that as I saw it the church as a whole was well over on the side of "No Involvement" particularly at the heart level. I said we in the campus ministry certainly could make the mistake of going too far the other way, but that I saw both problems as equally in need of attention. I proposed we all needed to be concerned about a healthy biblical balance. They never seemed to agree with my point, which still seems to me to have validity. The average church accepts something so far from the biblical plan that any movement toward it can quickly be viewed as something akin to unhealthy control.

I believe all the students who were with us would tell you today that we never taught anything but respect for the elders and other leaders. A year later we would be fired, but even at that time, we continued to teach the students to respect those who were over them in the Lord. I believe this message did get through because after we left, many who had been led by us and were loyal to us, continued to work under the leadership of the elders without bitterness or rancor (though there were struggles).

In the midst of all these events my family had a personal crisis. Our third daughter was born in February 1979. While she initially seemed as healthy as her two sisters, within twenty-four hours I was awakened by a call from Sheila that there seemed to be a problem with her breathing, and they were keeping her in the nursery for observation rather than bringing her for her scheduled feeding. They had assured Sheila that everything should be fine. But then, while I was teaching my New Testament class at the university, I got the message from Sheila that they were going to have to rush Corrie by plane to St. Louis Children's Hospital to deal with some type of serious heart problem.

I hurried to the hospital to briefly see Sheila and Corrie and then started a drive to St. Louis to hopefully be with our daughter. In those days before cell phones, I stopped two hours into the four-hour drive and called back to the hospital to ask Sheila if little Corrie had survived the trip. Sheila reported that she had indeed, and they had done an emergency procedure that had saved her life. The doctor would be waiting for my arrival to tell me more.

When I arrived, a pediatric cardiologist, Dr. Cathy Henry, met me and took me to a classroom in the Barnes Hospital/Washington University complex where she diagramed the problem on a white board. (Dr. Henry and her husband, a surgeon, would become good friends with us, eventually driving four hours to visit us in our home, and Sheila would get the opportunity to study the Bible with Cathy.)

Corrie's problem was diagnosed as transposition of the great vessels, a birth defect where the aorta and pulmonary arteries are switched. In 1979 corrective surgery on a newborn was not an option, but the procedure they did was designed to keep her alive for a year during which time she would hopefully gain enough weight to make her a candidate for corrective surgery. The bad news was that the failure rate for that surgery was about 30%.

Though there were various criticisms floating around about Crossroads-styled campus ministries (including ours), and our family was facing a serious personal challenge, I was not discouraged. Sheila and I were more spiritually and emotionally bonded than at any point in our marriage and were confident that God was at work. Sheila would be the one who would bear the greatest burden physically and emotionally from Corrie's health problems during the next year, but her faith had been energized. She looks back and reads things she wrote in her journal during that time is still amazed at the strength, grace and insight God gave her. Out of this experience she would do some powerful teaching among women.

It would be during this time that we would first connect with Roger and Marcia Lamb who were working in the church in Charleston, Illinois, with Kip and Elena McKean. Their son Michael was also a patient at St. Louis Children's Hospital battling leukemia. The Lambs and Joneses would be together many more times in years to come in ministry and in publishing.

In spite of tensions with the elders and other leaders, our ministry continued to go well, and in April '79 I took a bus full of students to attend the Rocky Mountain Evangelism Seminar in Estes Park. The Boulder church sponsored that event, and Tom had asked me to give two messages on "Create in Me a Pure Heart" from Psalms 32 and 51. I doubt that I have ever felt more deeply connected with messages I delivered. The response of the people was quite overwhelming.

Almost thirty years later I still have people tell me what those messages meant to them. I remember thinking that with so many people wanting to just lay their hearts open before God, this had to be a movement that God was blessing and would shape as he saw fit. The late Richard Rogers, well-known teacher at the Sunset School of Preaching in Lubbock, was my roommate at that event. It was our first meeting, and I was encouraged by our time together.

Five months later, in August of that year a significant group of us from Springfield came back to Boulder for the NCMS. Different people will have different memories of that week. Mine are all positive. Under Tom Brown's leadership, I felt the seminar had a great tone with Tom's heart coming through as usual. The men and women either from Crossroads ministries or those who were very positive toward those ministries (like ours in Springfield, Mike Fontenot's in Baton Rouge and a few others) were in the majority.

Tom had asked me to do a speech titled "Take Heed to Yourselves," and the emphasis was to be on how we as leaders need people in our lives helping us see our blind spots and sins. My positive feelings for this growing movement were increasing as I saw this as a group that wanted to live before others with some serious self-examination and openness—something not common in the culture of the Churches of Christ. However, I am sure that some of the brothers not from the Crossroads perspective did not share all the good feelings that I had. I know now that a sense that they were being shut out was growing.

What I remember was an event with an overwhelmingly positive and faith-building message. My most vivid memory of the 1979 seminar is sitting in the group, looking around the room at one point after someone's message and believing for the first time that I was with a group of men and women that were really going to take the gospel around the world. Once back home in Springfield, I shared that thought with Sheila. It was a moment we both would often recall in the years to come.

When Jesus and the disciples came off the Mount of Transfiguration, they returned to the difficulties of the real world, and so after back-to-back spiritual high points, appropriately enough there in the Rockies, I returned to begin what would prove to be a fruitful and yet very challenging year.

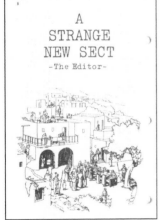

A
STRANGE
NEW SECT
-The Editor-

I wrote an article for the *Campus Journal* which described what could have been written by an investigative reporter had there been one in the first century looking into the growing Jesus Movement. I titled it "A Strange New Sect." It still makes interesting and quite convicting reading for me today, reminding me that authentic Christianity will always have elements that are troublesome to any worldly culture. The early church was a radical community living in response to scandalous grace that came from an offensive, stumbling block of a cross. It was community built around a crucified man who was worshipped as God, and it was an outrage to the world. (See this article reproduced in Appendix Two.)

I think my little attempt at historical fiction confirmed the convictions of some, but did little to reassure those who were concerned about our direction and nothing to lessen the criticism we would receive. They didn't buy the idea that a faithful Christian community will often be looked at as an extremist sect, though I am still convinced that is the case.

In 1979, one of our interns, Greg Jackson, and his wife, Theresa, accepted the opportunity to begin a campus ministry at Indiana State University. The following year, after time at Harding Graduate School, Larry and Sherry Sharp

would do the same thing at Illinois State University. Due to the growing concerns that our church leaders had about the direction of our work, in
Springfield we were not given the funding for more interns that year. They
were not eager to spread a philosophy of ministry which troubled them ("The
Crossroads Philosophy" as it was being described in critical articles in church
papers). The tension continued through the fall, and when university officials
began to express concerns to the church elders about our ministry, things
came to a breaking point.

On January 18, 1980, our daughter Amy celebrated her eighth birthday—
one our family will not forget. I had been to the campus and was returning
home. When I rounded the corner and started down the block where we
lived, I saw fire trucks in front of our house and watched an ambulance speed
by me leaving the scene. Smoke was pouring out of the house, but Sheila was
standing in the street on the lookout for me to quickly let me know everyone
was safe. The damage was extensive, and we had to find another place to live
for the next six weeks.

Two weeks after the fire and just a few weeks before Corrie's surgery was
scheduled, I was summoned to a meeting of the elders. The growing brotherhood controversy about campus ministries, pressure from the university and
their own personal doubts had caused them to make a difficult decision. They
were going to relieve me of my duties. The church there in Springfield had
enjoyed a harmonious relationship with the university for many years, they
explained to me, and they saw that our ministry was jeopardizing that relationship. One of the elders put it to me a bit different privately outside that
meeting. "Tom," he said, "I have been a Christian for more than twenty years,
and I have never been persecuted, and I don't want it to start now."

In that meeting I could sense they were conflicted. I had been in
Springfield almost nine years. All our children had been born there. I had
spent much time with these men in their homes. They told me how they
admired my life, but expressed that it just was not possible for us to stay. I can
still remember well some of their exact words. Whoever spoke for the group
said, "Tom you are the most committed Christian we have ever known, and
our campus ministry is perhaps second to none, but we are going to have to
ask you to go somewhere else and do what you are doing." I took that first
part of that statement as a bit of hyperbole, but it was clear from the second
part that our journey was going to lead elsewhere.

They knew Corrie's surgery was coming, and that after that it would take
some time for us to locate another ministry, so they agreed that I could remain
until the end of the school year, but with limited opportunities to speak to the

whole church. Because Dennis Files and Lynda Caine were so close to us and shared our approach to the ministry, the elders felt it would be necessary to dismiss them from the staff as well.

During those last five months our students continued to reach out, baptizing a number of people. Though we were all hurt by the elders' decision, we knew the validity of what we were doing would be undermined if we shut down or did anything that caused our students to be bitter. With the help of God and guided by 2 Corinthians 1:12, I believe we conducted ourselves in those last months not according to worldly wisdom but according to God's grace.

In March, Corrie underwent open-heart surgery. To the praise of God, the corrective procedure was a success. She would have to have annual check-ups, and avoid "run till you drop" sports like basketball, but would be able to go on to live a very normal life. Our gratitude was enormous.

The year before, when we were spending time in Boulder, we had been asked by the elders there to consider joining them to work with the adult ministry in partnership with Tom and Kelly Brown who were focused on the campus. Already knowing that support among the elders in Springfield was weakening, and believing that the situation in Boulder offered us a much greater opportunity to work in unity with an entire leadership, we were prepared to say that we would come.

However, as I met with a close brother one afternoon to pray, he asked if going to the high altitude was going to be difficult for Corrie. In the year before her surgery, she was functioning on only about twenty percent of normal oxygen intake. His question had not occurred to me or Sheila, but checking with the doctors, we were told that moving to a place with thin-air before her surgery would make her situation more difficult. For that reason we declined the Boulder offer.

However, Tom Brown told us that it was likely that no one would be hired for a year and that the opportunity might still be there after the surgery. Checking back with Tom almost a year later, I learned that the position had not been filled. As Tom made our availability known to his elders, we learned that one of them had become concerned that Tom and I thought too much alike and that it would be better to have someone working with the adults and preaching for the congregation who represented another approach. They would hire Kenneth Reid who had led the Bible Chair ministry for many years at the University of Alabama.

With the door in Boulder now closed, God would do what he often does—lead us to a most unlikely place.

We live in this world (where there is a certain system), and yet we are citizens of heaven (Philippians 3:20) and live by a totally different system. It is the right way to live. It is of God. But the world does not like it. It is offensive to those who have no desire to please God.

—From *Letters to New Disciples*, Chapter Eighteen,
"Opposition and Persecution"

10

Kirksville?

I remember my first thought when I heard that there might be an opportunity for us in the small northeast Missouri town of Kirksville. It was a one-word thought with a crooked symbol at the end: *"Kirksville?"* I had lived in Missouri for nine years, but had hardly heard of the place. I knew there was a university there, but I don't remember hearing anything about the church. Every year we in Springfield hosted the Mid-America Mobilization Seminar, and I believe that one of the elders from Kirksville came once or twice to one of those events, but I knew virtually nothing about the community. When I began to ask people what they knew about it, the most frequent answer was that it was the icebox of Missouri. Not exactly a heart-warming thought.

A couple of phone conversations and a trip to Kirksville completely changed our minds. Here in this town of 17,000, in the middle of acres of corn and soybean fields, seventy miles from the nearest shopping mall, was a little church of a hundred and twenty people eager to make a difference and a university campus (today known as Truman State) with the highest per capita ratio of international students of any school in the nation, due to low tuition.

The three elders there knew all about the controversies raging around campus ministry, but after spending time with us, wanted to bring us all (Sheila, Dennis, Lynda and me) in and put us on their staff. A wealthy and generous member of the congregation was willing to provide the additional financial support that would be needed.

Kip McKean, the young Crossroads-trained minister whom I had met in Gainesville, had begun a work in 1976 in another small Midwestern town, Charleston, Illinois. I had followed his work fairly closely and had taken students to two seminars that he had directed there. The success of his work on a small campus in a small town had given us a vision for what we might see accomplished. I am still grateful for his example.

We accepted the offer and moved in June 1980. Robert Wells who would go on to do mission work in Hungary, was already the full-time minister in Kirksville, but with great humility and kindness Robert allowed me to do the bulk of the preaching, and he demonstrated a remarkably teachable heart as this new staff (of three full-time people and two non-paid men, Mark Moore and Mark Palmer, who were like staff) moved in and were added to the work where he had been for a couple of years.

The Jones family 1980

We were joined by a number of students who transferred from Springfield. We spent an exciting summer, seeing a number of people baptized into Christ, and then headed for Baton Rouge, Louisiana, in August for the NCMS. Just prior to that seminar, I would be advised by one of our elders, a physician, to see a specialist in St. Louis. The doctor there confirmed what I was suspecting. He diagnosed me with "probable multiple sclerosis." Only time would tell for sure, he said, but my constellation of symptoms seemed to point in the direction of MS. Fortunately it would be another ten years before the illness would hit me hard, bring significant disability and be definitively diagnosed.

At the seminar in Baton Rouge, there was an air of excitement. Many campus ministries were thriving. Our dismissal in Springfield was being duplicated in other places, but there was a confidence that opposition and difficulty were always to be encountered if we were faithful. Kip and Elena McKean had just finished their first year in Boston, and his report of conversions at Harvard, MIT and Boston University increased the vision of most who heard him. I believe it was in his speech at that meeting that I first heard him talk about the seemingly impossible—reaching students in Moscow. We were still locked in the clutches of the cold war. It is hardly surprising that the group voted to have the 1981 meeting in the home of the Red Sox and Celtics (the Patriots would make a name for themselves much later).

The controversy in the brotherhood of churches continued, but we took heart—from God, from one another, and occasionally from a lone voice not in our movement. Reuel Lemmons, whom I had met in 1972 at my first Florida Evangelism Seminar was the editor of the *Firm Foundation,* and his weekly editorial is sometimes said to have been the most widely read piece in the Churches of Christ. With his picturesque speech he let it be known that he was never impressed with those that wanted to sit on the porch and throw rocks at those who were trying to do something. In one editorial titled "The Crossroads Controversy" he wrote,

Most of the criticism we have seen was purely rhetoric, by someone whose ox had been gored. When you boil out the inflammatory talk, and get right down to what is scripturally wrong with the congregation [at Crossroads], you may find a thimble full. You might find more in your own congregation.[1]

In Kirksville 1980–81 was a great year. Sheila and I, along with Robert and Cynthia, focused on the adults; Dennis and Lynda, now married, led the campus work, assisted by Mark Moore and Mark Palmer; and I did most of the preaching. Nearly fifty people were baptized into Christ that first year. Except for Kip's work in Charleston, this was unprecedented in small Midwest churches. Most amazingly, these new disciples came from twelve nations. (One of those from Hong Kong is now in Singapore and emails me quite often. His son was recently baptized into Christ.)

We could not help but remember what one of the elders had said during the interview process: "Come to Kirksville. We can reach the world from Kirksville." There were inspiring conversions among the adults as well as the students. We would later hear that our congregation had been held up in other places as an example of how adults and students could all share the same commitment and the same vision.

During these years many of us became accustomed to criticism and were convinced that much of it came from those who were involved in something far from New Testament zeal for mission and for relationships. Some of the charges against us were so outlandish or showed such a misunderstanding of New Testament practice that our skin became thicker.

In Kirksville, we were in a healthy church with a great balance of young and older and with elders who believed that being disciples of Jesus would always bring critics. When later the Boston Movement would receive criticism that was sometimes valid, it was easy for us to dismiss it, thinking it was the same as we had seen in the earlier days. No doubt this affected our ability to be objective and open.

In August 1981 Sheila and I would take the 1400-mile train ride from Kirksville (fortunately located near an Amtrak route) to Boston. Dennis and Lynda and two others training for the ministry would fly there and meet us. For the first time ever

National Campus Ministers Seminar
August 4-6, 1981 • Boston, Massachusetts

---

1. Reuel Lemmons, "The Crossroads Controversy," *Firm Foundation*, November 17, 1981. For more examples of his writing see Appendix Seventeen in this book.

the NCMS was held in a hotel—the old but beautiful Park Plaza in downtown Boston. I had been asked by Kip to do a message titled "If the World Hates You." My original plan was to include the text of this message as an appendix, but I have been urged by those I respect to make it a part of this chapter. It represented a conviction that most of us held deeply and that greatly influenced our thinking. As I recently looked back at my notes of that speech, I must say that I felt very sobered. In 1981 I was experiencing much opposition for my faith and had been for some years. Our church in Kirksville was often spoken against.

Today, in the wake of some trauma in the present ICOC fellowship, I, like so many have pulled back from some of the convictions I presented at the 1981 meeting, but more importantly have apparently not been living in a way that brings a strong reaction from the world. I see the need for some serious repentance. But here is the text of the speech.

If the World Hates You

This is the tenth National Campus Ministers Seminar I have attended, and this is the ninth time I have been asked to speak or to teach at one of these meetings. I want you to know that every year it becomes a greater privilege and more humbling experience. Every year I look out on more talent, more commitment, more purity of heart, and more faith in more lives than I have ever seen before. Every year I see more and more people whose faith and love and zeal and vision challenge me. And I would certainly come to these meetings just to see that and to grow from it.

I am sure that there are other committed groups of Christians that meet in other places under different banners, but I don't believe there is a group anywhere that I would rather be with. I love you. I see in you the heart of a disciple.

The desire for popularity while not found in everyone is something that quite naturally works in most people. Most of us want to be liked. We want people to speak well of us. We want the mention of our names to bring good responses and words of affirmation.

And since most of the world operates with a hedonistic ethic, many people will bend over backward to be popular and well-liked. Popularity brings pleasurable feelings, whereas unpopularity brings pain. When people want to maximize pleasure and minimize pain, they seek popularity.

The message of Jesus Christ that we are considering this week is an overwhelmingly positive message. It promises positive things and it delivers every time. It promises meaning and direction and relationships and ultimately a place with God forever. But there is one thing that Jesus never promised. He never promised us popularity with the world. In fact the only way to have popularity with the world is to get rid of those very elements of discipleship that make it powerful.

Our text for this message is found in John 15:16–23:

> "You did not choose me, but I chose you and appointed you to go and bear fruit—fruit that will last. Then the Father will give you whatever you ask in my name. This is my command: Love each other.
>
> "If the world hates you, keep in mind that it hated me first. If you belonged to the world, it would love you as its own. As it is, you do not belong to the world, but I have chosen you out of the world. That is why the world hates you. Remember the words I spoke to you: 'No servant is greater than his master.' If they persecuted me, they will persecute you also. If they obeyed my teaching, they will obey yours also. They will treat you this way because of my name, for they do not know the One who sent me. If I had not come and spoken to them, they would not be guilty of sin. Now, however, they have no excuse for their sin. He who hates me hates my Father as well."

Beginning with this text we want to look at several things about opposition and persecution.

No 'Iffy Matter'

First, we must begin with the fact that opposition for the Christian is not an "iffy" matter. A superficial look at this passage might lead to the conclusion that persecution and opposition might come to some disciples. After all, Jesus does say in verse 17, "If the world hates you." However, when we look more closely we see that there is really no question about whether or not the world will hate the disciples of Jesus.

There is no question about it, first, because the world hated Jesus first. That is a certainty. The world hated his message. The world hated his view of life. The outstanding representatives of the world acting on behalf of the world said, "Crucify him." So the only "if" involved in this thing has to do with whether or not we preach the same message and live the same life he lived. If we do, there is no question about us receiving the same opposition he received. Verse 20 is clear:

> "Remember the words I spoke to you: 'No servant is greater than his master.' If they persecuted me, they will persecute you also. If they obeyed my teaching, they will obey yours also."

Perhaps Matthew 10:24–25 emphasizes the same thing:

"A student is not above his teacher, nor a servant above his master. It is enough for the student to be like his teacher, and the servant like his master. If the head of the house has been called Beelzebub, how much more the members of his household!"

He says "If the world opposed and slandered me, how much more will they do it to those who are my servants." And we know how that "if" came out. They did call him Beelzebub, and guess what they will call us who are faithful to him.

Go back to John 15 and see, second, that there is no question about opposition coming for the Christian, because he is no longer like the world. Jesus says in verse 19:

"If you belonged to the world, it would love you as its own. As it is, you do not belong to the world, but I have chosen you out of the world. That is why the world hates you."

He teaches that when we are no longer like the world, don't belong to it and are not enslaved by it, the world will resent our defection.

How does the Soviet Union feel when some of her best athletes or dancers or musicians defect to the West? There is bitterness and hostility toward the defectors. The Western World is opposed by the Soviet hierarchy because the West represents values different from Soviet values. The values of the West, to be sure are not the values of God, but they are still very different from Soviet values. There is antagonism and opposition. And they hate those who defect. In a similar way, Jesus teaches that the world despises a defector. He makes it clear that the unpopularity of discipleship is due to the clash of values between God and the world.

The values to the whole world are threatened by the values of God. You can talk about the Western World, the Communist World or the Third World but the values of Jesus are a threat to each of those, because he calls people in all those systems to something totally different, to something revolutionary. The wisdom of man has always taken off in one direction and the wisdom of God has always led in a contradictory direction.

When men decide to stay in the world and operate by its wisdom, they will be threatened by the very presence of those who live according to the wisdom of God. And the people in the world oppose what threatens them.

Let me insert a footnote here, but one that I believe is important. When the world gets into the church, you can expect to see opposition to real discipleship coming even from within the church.

As far as I am concerned, this is the form of opposition that is most painful. It doesn't hurt me nearly as much to be slandered by someone in the world as it does to be slandered maliciously by someone in the church. It hurts so much more because I just don't expect any more from the world, but I expect more from those who have been washed in the blood of Jesus. And I think I have reason to expect more.

There is no form of opposition that is more painful than that which comes from within the body, but there is nothing new about that. And if it happens to you, don't feel something out of the ordinary is happening.

The world got into the church in Corinth, and those who had been led to Christ by Paul and those who had seen their names written in heaven because of him began to be his opponents. The world got into the church in Asia Minor, and the Apostle John describes a brother named Diotrephes who loved to be first.

Look at 3 John 1:9–10:

> I wrote to the church, but Diotrephes, who loves to be first, will have nothing to do with us. So if I come, I will call attention to what he is doing, gossiping maliciously about us. Not satisfied with that, he refuses to welcome the brothers. He also stops those who want to do so and puts them out of the church.

John wrote to the church where this brother was, but Diotrephes would have nothing to do with John. Instead he gossiped maliciously about him. That was bad enough, but he also refused to let certain brothers into the fellowship and he intimidated other Christians so they would not fellowship certain brothers.

And the key to all this is in the statement: *"He loves to be first."* Diotrephes operated according to the world's values. He looked out for Number One. He knew nothing of God's values that call us to die to ourselves and our self-centeredness. When the values of this world still live in those who claim church membership, you will certainly see those people oppose authentic discipleship, and sometimes their attacks will be more bitter and more vitriolic than those who come from the world.

But opposition is not an "iffy" matter. It will come from the world, and it will come from a worldly church that speaks of the cross but has not died on it with Jesus Christ. The only "iffy" matter is our discipleship. *If* we live the life and preach the message, we will be opposed from without and from within.

You Can't Be Loving Enough to Avoid It

There is a second point I want us to see in John 15 and other places: You can't be loving enough or kind enough to avoid opposition. No, instead it is real love that will bring opposition. It is interesting to notice several of the "persecution texts" in the NT and give particular attention to the contexts in which they appear.

Here in John 15 Jesus says in verse 17, "This is my command: Love each other." He follows this immediately in verse 18 with "If the world hates you, keep in mind that it hated me first."

In the Beatitudes in Matthew 5, Jesus describes this new attitude of heart and mind that will be in a disciple. He will be poor in spirit, repentant over sin. He will be meek (teachable and open). He will long for righteousness and pursue it. All that will lead him to show mercy to others from a pure heart. He will use his life to bring men and women to peace with God and with other people. But then right in this context comes the last beatitude: "Blessed are you when you are persecuted for righteousness sake." The merciful peacemaker's life leads to persecution.

In 1 John 3:11–12 we read:

> This is the message you heard from the beginning: We should love one another. Do not be like Cain, who belonged to the evil one and murdered his brother. And why did he murder him? Because his own actions were evil and his brother's were righteous.

The love Christians will have is once again connected with the hate the world will have for Christians.

What is all this saying? You cannot be loving enough or meek enough or pure enough to avoid opposition. No, it is these very qualities of Christ in us that will judge the world and provoke the world.

Several years back we had the song "What the World Needs Now Is Love, Sweet Love." The world may welcome its own version of "sweet love," but it is often offended when it sees the tough love of Jesus Christ that refuses to heal the wound lightly and refuses to say "Peace, peace" when there is no peace.

All of us in this seminar need to grow in our love. We have been called to love like Jesus and none of us is there yet. We need to become more sensitive to people. We need real compassion and real sensitivity and real gentleness. But, we should never think that growing up in that love will make us more popular with the world or with a worldly church.

The more we live the first seven beatitudes, the more certain it will be that we will have the opportunity to live the last one—and be persecuted for righteousness sake.

Opposition Does Not Prove Our Genuineness

Third, we need to be reminded that opposition alone does not prove the genuineness of our discipleship. I feel sure we all know this, but in my mind this message would not be complete without a discussion of this point.

All who seek to live a godly life in Christ Jesus will be persecuted (2 Timothy 3:12), but it does not follow that all who are persecuted are living a godly life in Christ Jesus. Sometimes opposition may come from within and from without the church because we are hypocritical, because we don't watch our lives and doctrine closely, because we are self-righteous or rude or inflexible in matters of opinion.

Peter reminds us in 1 Peter 4 that we will be opposed, but he also reminds us to make sure that when it comes, it comes because of righteousness and not because of something else in our lives that even the world recognizes as bad.

> Dear friends, do not be surprised at the painful trial you are suffering, as though something strange were happening to you. But rejoice that you participate in the sufferings of Christ, so that you may be overjoyed when his glory is revealed. If you are insulted because of the name of Christ, you are blessed, for the Spirit of glory and of God rests on you. If you suffer, it should not be as a murderer or thief or any other kind of criminal, or even as a meddler. However, if you suffer as a Christian, do not be ashamed, but praise God that you bear that name. (1 Peter 4:12–16)

How should we apply this to our lives? When opposition or insult comes, we need to examine our lives first to see if there is anything ungodly in us to justify the things being said. Sometimes we may find some truth in what the critic is saying. If so, we should deal with that, but all the while realizing that opposition will still come, but now for the right reasons.

Opposition or persecution is one of the marks of genuine discipleship. When found in concert with other biblical qualities (like the first seven beatitudes) it is an indication of something genuine. By itself, it may not say anything except that a person has a character that is offensive even to the world's low standards.

An Opportunity Not Just a Problem

Fourth, opposition, insult and persecution must be seen by Christians as an opportunity, not just a problem. When Jesus talks about our responses to persecution he says something incredible. He says "Rejoice in that day and leap for joy" (Luke 6:23).

John R. W. Stott in his book on the Sermon on the Mount says,

When Christians are persecuted here are some of the things they must not do: (1) retaliate like an unbeliever, (2) lick their wounds in self-pity, (3) grin and bear it like a Stoic, or (4) pretend they enjoy it like a masochist. Instead they must rejoice because of heaven. Not just because they are going there (although that is important) but because of the way heaven can use these persecutions on earth to advance the Kingdom.

Christians should never go out trying to provoke persecution, but they must never fear it because opposition and persecution just give Christians that much more opportunity to show the world how different they really are. Jesus showed the world the difference all the way through his life and ministry, but never do we see just how different Jesus was than when they tried him in their kangaroo court and mocked him, spit on him and tortured him to death.

The way he handled all of that persecution, insult, spitting and those caustic comments just caused his light to shine that much brighter. There was no spite, no bitterness, no resentment—only forgiveness in his heart.

We should not be misled by the word "rejoice" here in Luke 6. Persecution is not fun. It is no fun to have stories circulated about you that bear little resemblance to the truth. It is no fun to be hated. I remember the first time anyone ever looked me in the eye and told me they hated me. That statement came after working with an individual for a long time and doing all I could to get this person to deal with the real problem in her life. It was not fun to hear those words. I did not get over it quickly. The fact is I still have not gotten over it.

But, I am thankful to God that I knew enough about his Word to know that this kind of response was promised to me. Just about the only thing promised more in the NT than persecution is the power given to Christians in the midst of such trials. When we hear the promise of persecution, we also need to hear the promise that God will use those things to shine his light even brighter.

Persecution is an opportunity. Otherwise Jesus would never have commanded that we rejoice in it. Rejoicing is done either because of something that God has done or in anticipation of something he is about to do. When we are persecuted, we should rejoice for both reasons. We rejoice because our lives and our message have found their mark and the world is convicted. We also rejoice because God will take our suffering and make his power perfect in these trials.

Persecution is not only an opportunity to shine brighter. It is an opportunity to be reminded that our citizenship is in heaven and that the world is not our home. The Christian who never catches opposition and is always popular and accepted may get real comfortable here in this world. But when we are catching the world's flack, it is a reminder to us that we are aliens and strangers in this world. And I need to thank God every time I am reminded of that.

No Opposition? Need to Ask 'Why Not?'

Finally, if you never receive opposition for your faith, the Bible would give you plenty of reasons to ask "Why not?" If you are never receiving any opposition, and no one insults you or slanders you, your Christian life is abnormal and needs to be examined.

Look back to 1 Peter 4:12–13:

> Dear friends, do not be surprised at the painful trial you are suffering, as though something strange were happening to you. But rejoice that you participate in the sufferings of Christ, so that you may be overjoyed when his glory is revealed.

What is Peter saying is the normal experience? Then what would be the abnormal experience? If I live my life day after day, supposedly as a Christian and everyone likes me and no one feels threatened by my life and no one feels the need to oppose me, what does that say about my life? It says that I must not be exposing much darkness in people's lives. It says I must not be that different.

Brothers and sisters, this does not mean I need to go out and try to get someone to persecute me! It simply means I must need to shine my light brighter in the world of darkness, because no opposition means something abnormal about the way I am living my life in Jesus.

It is not surprising when Christians are opposed. It is surprising (and of concern) when Christians are not doing enough to disturb the world and convict the world. It is surprising when a church never does anything to upset or disturb the people of the world. That church has figured out how to do something that Jesus Christ never figured out. The scandal of many churches is that they are so popular with the world, which is full of darkness.

Brothers and sisters, we don't need to become paranoid people who center our lives on the fact that we are going to be persecuted. The center of our message needs to be Jesus Christ and his word which changes people's lives. At the same time, we must not be naive, forgetting what the world did to our Savior. We don't need to go around asking each other "Did you get persecuted today?" and we don't need to get together for the purpose of comparing persecution stories.

We must have a calm, quiet awareness that every single authentic Christian life will be unpopular with the world. We should not hope for people to oppose us, but we must be sure that some will. We must not go fishing for persecution, but we must not fear it, and we must joyfully accept it when it comes.

If this group fans out from this place to this nation and to this world and preaches the whole will of God, we will be opposed. We will be strongly opposed, and that will be a normal thing. I don't think we have seen anything yet compared to what we will see.

But we must count it a privilege and an honor to suffer any insult or injury in order for the name of Jesus to be known in more lives.

I recall a conversation with Chuck Lucas after this message in which he shared with me how the constant opposition to their ministries was wearing on him. A few months later he would make an appeal to the churches that he hoped would change the climate.

As I reflect on these events, I must apologize to the campus ministers who were not closely affiliated with the Crossroads Movement, because I have hardly any memory of how many of them were present at the Boston seminar, although the number had to be small. One indication of where things had come is that Terry Smith who had hosted and directed this event just three years earlier, and had been my friend for twelve years, was living and ministering in Burlington, a Boston suburb, but did not attend the seminar. Sheila and I did go to their home before we returned to Missouri, but while I don't remember what was said about their decision not to attend, I know they were feeling the prevailing view was that unless you did things the Boston and Crossroads way, you could not possibly be doing it right. In spite of this, the Burlington Church and the Lexington Church (which became Boston) did continue to hold some joint events until sometime in the mid-80s.

Chuck's appeal for unity with all the Churches of Christ came in the form of a lengthy article that appeared in the November 17, 1981, issue of the *Firm Foundation*. In a quite remarkable piece titled "An Open Letter to the Brotherhood of Churches of Christ" Chuck told of meeting with all the Crossroads-trained ministers to discuss issues relating to the current controversy and he made three points:

> (1) I assured them that I have never wanted and do not want in any way to direct or to exercise undue influence over them or their ministries… They must be completely responsible and submissive to the elders of the local congregation.

(2) I expressed my desire to be more approachable and for them to feel a greater freedom to challenge me as I have challenged them and for all of us to be more open to different points of view, without allowing any differences to affect our relationships with one another.

(3) Aware that some have perceived a spiritual arrogance, exclusiveness, or elitism among us, I urged that genuine humility be characteristic of our lives and that we give greater diligence to admitting our wrongs, our failures, and mistakes. I urged greater dialogue with every segment of our brotherhood and a renewed effort to bring about reconciliation wherever disunity exists.

This was followed by a section in which Chuck stated twenty things that he believes and twenty-eight things that he does not believe. Most notable in the latter list would be these two statements:

(1) [I do not believe] that any hierarchy should exist in the church other than the spiritual leadership set forth in the scriptures and (2) [I do not believe] that baptism should be withheld from penitent believers until human demands or standards are satisfied.

He continued by holding up the good that has been accomplished at the Crossroads Church and in those churches staffed by Crossroads-trained campus ministers. He ended with this plea:

We beg the entire brotherhood of churches of Christ to open wide your hearts to help us. Help us to overcome our imperfections. We need you and we believe that we have much to offer as well. We desire to work together in the spirit of Christ to accomplish his mission and purpose for our lives and his church on this earth. We want the world to know that we are his disciples by our love for one another. Public condemnation of other Christians and congregations is totally out of place...The great need at this time in our brotherhood is to heal the wounds that exist, restore the kind of unity for which Christ prayed and to love one another fervently, for love never fails.

While I was fully on board with the new wave of ministry and found it to fit with my own deepest convictions, I had not lost sight of the need for reaching out to other brothers. I am sure Chuck's letter encouraged me to think even more that way. At the end of the Boston conference, I joined Mark Mancini, converted and trained by Kip in Illinois, and the campus minister in Columbia, Missouri, in inviting the group of campus ministers to Missouri in 1982. The event would be hosted by the church in Columbia, but Mark and I would co-direct it. The vote went to us (it was probably uncontested), and we began to prepare for the event.

The next year Sheila and I met several times with Mark and Connie

Mancini to plan for the 1982 NCMS. It was my desire to make a concerted effort to include various segments of the Churches of Christ and change the view that this movement had no room for the thinking of others. Mark, who I assumed was in regular touch with his mentor, Kip, was agreeable to this approach as were the elders of the church in Columbia. In retrospect, I would guess that both Mark and Kip had been influenced by Chuck's appeal for all churches to reach out to each other. It was a joy to work together with the Mancinis.

The program we put together was under the theme "What the Spirit Says to the Churches," and the main speakers included Bill Smith, from the White's Ferry Road Church in Louisiana; Pat Hile, a long-time missionary to Guatemala; John Morgan, one of the elders in Kirksville; Steve Gooch, a Crossroads-influenced campus minister; the late Calvin Conn, a long-time campus minister and an elder; and Dr. Tom Olbricht, who had given those memorable lectures in Albuquerque nine years earlier.

HEAR WHAT THE SPIRIT SAYS

Twenty-fifth
National Campus Ministry
Seminar
August 3 - 5, 1982 Columbia, Mo.

Under the Oversight of the
Stadium Blvd. Church of Christ
Columbia, Missouri

1982 National Campus Ministers Seminar brochure

A photo taken at the close of the week appeared in the next issue of the *Campus Journal* and shows Sam Laing in the middle and me standing by Dr. Olbricht (see page 81). It would be the last time Dr. Olbricht and I would see each until I discovered twenty-two years later that we lived only an hour from one another in New England. The renewal of that relationship has been a happy one indeed.

At the conclusion of the Columbia seminar, I honestly believed God had answered our prayers, that we had turned a corner, and that unity was a real possibility. I would write in the *Campus Journal* that this week was so encouraging to me "because I saw many who decided to stop putting labels on each other and work for understanding." I went on to say, "It was encouraging because I sensed that people from all backgrounds and training were there to learn from one another. It was encouraging because the result was a beautiful unity."

Again, I am sure others will have different memories, but it seemed to me that we had come a long way in five years from that difficult week in Lubbock.

When the selection of the next seminar was made at the close of the week, the invitation of the Northwest Church in Seattle, Washington, was accepted. In March 2004 Tom Olbricht pointed me to a Web site promoting the NCMS for that year. I had not realized that those in the Churches of Christ had con-

Fall 1982 *Campus Journal* Cover

Editorial in Fall 1982 *Campus Journal*

1982 National Campus Ministers Seminar
Columbia, Missouri

Pictured are about half of those who attended the seminar in Columbia, Missouri. Many current leaders are recognizable. A picture was taken of the other side of the auditorium, but the quality was too poor to reproduce. Bruce Williams and Sam Laing can be seen in the center. Tom Olbricht and I are to the far right.

tinued that meeting. I found that this site contained a list of the places where all of the seminars had been held from 1959 to the present with some annotations. It has this note about the plan to have the 1983 seminar in Seattle: "The Seattle seminar broke the string of seminars since 1979 dominated by Crossroads/Boston."

To be accurate, here is the list of the eight seminars from 1976 to 1984:

1976 – Crossroads in Gainesville, Florida
1977 – Broadway in Lubbock, Texas
1978 – Harding College in Searcy, Arkansas
1979 – University of Colorado in Boulder, Colorado
1980 – L.S.U. in Baton Rouge, Louisiana
1981 – Boston, Massachusetts
1982 – Columbia, Missouri
1983 – Northwest Church in Seattle, Washington

Out of eight years, the seminar went to three locations led by Crossroads-trained ministers, to three places with no-Crossroads influence and to two others led by those of us (Mike Fontenot and me) who were not Crossroads-trained but where certainly supportive of that direction for campus ministry. However, it is an accurate observation to say those related to the Crossroads ministry had become the majority at these meetings and could easily determine where the locations for the seminars would be.

The same note on that 2004 NCMS Web page goes on to say: "Mike Buckley reports, 'They [Boston folks] allowed us [Seattle] to host it because we had a lot of baptisms the previous year. Some of the speakers were criticized by Boston folks, however, because they had not baptized a high enough quota of people.'" I am sure that was Mike's perspective. My memory of the selection of Seattle is quite different. When I read his statement, however, I realized regardless of what we remember, that after twenty years there was still a wound here that needed to be healed, and I began to pray that I might play some role in seeing that healing take place.

The school year 1982–83 is memorable for me for several reasons. In January '83 the "no fly" boy would take the longest train ride of his life (nearly 2,000 miles). After boarding a train on a frigid and snowy night just outside of Kirksville at the Amtrak station in the little burg of LaPlata, I would arrive in Los Angeles twenty-four hours later, after a spectacular ride through Colorado, New Mexico and Arizona. I was able to sleep all night as the train carried us across the not-so-spectacular landscape of Kansas (apologies to my friends who live there).

Once in Los Angeles I had a few hours before boarding a train for San

Diego. I rented a car for a drive out to Malibu to get a look at Pepperdine University. I still wonder to this day how anyone gets any studying there with that stunning view of the ocean.

My train trip down the coast to San Diego was beautiful with the tracks running almost on the beach at times. I was coming to San Diego for a conference being sponsored by the Poway Church, being led by a Crossroads trained minister, Andy Lindo. Andy's wife, Rita, had been one of the three Gainesville students I had first met in Abilene in '74, and I had seen the Lindos through the years. Andy had asked me to come and speak at their conference which was to focus on the Book of Ezekiel.

San Diego, 1983, with Gordon Ferguson and Jerry Jones at Southern California Christian Conference. Poor quality picture but one that brings a special memory.

As you probably have seen by now, the Lord always provided me with interesting roommates for these events, and this time the selection would be even more significant. Jerry Jones, whom I had already met, was on the program, but Gordon Ferguson and I met there for the first time. We would lie awake talking and dreaming until almost 4:00 one morning. To paraphrase Humphrey Bogart in *Casablanca*, it was the beginning of a beautiful friendship. Four years later, the Joneses and Fergusons would both move to Boston and spend sixteen years together enjoying and benefiting from a special relationship—a real gift from God.

At that conference I was asked to speak on the sovereignty of God from the book of Ezekiel. My study for the message led me to say, "God can do anything he wants, any way he wants to do it, with anybody with whom he wants to do it, any time he wants." I believe this and stand in awe of this truth, but I am still seeking to understand all it means and all the ways it needs to affect our thinking.

Once back in Missouri, I began to prepare for another speaking engagement at the Midwest Evangelism Seminar in Chicago. There Jerry Jones did two messages on "Jesus, the Discipler," and I did two on "Timothy, the Disciple." Within a few weeks I was hopping the train again, this time to Ft. Collins, Colorado, where Ronnie Worsham and Mike Rock were leading the campus ministry. I was beginning to get used to those beautiful spots in Colorado.

I describe these different speaking engagements for one important reason.

While I was going here and there and getting lots of encouragement in other places, the ministry back home had slowed down considerably. I don't believe we were a statistics-driven group. I had never been trained to think that way, although I would not deny that eight or nine years of tracking baptisms in the campus ministry churches had some effect. However, it was evident to me that the church was not as healthy as it once was and that was certainly being reflected in the smaller number of people being reached.

More than that, I felt I was not personally the example that I needed to be on a number of fronts, and so when I returned from Colorado, I made a decision unlike any I had ever made, and that was not to accept any speaking engagements for the next year, in order that I might focus on my own life, local ministry and heart. Though Sheila had frequently spoken at women's events and for women's classes at seminars, she had come to this same conclusion in her spiritual life.

In August '83 when the NCMS was held in Seattle, others from our ministry attended, but the rail connections to Seattle were convoluted, and the thought of another cross-country train trip was a bit too much. While I was not there and don't remember what was reported to me about it by others that went from our staff, Gordon Ferguson, who lived in Tacoma at the time, was asked to be the close-out speaker. When I asked him to give me his recollections of the event, he spoke of the tension I had become accustomed to between the two groups that were represented and how Milton Jones, the leader in Seattle, was working to keep unity. It was Gordon's observation that Milton was closer philosophically to the Crossroads ministries but closer relationally to the men who had roots in the Bible chair ministries. Of course, I could remember some of those early years when that was my same position.

After one message by a well-known Churches of Christ leader that Gordon felt was aimed squarely at the Crossroads-trained folks, Gordon remembers how he tried to close out the meeting with a message from 1 Corinthians with words he hoped would help unify the group. Gordon recalls, "At the end, a number from both sides expressed appreciation for the thoughts and the challenges, but it didn't go far afterwards."

In July before the seminar, I had submitted to the board my resignation as editor of the *Campus Journal*. I was increasingly involved in ministry not directly focused on the campus and saw in Milton Jones one who was in a better position to fill this role. I, too, had observed what Gordon described about Milton and felt he stood the best chance of keeping the different elements among campus ministry united. The CJ board was predominantly composed of non-Crossroads men, and the board, as I recall, quickly approved the selection of Milton. I edited the Fall '83 issue after the seminar and wrote my final editorial.

I reminded readers of what amazing things had happened in just twelve years:

> Who would have thought in 1972 that the National Campus Ministers Seminar would be held in Boulder, Colorado, in Boston, Massachusetts, and in Seattle, Washington, because of the great works going on in those places?

I sought to end my tenure on an irenic note. I listed three groups that we needed to appreciate:[2]

(1) *Those who gave stability and credibility to campus ministry.* I mentioned men like Stephen Eckstein, John Wilson and Kenneth Reid, all men who were vitally involved in this work well before guys like me came on the scene. I wrote,

> These men did not use the campus ministry as a stepping stone to some more glamorous positions, but spent many years in campus ministry because they believed that working with students would make a great difference in the church's future... Without [the] stability [they provided] campus ministry would not have been around long enough to outgrow some of its weaknesses.

(2) *Those who brought a change of emphasis to campus ministry.* Here I specifically mentioned Chuck Lucas and the Crossroads ministry. I first described the fortress mentality that was in many campus ministries in the earlier days, and then added,

> Our brother Chuck Lucas will tell you today that he made some mistakes in trying to penetrate all this and convince us that faithfulness to Christ meant we needed to make changes in our emphasis, but I, for one, am grateful that he persisted in those efforts.

I described the great number of people that had been reached and the great cities that now had thriving churches. I ended with this thought:

> There have been, according to some reports, abuses that have taken place in the new wave of campus ministry, but I remain a strong believer that there has been far more that has been Biblical, balanced and much needed.

(3) *Those who have lifted up our eyes and helped to see the tremendous opportunity that we have to export what we have in Christ to other nations via the cam-*

---

2. Looking back it is easy for me to see now that I should have paid tribute to those who started Campus Evangelism (CE) and planned a number of seminars that gave campus ministry a new thrust.

pus ministry. I quoted first from the final editorial John Wilson wrote when he stepped down as *CJ* editor in 1975. These were his words:

> Now I hope to see the ministry become international. I believe we are on the verge of developing an approach to campus work which will work anywhere in the world. We can begin to dream about a movement among students that will result in establishing the church where it has never been or where its growth has been painfully slow.

I then pointed out that these things, eight years later, were becoming a reality and mentioned the names of Kip McKean, Dave Valiente and Mike Fontenot. I added these words which today give me chills:

> If Milton Jones serves as editor for this publication for ten years and then writes his farewell editorial, he will probably write about the ministries in London, Sydney, Tokyo, Paris, Munich, Lagos, Bombay, and perhaps Moscow and Peking.

At the time I wrote this in 1984, most of those cities had been targeted by the Boston Church. But I was stretching my vision to think of Moscow and Peking (now we say Beijing). Within ten years there would be church plantings from Boston or Boston plantings in all those cities except Beijing. The planting to Moscow that would grow to thousands of followers throughout the old Soviet Union would astonishingly happen in less than ten years—in 1991! By 1994 there would be a thriving church in Hong Kong, which would soon be absorbed into mainland China, making the outreach to Beijing possible.

I ended that final editorial with an affirmation of the great potential of campus ministry and an appeal for unity: "Jesus didn't pray for the unity of believers on the night before he died," I wrote, "because he couldn't think of anything else to pray for. Unity is crucial."

Though I was leaving the *Campus Journal*, I would stay interested in campus ministry and was invited in August '84 to do the opening message at the NCMS to be held in another Columbia (this time the South Carolina capital). The ministry there was led by Randy McKean, and the elders were Bill Hooper (now an elder in Dallas) and the late Calvin Conn, a long-time friend. This was one of the first speaking invitations I remember accepting after my decision in the spring of '83 to devote myself to my local ministry.

I was asked to speak on the topic of "Restoration and Campus Ministry," and I devoted a good portion of my message to the idea that biblical Christianity is non-sectarian. I was beginning to explore the implications of that idea and gave some examples of where my thinking was leading me. Others would later tell me that they had trouble reconciling that message with my decision three years later to go to Boston. That is a question I will come back to later.

The most memorable speech of the seminar was likely one given by James Lloyd of London in which he challenged the materialism of American Christians. This is a message we continually need to hear.

It is obvious that God has put spiritual leaders in place for some very important reasons. He has given them serious and often sobering responsibilities. They will have to give him an account of how they led those under their charge. But what is clear from these texts is that the basic attitude of every disciple toward leadership is to be a positive and supportive one. That does not mean you should never ask questions or give input; it does mean there is no place in the kingdom for the critical spirit who picks at actions, second-guesses decisions, or has a rebellious attitude.

–From *Letters to New Disciples*, Chapter Ten, "Working with Leaders"

11

From 'Bama to Boston

After the Columbia seminar, Sheila and I drove to Birmingham, Alabama, to "scout out the land," as we had already made plans to leave Missouri the next summer and plant a new multiracial church in our home state, and the former symbol of segregation, with the help of people from several ministries. In June 1985 our family said our good-byes to many special friends in Kirksville, especially Lanny and Beth Morley and Glenn and Andrea Browning, who had been such great supports to us and with whom we had spent five encouraging years. As always, there had been some struggles, but we were very grateful for the love and partnership that we had found there.

We arrived in Birmingham and assembled our team of twenty-four Christians. As God would have it, twelve were white and twelve were African-American—in a city where finding such a group on a Sunday morning is still most unusual. My co-leader for this planting was John Causey, who had been the first person baptized in the Indiana State ministry started by my friend Greg Jackson.

In August of that year the NCMS was held in New York City. My health was not so good and the move had been hard. I didn't make the trip, but others from our ministry did. I can recall no details that were reported to me about the event. I would later learn that those who did not feel a kinship with Boston had started an alternate seminar. According to the campus ministry seminar Web site I referred to earlier, the other meeting that year was held in Arlington, Texas.

In 1986 the NCMS name was changed to the International Campus Ministers Seminar and was held in San Francisco where Tom Brown was then leading. In the midst of health and emotional challenges, and with the event a world away for one who was not flying, I did not attend. It was eighteen years later in 2004 that I first became aware of what a painful event that was for all who had not fully thrown their support behind the Boston approach.

To help you understand that event in 1986, let me describe some information I only gained recently. In February of 2004 reconciliation talks were held at Abilene Christian University between leaders from the "mainline" Churches of Christ and leaders from the International Churches of Christ.

After that meeting Dr. Jack Reese of Abilene and Gregg Marutzky, who was at the time the lead evangelist for the ICOC congregation in Dallas, contacted me about attending a meeting in Morgantown, West Virginia, with a few campus ministers from Churches of Christ who had felt alienated from our movement. Milton Jones was to be one of those men, and I was eager to see him. It was at that meeting that I heard from Milton and Mike Buckley about their experience at the 1986 seminar. Though Tom was hosting it, Kip seemed to these brothers to be in charge.

Milton remembers well that the theme of the seminar was "Doulos and Diakonoi: Servanthood." Milton and Mike both described how encouraged they were on the first day when they heard speeches by Tom Brown and Sam Laing that emphasized the idea of servant leadership. On the second day of the event Kip spoke, and as they heard it, basically said, "All those who are faithful and want to evangelize the world must align with Boston." In Milton's mind this was the end. Milton remembers getting up and leaving in the middle of the speech with several others, feeling that what he was hearing was so far from the gospel.

Milton felt betrayed. He was one of the few people in the mainstream of the Churches of Christ still standing up for our movement. This had made him the object of much suspicion and criticism among those churches, and now he felt he was being pushed out of fellowship with our group. Later that year Milton would hear that there was a meeting of Boston leaders where plans were made to come to Seattle and "take captive" members of the Northwest Church. The goal was to make them part of a new Seattle Church of Christ.

Eventually Milton felt he lost everything. He felt that Boston took his key leaders, including Preston and Sandie Shepherd. Milton had wanted to be the one who would help us all stay together, and now he felt it had all fallen apart. He describes himself as going through a complete break down that lasted for several months. I consider Milton a man of great faith and integrity, and it grieves me to know the way he was treated. Gregg Marutzky, Sheila and I agonized as we heard Milton recount some of these memories. Gregg apologized with tears. Had I been aware of what Milton was going through in 1986, I would hope that I would have spoken up, but then while one Jones was going through a painful August in Seattle, the one in Alabama was in maybe the toughest shape of his life for entirely different reasons.

After fifteen months in Birmingham several factors led to a decision for our family to move to Huntsville, Alabama. By this time, I was consistently dealing with depression which had reoccurred in my last two years in Missouri. I finally sought some medical help, but it brought little relief.

Consistently being in a dark place hardly made me fit for leading this church planting. Thinking about my failure only took me in deeper. In those days, however, this was not something which someone in a church leadership position dared talk openly about. (Since depression became a recurring issue in my life, I have added an appendix giving my thoughts on it. This is reprinted from the book, *A Man in All Seasons, Volume One,* and can be found in Appendix Ten.) In addition to my problems, our oldest daughter was the only teen in the Birmingham congregation and needed relationships.

Finally I was open with the leadership of the Central Church in Huntsville, where the lead evangelist was Thom Bogle, a Crossroads-trained minister. Thom and the elders encouraged us to join their staff, and I will always be grateful for their support as we went through a tough time. The church in Huntsville had been one of the main supporters of the Birmingham planting, and they helped find someone to replace us. They would find that help in an unexpected place. You know the world has changed when the church in London sends someone to provide leadership in Alabama.

During this time I was beginning to hear of more and more leaders particularly from Crossroads-related churches who were moving to Boston to receive training so they could be sent out on some of the many plantings that the Boston Church had scheduled. This was not something I ever thought I could do. Many of the questions that I had once had about Crossroads now surfaced again in new and more serious forms in regard to Boston, and I could not see myself ever fitting into what appeared to be a rather massive system that was developing there with a lot of power being located in one man.

The year in Huntsville was a better one for our family. In a role with less pressure, I began to enjoy teaching and leading again. The church in Huntsville had developed a close relationship with the church in London (thus the help from there for Birmingham, Alabama). Financial support was being given to London, and James Lloyd and Douglas Arthur were in regular communication with Thom Bogle. Different leaders from London passed through from time to time. The reports of rapid growth in England were inspiring and encouraging.

At one point, the elders and evangelists of the Huntsville church invited James Lloyd to come and spend a week with us and evaluate our ministry. The result was a recommendation that Thom Bogle move to Boston. From a cynical point of view that likely will seem like some sort of a Boston power play, but there were actually solid reasons for this decision.

In August 1987 a leadership conference was held in Atlanta that basically replaced the Campus Ministers Seminar among the Boston-related churches.

The conference was hosted by the Atlanta church where Sam Laing was by this time the evangelist, but it was primarily directed by the leadership from Boston. It was made even more clear at this meeting that Boston was calling other churches to more formally connect with them, and it also seemed more clear that those who did not, would not have any real support or fellowship from Boston.

Burned by some attempts to work within existing churches, Boston had decided to be a completely separate movement without connection to others. At best, this was a mistake. At worst, it was a sin. In either case it led to a form of sectarianism and this is now seen clearly by most who remained with the movement.

With the Bogles having moved to Boston, the church in Huntsville was trying to make a decision about a lead evangelist. Boston communicated that they were willing to send someone in, and a name was actually given to us. Douglas and Joyce Arthur (not the suggested couple) came from London and spent a week with the elders and staff talking through what a move in this direction might mean. The elders wrestled with this decision, eventually concluding not to have a Boston-trained leader come. With the Bogles gone, the remaining staff of four couples had a decision to make. As I recall, the elders wanted us all to stay. I was offered the role of lead evangelist. If Sheila and I wanted to go to Boston, we were told by the church there that support would be available for us.

The decision was not an easy one for us, or I should say for me. I did not feel ready to be the lead evangelist in Huntsville, believing that the elders were embarking on a lonely road and were being prideful to think they could lead the ministry without outside help and input. (At this point I can understand more about the concerns they had about the control that Boston would exercise.) At the same time I also was not sure that I could be in Boston with the questions and fears that I had.

I felt considerable angst (something I can do "well"), wrestled in prayer, and marvel to this day at what happened next. One of the elders communicated with us that Dr. George Gurganus and his wife, Irene, were going to come through Huntsville the next weekend, and George had been asked to preach for the church. I had first met George in Abilene in 1974 at the Missions Seminar and had been with him several other times. I knew how respected he was throughout the country. I had never known he was from Alabama but learned that he was in the state to visit family before heading back to Boston. He and Irene had visited the Boston Church, seen the vision for world missions and shocked a lot of people by leaving their retirement home in the Missouri Ozarks and moving to be with the Boston Church.

Sheila and I and the Huntsville elders and wives spent an evening with the Gurganuses hearing about their experience in Boston. They had decided to move there and prepare to go back to Tokyo with the team the church would send out. While George could not relieve me of every concern I had, the many positive experiences he reported gave me reassurance not only that the Boston Church had great plans for world evangelism but that the situation there was one in which I could work.

Before saying we would move to Boston, however, I wanted to check out one other possibility and that was going to the Atlanta church which had cast its lot with Boston. In Atlanta we would not be so far from my parents for whom I am the only child. I talked it over with Boston elder Al Baird and shared with him a desire to be in a place where my oldest daughter would get her needs met. He told me that would be Boston, as it would be several years before Atlanta had a strong teen ministry. That settled the issue for us.

It was now clear that the entire staff in Huntsville would be leaving to go to other discipling ministries (as the movement churches were being called by this time). No one had confidence that we could continue to fulfill our ministries by staying in a church that was going to become something of an island. Brad and Lori Bynum decided on London. Alan and Deedee Allard, Chicago. The two singles leading our teen ministry were going to Boston, as were we.

A very difficult open meeting was held with the church as we explained the events of the previous few weeks and the reasons for our decisions. During that meeting I felt my left leg grow numb. It would remain in this condition for six weeks, well after we moved. This was the beginning of a series of MS attacks.

It was difficult for us to leave Huntsville because though we had come to a different conclusion from the elders and their wives, we had grown close to them and had come to love them very much. And we certainly felt their love for us.

I know that for some who had known us through the years, our decision was an enigma. How could someone who in 1984 gave a passionate speech about the dangers of sectarianism, definitively make a move in 1987 to unite with a movement that in the minds of many people took sectarianism to a whole new level? To try to answer that question, hopefully will expose more than just one couple's life choices, but will shed some light on the history of two movements.

The first answer has to do with great disappointment that I and others experienced with the mainline Churches of Christ. I read recently on a Web posting, someone's observation, which I unfortunately did not document, that "nominalism" and lukewarmness in the mainline church created the ICOC. In this statement I believe there is a world of truth. Many of us did read the Bible on our own in the '60s and '70s, and we did find there, in Phillip Yancey's words, "a Jesus we never knew." We found a Jesus who issued a radical call to discipleship. We found a Jesus who was revolutionary. We found a Jesus who intended for his gospel to be preached around the world and who expected those of us who followed him to take it there, whatever it might cost us. In a world of political revolutionaries, we found a man to follow whose purpose was higher and whose impact would last far longer, but whose call was radical and total.

But then when this Jesus we had never heard about in our traditional churches was proclaimed, the reaction, in our view, was as negative as it was swift. The Jesus we never knew was a Jesus that most people did not want to know. Most church members were involved in pursuing the American dream and were happy with the comfortable Christianity that allowed them to work Jesus in around the edges of their lives. It was an approach to Christ that allowed people to hold on to their pride, their materialism and their racism.

Particularly, in Churches of Christ, the majority had become accustomed to some negative reactions from the world around them, thinking as they did, that they were the only Christians and the only religious people headed for heaven. However, it seemed most were content with a commitment to fairly external things that they believed marked them as a New Testament church. Talk of the radical changes that Jesus called for in people's lives made a large number of people more than a little uncomfortable.

In the Crossroads, and eventually the Boston, Movement some of us found the one place we could go where Jesus' high call was held out as "the normal Christian life," to use the language of Watchman Nee. In this movement the standard—the norm—was a high degree of commitment. In the Crossroads Movement, the call had been for all to make Jesus Lord. In the Boston Movement the message was for every member of the church to be a disciple, looking at all that Jesus said was involved in that term.

Our decision to align ourselves with such a movement did mean separation from other believers. That seemed inevitable and a fulfillment of Jesus' promise that a radical commitment to him would alienate us from some of our closest relationships. As painful as it was, it seemed that such separation was part of the cost of discipleship that Bonhoeffer's book had called me to consider twenty years earlier. Whatever sins and mistakes would later be revealed in the Boston Movement and the International Churches of Christ, calling people to a radical commitment to Jesus was not one of them.

In August 1987, I traveled by train from Atlanta to Boston to attend the World Missions Seminar. Sheila had flown on ahead of me to be with her sister, Emily, who along with husband, John Bringardner, had just relocated to Boston from Tallahassee. I can still remember a seven-word phrase I wrote on my legal pad while watching the North Carolina countryside pass by: "The grace of God and hard-line discipleship." I was convinced that both were vital, and on that train ride I remember thinking it seemed the only place where I could preach and practice both was in the churches connected with Boston. Whether or not that was true is an open question, but at that point I was coming to the conclusion that I needed to be with them to be faithful to both issues.

Now, almost twenty years later, I still wrestle with that matter. As I write this, a number of conversations have taken place between those of us in the International Churches of Christ and those in the mainline Churches of Christ (as well as Independent Christian Churches—also out of the Restoration Movement). These have been healthy and needed. I am certainly open to dialogue with many other groups as well. I am sure those outside our churches have some reservations as they talk with us. I have my own concerns as we open these conversations. The one thing I probably fear the most is that increased connections with those in other fellowships may lead us back to that comfortable Christianity that is so at odds with the Jesus of the New Testament.

This is not to say that there were not Christians in these churches who loved the lost and longed to see an effective outreach to their communities and to the world. But, in my experience, these Christians were in the minority, and what I had not personally seen was a group of elders and leaders who were boldly leading their church beyond the borders of the status quo.

From the observations and concerns that I currently read in the *Christian Chronicle* and other mainline publications, I see that what we sought so earnestly to get away from is still far too prevalent in the churches we left. How that will be resolved is a matter of much prayer for me. I do know, however, that a commitment to the high standard of discipleship was one of the prime reasons that we threw our lot with Boston in the first place. That our decision placed us in a group that was increasingly viewed as sectarian and elitist was troubling to me, but at the time seemed to me to be an unavoidable part of the cost of serious commitment to Jesus.

The second reason I believe we united with the Boston Church was because of the vision and plan they had for world evangelism. I also believe that is the reason some of us remained in denial when things that we knew in our gut were not right began to happen. We didn't know anywhere else where a plan to reach the world was working. Though we had seen growth in our ministries in the places we had been, I still had a strong sense that the grace of God needed to go outside our American culture and touch the world. I had been associated with missionaries in Churches of Christ for many years. I knew how many men and women there were who had put their lives on the line to take the gospel other places, but the results, it seemed, were always so meager.

By the time we made our decision to move to Boston, the church there had already planted a church in London that was experiencing growth like we had never heard of in a foreign planting. Churches had also been planted in Paris, Bombay, Hong Kong, Tokyo and Johannesburg. Plans were laid for plantings in dozens of other major cities around the world.

The vision John Wilson had written about in his last *Campus Journal* editorial ("Now I hope to see the ministry become international") and the conviction I had sitting in the Campus Ministers Seminar in Boulder in 1979 ("We really will go to all the world."), seemed to be coming to fruition. Steve Johnson and Sherwin Macintosh wrote a musical in 1987 based on the book of Acts with the title *UpsideDown*.[1] One of the scenes has Gamaliel singing "You Might Be Fighting God." That was the last thing I wanted to be doing. If God was moving to get the gospel out to the world and if he was using the Boston Church, I wanted to be part of it.

Were there things that concerned me? Sure, primarily some things about how Kip was leading. But I remember lying in bed as a guest in the Bringardners' house in Andover, Massachusetts, after the 1987 World Missions Seminar and thinking that had I been among the first disciples of Jesus, I am sure there would have been things about *his* approach that would have concerned me as well.

After events of 2002–2003, that I will describe in Chapter Thirteen, forced the whole movement into a time of reassessment, we often emphasized the mistakes and abuses that developed. However, an experience I had just a few weeks before writing the first draft of this chapter while still living in Boston put some things in perspective for me. Four evangelists from our European churches came to Boston to talk with us about the condition of our mission efforts in Europe and what plans we could make for strengthening those works in a new day when the old ICOC structure was no longer in place. A team of leaders from Boston met with them for two days, and then the group

---

1. One of the remarkable elements of the Boston Movement was the production of such quality musicals and dramatic presentations. DVDs and CDs of *UpsideDown* still sell consistently through DPI and still move and inspire many hearts.

met with all the elders, several evangelists and some members of the Boston Church board.

As I listened to these four men share their hearts for Europe and their gratitude for the Boston Church, I was deeply moved. All four men had been led to Christ in our movement and had been raised and trained to be evangelists. Their maturity, their wisdom, their love and their commitment were evident to all of us. In spite of our mistakes, there are now twenty-eight churches in twenty-six European countries where men and women like these have seen their need for Jesus in the midst of a culture where an empty, agnostic way of life is handed down from generation to generation.

I have names and email addresses for Christians in Paris, Berlin, Geneva, Bucharest, Budapest, Zagreb, Warsaw, Prague and twenty other cities. While in Boston I prayed each day for a different European church and sent them notes of encouragement. Again, I would say, whatever the mistakes have been in the International Churches of Christ, having a passion for world evangelism has not been one of them.

That God has now moved us to open dialogue with others is of great encouragement to me. It is something I have welcomed and embraced. Somewhere along the line we began to identify the kingdom of God with this movement. That was never something I believed, but I certainly became part of a church culture where it was the assumption. That was our mistake—and a huge one—but one we have acknowledged and can correct. For any one group to teach or even to subtly send the message that it has a corner on God's grace or God's truth is as foolish as it is wrong-headed. May God forgive any of us who taught or tolerated that idea.

However, my prayer is that the two things that I believe led many of us to unite in what would become the ICOC, would still be given the highest priority as we talk and move forward. (1) God's grace is indisputably radical and the response to it must be equally radical. "Love so amazing, so divine, demands my soul, my life, my all." (2) This grace must go to all nations, and we must be committed to taking it there.

If you need an example of perseverance, you need look no further than Jesus. At some point, you will be severely tested. It may seem that all the demons of hell have been marshaled to try and pull you out of the kingdom. It may seem the enemy is employing a full-court press. But like great heroes of the faith who have gone before you, you can make it. You can fix your eyes on Jesus and say "I will never quit." The man or woman who emerges on the other side of those trials and battles will be a wiser and spiritually richer person. Never quit.

–From *Letters to New Disciples*, Chapter Seventeen, "Hitting the Lows"

12

The Boston Years

Our move to Boston in October '87 was our fourth in three years. This was not exactly the way we thought it should be done with children in school. There would be two more moves in the next three years, within the Boston area, making it six moves in six years. I know it was tough on our girls. All three of them went to a different school every year for a five year period. These were times when we felt like we were living out a bit of Hebrews 11:38. What does it say? "They wandered in deserts and mountains, and in caves and holes in the ground." Well, that wasn't exactly our situation, but it felt like it at times to soft Americans.

There will probably never be another ministry situation like the one we found ourselves in when we got to New England. The Boston Church staff meeting was a veritable "who's who" from the campus ministry seminars. It seemed that most everyone I had known from the Crossroads Movement was now there.

I would later tell people that God brought me to Boston maybe the only way I would have come—on a stretcher. I had my doubts and concerns, but I also had some serious needs. However, once I was there, I would ask God more than a few times why this was the right place. My health was not good. My legs had grown more problematic. My battles with fatigue were becoming more disruptive. My confidence which had been growing in Huntsville was now low as I compared myself to all the younger, high energy and ambitious leaders that had poured into Boston. Depression had returned. With all this going on in my life, I found the pace of the ministry dizzying.

The high-performance atmosphere of the Boston Church staff would have seemed to make it a most unsuitable place for someone like me. And, yet, God provided, as is his nature to do. In the midst of a frenetic ministry pace that looked like it might crush me, he provided angels of mercy in the forms of Wyndham Shaw, J.P. Tynes, Gordon Ferguson and Cecil Wooten. Sheila, of course, was always there through thick and thin. All of them in different ways were faithful friends who saw me at my lowest but helped me remember God's faithfulness and my chosenness.

My Approach in This Chapter

In describing the years we have spent in Boston I will not try to detail every year as I have with the events leading up to our union with the Boston Movement. Instead I want to share some broad perspectives about both our personal experience and the experience of the church. I have told several people that in my mind each year from 1969 to 1987 had its own unique identity, so much so that someone could pick any year during that span, and I could quickly tell of events and people that had impact on me and the movement. However, the eighteen years in Boston are all very blended in my mind, which is the primary reason this chapter will be different from the others.

Some of my early readers of this material wished for more details about the Boston years. I certainly understand that. However, not only is this book long enough already, but I feel that others will be able to share more informed perspectives on such details, and I hope that in due time they will do that.

Boston and Crossroads

Those who have tried to follow the movement's development carefully will surely have questions about what happened to the relationship between the Boston Church and the Crossroads Church and Crossroads Movement that spawned it. While I must leave any detailed discussion of this to others much more intimately involved in the dynamics between the two churches, I will make some observations.

I know that as Kip's influence and that of the Boston Church grew in the early '80s, Chuck's role as a mentor for Kip seemed to be diminishing. The center of the movement was no longer Crossroads but Boston. Chuck and many who were peers of Kip at the University of Florida began to feel their efforts were being devalued (much as those campus ministers felt back in 1973; see Chapter Four). Kip saw himself as the real reformer, and for him the history of the movement started as he came to Boston and met with the famous "thirty would-be disciples" in a Concord living room. He would emphasize this idea repeatedly in speeches on almost any topic.

When Chuck was asked to resign by the Crossroads elders in 1985, this seemed to validate Kip's thinking and his revisionist history. In comments drawn from an interview with Kip, Foster Stanback implies that Chuck's resignation led many Crossroads-trained ministers who might have had concerns about Kip, to give those up and seek direction from Boston.[1]

---

1. C. Foster Stanback, *Into All Nations: A History of the International Churches of Christ* (Houston: Illumination Publications International, 2005), 43. This book is a useful resource in understanding the Boston Movement, but I must tell the author I was never the campus minister in Baton Rouge, Louisiana. That was my friend, Mike Fontenot—a true Cajun and Bayou Bengal.

With Chuck's departure from Gainesville, the church there gradually began to experience decline, certainly in no small part due to the fact that a good number from there moved to Boston or Boston-related ministries. Eventually the Crossroads Church would disassociate itself from Boston due largely to the view of church government being espoused by Kip and supported by others. It would finally reconcile completely with the Churches of Christ.

Repentance and Baptism

After our move to Boston, I was first linked in a discipling relationship with my old friend Wyndham Shaw, who had moved there from Charlotte several months before we did. He was understanding, supportive and encouraging. In the Boston ministry everyone who came in had a talk with an existing staff person regarding their conversion and their commitment. My talk was with Wyndham.

Since I was baptized at a young age in a Church of Christ congregation, I suspected that questions would be raised about the validity of that experience. Wyndham, however, just wanted to know why I felt good about it, and when I shared with him the thinking I had done through the years, he accepted that and said that if I was at peace, then he could be. Neither he nor anyone else ever brought the matter up again. That I suspect will be a surprise to some people who knew of others who had been grilled pretty hard about their baptism.

Some weeks later Wyndham and I were studying the Bible with a non-Christian named Dave. I remember later being concerned that the study we had done might lead Dave to think that he had to do a list of things in order to become a disciple. I was eager to get back with him and let him know that the key issue was his having a repentant heart, not a list of accomplishments or even changes. As soon as I had that thought, another followed it, quite unexpectedly. "But, Tom," I thought, "did you really have a repentant heart at the time of your baptism twenty-eight years ago?"

Through the years I had studied with and baptized many people, and as I did, I had often thought through and evaluated my own experience, feeling that I had done what I did with the faith that I had, and would have been unfaithful to God at that time if I had not confessed my faith and been baptized. This was the first time, amazingly, I had ever seen it from this perspective. I took time to pray, read Scripture, and consider what I needed to do. Eventually I got back with Wyndham to let him know that I believed I needed to be immersed *now with the right heart*. He assured me the decision was mine.

Looking back, I believe I first clearly saw my need for repentance with some depth of understanding in 1967. I saw my sin and the cross far more clearly in that "conversion" in 1977, and the godly sorrow I experienced then led to genuine repentance. From today's perspective it seems that I might have considered being immersed again at either one of those points, but then in those days I don't remember that even being a consideration. Certainly no one ever suggested I consider it.

In 1987, I was convinced that I had been living with a deeply repentant heart for at least ten years if not more. However, I felt the need to be baptized knowing clearly that my heart was repentant. It was not a normal conversion experience like we find in the early days recorded in Acts or as some people have today. I had been living with a converted heart for a long time. But, nonetheless, entirely at my own initiative and from conviction, I was immersed in the name of the Father, the Son and the Holy Spirit on December 30, 1987.

Earlier when we were still in Huntsville, many of the women came back from a Boston event describing a women's leader who had been baptized after years in the church. Anxious to prevent a rash of "re-baptisms," I had written a paper titled "My Baptism: Was It Valid?" It cautioned against trying to have a perfect baptism and warned that there is no such thing as perfect repentance. I still believe everything I wrote was true.

After I was immersed in Boston, I know there were those who concluded that my baptism likely happened under duress from the Boston leadership, but that was far from the truth. I am sure that others will have various opinions about what I did. I only know that quite unexpectedly, I found myself confronted with something significant that I believed needed to be corrected.

Was my baptism as a junior high student an authentic experience? After years of explaining why I thought it was, I concluded in 1987 that what I did at that young age was just too far from the New Testament experience for me to feel great about it. God only knows. This much I have come to believe: *we must leave to any person who has been immersed the decision about the need for it to happen again.* We should teach and explain the Scriptures, and raise questions when our gut tells us something, but ultimately it is not my place to tell anyone "I believe you need to be baptized again." That is their decision, and theirs alone to be made before God.

But, some of you will ask, was God working in my life through all the years before 1987? I am absolutely convinced that he was. There is no way I can deny all the ways I had experienced his love, his power, his guidance and his discipline. How do I explain that? I will leave that to someone else. Who knows, maybe my earlier adolescent baptism was genuinely into Christ because I acted obediently with the faith I had.

Some will no doubt say, while you felt no pressure from Wyndham, you were in an atmosphere where people all around you were being baptized again. Are you sure you didn't do it because of that? I don't think that was true, but how well do we know ourselves? Anything is possible. Only God knows our hearts. I do know I just wanted to be faithful.

My conviction is that every person needs to be shown the heart of the gospel and needs to respond to it with faith, repentance and baptism. This is what I have taught to every person I could for the last forty years. (See Appendix Eight for my chapter on baptism from *Letters to New Disciples*.) I could never be a part of any ministry where that is not the way people are taught to respond to the good news of God's grace. It is absolutely the best when all those experiences come together in a clear and definitive way as a person leaves the world and comes into Christ.

However, it is my view that not everyone's experience will fit so neatly into the pattern we think we see in Acts 2, 8, 9 or 16 in those formative years of the early church. Mine certainly does not. In truth, Acts 2:38, Acts 8:12–17 and Acts 10:44–48 don't really represent such a neatly repeated pattern after all, and it takes a bit of theological gymnastics for us to get them to all fit a formula. Just compare them carefully.

More and more, I am convinced that God looks on the heart and that his work can't always be put in the kind of box that logicians (and some of my engineer friends) love. I came to see different matters more clearly over time and attempted to respond with humility and faith with each new understanding. I am convinced that God rewards those who diligently seek him and that my faith, flawed and faltering though it was, but working through love, brought me into God's grace as faith is wont to do.

Having described this, I will address one question that some will ask: Were there many unnecessary "re-baptisms" in the Boston Movement? As I hope my own situation illustrates, every person's circumstance is unique, and we should not judge anyone's experience because of a general pattern of abuse. That said, I do believe the answer to the question is "most likely" or "almost certainly," and I think most leaders in the ICOC fellowship would agree with that. There was a serious misinterpretation and misapplication of Matthew 28:18–19 that led people to believe that they had to have all sorts of things in place prior to baptism and focused too much on man and not enough on man's Savior. To say this another way, there was too little understanding, in my opinion, of salvation by grace through faith, but I have addressed that in another book.[2]

My confidence now is that God's grace is wide enough and deep enough to take all our faltering steps into consideration and bring us to himself as we seek him with humble hearts. If we think that the God who loved us so much and gave his Son for us while we were yet sinners, will see in us a surrendered and broken and contrite heart and, yet, fail to save us because of a technicality or an honest mistake in lining all the theological dots up just in the right way, it would seem we have missed the heart of the gospel. I have been given more training and opportunities to study the Scriptures than the average person, but even with that, I have trouble lining up all the dots. If that is true for me, would it not be even more true for the average Christian? I believe that a safe, nonjudgmental discussion about such matters is badly needed today in all wings of the Restoration Movement. I don't believe we should fear going there.[3]

Publishing Ministry

While I know that there are many who need to find healing from a variety of personal hurts that came as the leadership styles and personal discipling within our ICOC churches moved in some unhealthy directions (and I don't want for a minute to minimize the hurt they experienced), I would not be one of those people. I came to Boston as a bruised reed and dimly burning wick, and the leadership there did not snuff me out (Isaiah 42:1–3). I was physically and emotionally fragile, but through the care and encouragement of such men as Wyndham Shaw, Gordon Ferguson, J.P. Tynes, Cecil Wooten, Roger Lamb, Randy McKean and Dan Bathon and the faithful love and support of my wife, Sheila, I eventually regained a new vision for my life.

After working with various Boston-related publications for four years (including the *Boston Bulletin*, *Discipleship Magazine* and *UpsideDown* magazine), I was given the opportunity to begin a publishing ministry that would produce books and other resources for our churches. The Boston Church provided the initial funding for what would become known as Discipleship Publications International (DPI).

At the beginning of our second year of operation, Sheila was able to join me at DPI, and we worked there as a team until I had to step down for health reasons. (She, however, is still there, doing a great job keeping some wonderful things going as the managing editor.)

---

2. Thomas A. Jones, *Strong in the Grace* (Spring Hill, TN: DPI, 2004).

3. A book I believe can prove useful in this discussion, *Down in the River to Pray*, by Hicks and Taylor, is reviewed in Appendix Nine.

With a clientele composed primarily of the fast growing and multiplying churches in our movement, we experienced a remarkable ride. I had always wanted the first book I worked with to focus on the cross of Christ. It is

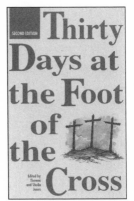

tremendously gratifying to me that the first book we published, *Thirty Days at the Foot of the Cross* (an anthology), is still one of our strong sellers fourteen years later. Beginning with that book, in just over ten years DPI would publish more than 130 titles and print more than two million volumes, plus produce a children's curriculum with pages equal to another fifty books.

The books produced by DPI were translated into more than fifteen languages, and operations similar to DPI were set up to publish and distribute our books in French, German, Spanish, Chinese, Portuguese and Japanese. Our staff at one point totaled twenty-five people.

There are two things about the DPI operation that are worthy of special note. The first is that this publishing ministry never became, in the terminology of our church culture, "a kingdom entity." There were significant funds that every church in the ICOC sent to Los Angeles for the support of various "kingdom projects"—such as the law and media department. This department included the operation of KNN, which produced regular videos for our churches. However, DPI never received any of those funds. Instead, the primary funding came from the sales of books and other resources, with the Boston Church providing help when cash flow was strained.

The second matter is related to the first. In the eight years I served as editor in chief and in my last year as senior editor, never once was any direction given from anyone in the leadership of the ICOC or the Boston Church about what we should or should not publish, and I cannot remember a single time when I received a phone call or email from any leader questioning or opposing something that we had put in print. That was true, even though books we published often challenged some of our tendencies, like too little emphasis on grace and a lack of humility and a servant spirit among leaders.

Had DPI moved its operations to Los Angeles and become a kingdom entity, that might have been different, but I appreciate the leadership we had in Boston at the time that believed it was important that DPI be able to maintain editorial independence.

From the first book that we published, *Thirty Days at the Foot of the Cross*, to one of the last that I edited, *Golden Rule Leadership*, we were given freedom to publish whatever we believed was most needed. As a result, I believe, most of what was published in ten years was not tied to some areas of emphasis that would later be repudiated or to some current agenda.

It is true that DPI published and distributed the "First Principles" studies (for evangelism) written by Kip McKean that have now been replaced or significantly revised. While we did not author these, it is true that we did not challenge some of the assumptions and implications in them.

However, in 1988 shortly after moving to Boston, Sheila and I were in the last class on "First Principles" that Kip taught there. After his class on "Discipleship," I did ask to meet with him and let him know that I could not teach the material as he had done, feeling his approach made some unwarranted and improper uses of Scripture. He asked me how I would teach it. When I explained, he encouraged me to do what I felt was best. Once DPI began, we did make some changes in that one study before publishing more copies.

Because of my role in the Boston Church, I was not in the primary leadership meetings and did not have a great deal of contact with Kip. However, in all my interactions with him I never remember a time when I was not treated with respect.

Regarding DPI, I know that there were things in some of our books that we would say differently today, but for the most part I believe we kept a solid biblical base for the things that were written and that most of the materials are quite free of language that would communicate a sectarian bias. As we have moved into a different era, the content of many of our books has made it possible for DPI to continue to have good sales of materials published years ago.

Working with DPI was one of the greatest experiences of my life, and I will always be grateful to Randy McKean and Dan Bathon who were primarily involved in making the decision to give me this opportunity. Working with writers like Douglas Jacoby, Sam and Geri Laing, Mike Taliaferro, Henry Kriete, Steve Kinnard, my very special friend Gordon Ferguson and many others was a joy. There were few weeks when phone calls or emails did not come from far-flung places telling us how the message of one of the books had changed someone's life, helped someone stay faithful to God, or given someone the encouragement that they needed for a challenge.

I have often been told that DPI also played a major role in maintaining the unity and connection of our churches. In what we called "The Daily Power Series" we produced a series of twelve books (covering subjects ranging from the cross, prayer, the church, ministry to the poor, to the promises of God). The series likely involved a hundred or more contributors from around the world. Most of these volumes resulted in sales of 15,000 to 20,000 copies, and believers in many countries read inspiring chapters from Christians from every inhabited continent with some of the books being translated into various languages.

In the wake of the many changes in our churches, DPI's survival was in real question for a time. However, Kelly Petre, who replaced me as editor in chief, led DPI through a difficult period (until the financial challenges resulted in his moving to another career). Sheila was able to remain the only fulltime staff member, and transitioned from associate editor to managing editor (and is in that role at this writing).

Korean translation of *Thirty Days at the Foot of the Cross*

Because of Kelly's and Sheila's efforts most DPI books remain available and new titles are being published on a regular basis. We remain optimistic that the work will continue, now under an independent board no longer formally connected with the Boston Church. However, our relational connection to the Boston Church remains strong, and we will never forget the support they provided to our publishing efforts.

Use of Scripture

One of my real concerns prior to moving to Boston had to do with the use of Scripture by the ministry there. To be more specific, my concerns had to do with Kip McKean's use of Scripture, for however he interpreted Scripture became the way the whole movement taught it. The only way I could remain with the Boston Church was to be able to express the problems I found in certain teachings. I did that with Kip, and I did it with others when I felt the need to do so. When I have told others that I was always listened to and often saw changes, some have shared with me that this was not their experience.

One issue that I never heard openly addressed in the Boston/ICOC movement was that of hermeneutics.[4] However, there was, as there must be, a hermeneutic at work. Scripture was interpreted particularly in the "First Principles" evangelistic Bible study series according to what I would call a very *pragmatic* hermeneutic. In other words, Scripture was interpreted, primarily

---

4. *Hermeneutics* refers to a specific theory or method of interpreting certain texts, particularly religious texts. A simplistic hermeneutic was being used in churches of my youth when the teacher would read a biblical text and then say to the class, "It means what it says and says what it means." While that may have sounded like an uncompromising commitment to the Scriptures, it was not much help when one read, "If your hand causes you to sin, cut it off" (Matthew 5:30) or "If anyone comes to me and does not hate his father and mother...he cannot be my disciple" (Luke 14:26).

by Kip, in accordance with what worked best in the ministry to accomplish the goals he believed were most important.

As an example, in the study of "The Kingdom of God" in the evangelistic series, the kingdom was seen as simply the church (an idea also found in the Churches of Christ from which we came), so the admonition to "seek first the kingdom" could be used to convince the person studying that he needed to attend all the services of the church. As I have written in *No One Like Him*, identifying the kingdom as only the church is most problematic. The same thing could be said, but even more strongly, of using John 15 ("abundantly fruitful") to say that every member of the church needed to be seeing many conversions from their personal ministry.

However, my guess is that this *pragmatic* hermeneutic was a completely unconscious thing with Kip, and not any effort to purposely misuse the Scriptures. Nonetheless, I saw this tendency leading to various doctrinal positions that became quite important in the movement.

Perhaps the most notable, at least for me, was Kip's insistence from Acts 11:26 (a non-doctrinal, historical observation) that "disciple = Christian = saved." This was one of my problems with the aforementioned "Discipleship" study in the evangelistic series. How that formula was extracted from this text went something like this. In his training class, Kip would address his prospective fictitious disciple with these words: "Joe, would you agree that a Christian is saved?" (A non-biblical cultural assumption.) "So if disciple equals Christian as we see in Acts 11, who are the only people who are saved? Only disciples are saved." In my view, the interpretation of the passage came from the outcome you wanted to achieve with the person you were studying with.[5]

In addition to my meeting with him in 1988, he and I had at least one other long phone conversation and possibly two about this text as he wrote his first article on "Revolution through Restoration" (1992). I agreed with Kip that one could not be saved without a disciple's heart that submitted to Jesus as Lord, but I objected to using this text to develop a formula that it was not written to any way imply. As far as I was concerned the end did not justify the means, and Scripture must always be used contextually according to sound principles of interpretation.

---

5. First, we must note that Acts 11:26 simply says that the disciples were first called Christians in Antioch. There is no doctrinal statement here. It does not say God called them Christians. It is almost certain that they were given this name by unbelievers. Luke is just making a historical notation that Antioch was the place where this moniker was first used. Second, we must say that most religious people in American culture would agree that "Christians" are saved. But how valid is it to make a theological point by starting with a cultural assumption based for the most part on biblical ignorance?

I shared with Kip that the use (or misuse) of Acts 11 to teach that disciple = saved, created another problem and that was that it contradicted his own teaching from Matthew 28 that only disciples were to be baptized for the remission of their sins. You ended up with a message that said you must be a disciple before you can be baptized to be saved, *but* disciple = saved. That, in effect, meant that you must be saved before you can be baptized to be saved.

It was not surprising to me that a misinterpretation of both texts would lead to a contradiction and something that was, to me, embarrassingly nonsensical, but Kip never saw it as I did. He repeated the formula with a slight change in the "Evangelization Proclamation" signed by the world sector leaders (February 1994), stating in that document: "In the next few months the Bible doctrine from Acts 11:26 of Saved = Christian = Disciple was crystallized." I wrote to Randy and Kay McKean, the world sector leaders for our Europe and New England world sector, expressing my concern. I have included that letter as Appendix Thirteen because it contains a more detailed discussion about the use of Scripture.

The influence of Kip's hermeneutic was a phenomenon either too little recognized or too little acknowledged, and I am not sure that even today enough of our ICOC leaders see how it affected our teaching.[6]

Once Kip had moved on to L.A., it seemed to me that others in Boston felt more freedom to study the Scriptures carefully and use them more carefully in context. The teaching of Gordon Ferguson no doubt had much influence on that. Others, including me, had opportunities to teach expository lessons from such letters as Ephesians that gave us the chance to help the church see the Scriptures in their richness and not just as isolated verses to bring about conversions.

One of the things that always troubled me was that Galatians 5 was known by many believers as the passage that talks about sin since it was used primarily in the "Light and Darkness" study to help someone see the extent of their sinfulness. Galatians 5:19–21 is sure enough there and needs emphasis, but Galatians 5 is primarily a chapter about *freedom* from the law (and consequently all systems of performance) not a chapter primarily about *sin*.

---

6. Having commented on the hermeneutic found in Boston, I should also be quick to say, we must be equally critical of a pragmatic hermeneutic found in popular evangelical circles. They go for a quick result, namely "decisions for Christ," and that decision is often a shallow one to pray a quick prayer. There is normally no contemplation of and commitment to repentance and dying with Christ in baptism. One of their own, the renowned Robert Webber who died in 2007, has a written a frank critique of an approach that turns the biblically rich experience of baptism into something that "no longer has any meaning" (Robert Webber, *The Divine Embrace* [Grand Rapids: Baker Books, 2006], 74.)

One of the great weaknesses I observed in Kip's training of younger men was how he modeled for them topical sermons that pretty much allowed the speaker to go anywhere he wanted to go. Often the first letter of every sermon point would spell some word like "radical" or "faith." Sermons were not constructed from the careful exposition of Scripture but by finding words that fit the acronym you wanted to end up with and then finding texts to help make the points. On the day I wrote this, I happened to come across a Web site as a result of Google search that led me to one of the new churches Kip has recently started. The article on the site featured a sermon by the evangelist. Here was the outline of the seven-point message:

"Delivered from the Lion's Mouth"
1. My Lord is a warrior
2. Incredible strength
3. Rescued
4. All about the Lord
5. Consider their exploits
6. Listen to the word
7. Eternal life

Do you see it? The first letters of each point combine to spell "Miracle." As a result of this legacy, to this day I find that even some of the best speakers among our churches seem to have very little knowledge of how to deliver expository sermons (the efforts of Gordon Ferguson not withstanding—his book on preaching was one of the early DPI publications). I believe this will change and, in fact, I am already seeing positive signs.

Personal Ministry

In the years we were with the Boston Church we did not see the growth we expected when we moved there. Around the world, for many years, there was spectacular growth in places like Manila, Moscow, the old Soviet republics, Mexico, Sao Paulo and Bogotá. In places like Hong Kong, Tokyo, Berlin and Eastern Europe, growth was slower but strong and sustained. However, in the last twelve years we were in Boston, prior to the massive changes that came to our churches in 2003 (see Chapter Thirteen), I suspect that growth in any of those years was never more than five percent, if that. The trauma of 2003 resulted in a loss of membership in most all the churches, including Boston.

Though Sheila and I both were very involved in the publishing ministry, like everyone else in Boston, we also were focused on having a local ministry.

At various times we led house churches and family groups, and had the opportunity to study and lead a number of people to decisions of faith and baptism into Christ. Much of our ministry focused on discipling and maturing individuals and working with marriages and families.

In 1996 after working through a number of reservations mostly related to my health, I accepted the appointment as a region elder in the Boston Church. At that time, the thinking was that certain elders because of energy, availability and experience should serve as elders over the entire Boston congregation, but others should serve as elders in one of our regions. In the West Region, with about 500 Christians, I served alongside two other elders and friends: Stan Morehead and Jack Frederick.

The Overcomers Ministry

Because of my ongoing battle with MS, which had progressed significantly in the early '90s, the Boston leadership felt I could serve well as an elder with a special focus on the physically challenged ministry, which had been started in 1988 by Bill Sullivan, another Boston disciple with MS. As a result, for eight years my work as a shepherd not only entailed work with our region but also with the "PC ministry" (eventually called "The Overcomers Ministry"). My reporting on the Boston years would be incomplete without more elaboration on the impact of this ministry. If any readers are tempted to skip this section to get on to more relevant history, I hope they will not. There are lessons here for us all.

As was the case with others, I reluctantly attended my first physically challenged ministry devotional in the early '90s. It seems that there is something in most of us that does not want to admit that we really have a special problem. I think I also had the fear that being around a lot of sick and disabled people would not be encouraging. In this case, I could not have been more wrong. I have said on many occasions that I have never met more inspiring people than those I came to know and love in this ministry.

Like the paralyzed man who came to Jesus through the roof with the help of his friends and like the woman with the bleeding disorder who touched the hem of Jesus' garment, these were true Jesus people. Whatever difficulties we had in the Boston ministry, it was always a huge plus to me that almost all of these who were sick and disabled had been brought to Jesus through the evangelistic outreach of the Boston Church. Others would do well to ask how this is going in their churches.

In Boston there is Phil Pineo, a quadriplegic, paralyzed as a young man in a diving accident. I remember first seeing Phil maneuvering his electric wheelchair through a crowded service at the Boston Garden using his mouth and the little straw on his chair. Christians had shared the gospel with Phil in the late '80s, and he was a stalwart in the PC ministry.

There are Rich and Karen Nurt. Before their marriage, Christians had reached out to Karen, who has a rare and progressive form of Muscular Dystrophy. Rich has post polio syndrome, having contracted the disease as a child as a result of a vaccine gone wrong. He became a Christian in 1982. Both Rich and Karen are in wheelchairs, but both became vibrant disciples.

Sheila and I had the privilege of counseling them as they fell in love, and I had the honor of performing their marriage ceremony. Of the many weddings I have been asked to conduct, this one will always be one of the most special. Of course, they both were in their wheelchairs. I, as one with MS, was seated on a chair between them. Phil Pineo, Rich's long-time friend and mentor, was the best man, of course, in a wheelchair. Rich and Karen's first dance was one for the ages. They have just celebrated their tenth wedding anniversary, and they continue to share their faith in Jesus wherever they are, reach out to others who are physically challenged and have impact on the lives of many even as Karen's health declines. I am one of those many.

Then there are the O'Neils—Dru and Paul. Dru has suffered from so many debilitating and challenging physical problems that you need a scorecard to keep track. Her battle with diabetes caused her to lose her vision. She has had a kidney transplant and surgeries for cancer. Paul has good health, but together they have faced their trials with faith and humor, and have been an inspiration to many. Not so long ago, they planned and led the first retreat in the ministry just for people with physical and emotional challenges.

I could write of others like Cathy, Larry, Courtney and Michelle, and how God used Bill Sullivan and Steve Rankel to spread the idea of a ministry like this to other churches, but I will conclude my comments about this ministry with a few words about Mark Matthis. Another severely disabled man, Mark also became a follower of Jesus in the '80s through the outreach of Boston disciples. He worked with Bill Sullivan to establish the physically challenged ministry. In 2003 he developed cancer and was an inspiration to us all as he faced his death with a confidence that Jesus is the resurrection and the life— the ultimate overcomer.

Mark and several others I was privileged to know in this ministry have now graduated to glory. They fought the good fight, kept the faith and finished the race. We look forward to our coming reunion with them. Of one thing I am fairly certain: When we finally get to that eternal city, some of these brothers and sisters who endured such suffering in this life with grace and faith will be among its leading citizens.

Some years ago I came across an amazing prayer of surrender from French mathematician Blaise Pascal (d. 1650), written as he dealt with his own deteriorating health. It has inspired me often. He prayed: .

> Take from me, O Lord, that self pity which love of myself so readily produces, and from me the frustration of not succeeding in the world as I would naturally desire, for these have no regard for your glory.
>
> Let me no longer wish for health or life, but to spend it and end it for you, with you, and in you. I pray neither for health nor sickness, life nor death. Rather I pray that you will dispose of my health, my sickness, my life and my death as for your glory, for my salvation, for the usefulness to your church and your saints, among whom I hope to be numbered.
>
> You alone know what is expedient for me. You are the Sovereign Master. Do whatever pleases you. Give me or take away from me. Conform my will to yours and grant that with a humble and perfect submission, and in holy confidence, I may dispose myself utterly to your purposes.
>
> May I receive the orders of your everlasting provident care. May I equally adore whatever proceeds from you.

In the ministry with the physically challenged, I knew many with Pascal's heart, and in their lives I have seen what Elisabeth Elliot called "the very guts of faith."[7]

There was one special place where our publishing ministry and our ministry to those with physical and emotional challenges came together. For years I had thought about different books that I hoped to write. The first one I actually published was not one of those I had planned. In *Mind Change: The Overcomer's Handbook* I shared spiritual lessons I had learned in dealing with both depression and MS and applied those lessons to various challenges that we all face. I expected that the book would resonate mostly with those who were older or were facing physical difficulties.

I was quite surprised to get letters and emails from literally all over the world from people of all ages and people with no health issues. I remember particularly a letter that came from a college student

7. Elisabeth Elliott, *A Path Through Suffering* (Ann Arbor, Michigan: Servant Publications, 1990), 66.

in Tokyo who shared with me how the book had helped him in various spiritual battles. A young woman from Scotland wrote about how she had torn out the "power thoughts" at the end of the book and taped them to her ceiling so she would wake up and focus on them first thing every morning. A women's leader I met recently said to me, "That book saved my life."

As I write this, the revised third edition of *Mind Change* has just been released. In dealing with my own illness and in working with those in our Overcomers Ministry, I have seen the truth that God's grace is sufficient and that he does indeed make his power perfect through weakness.

Ministry to the Poor and the Needy

When Douglas Arthur came to Huntsville, Alabama, in August 1987 to spend a week there trying to help the church sort out what it would do next, he shared with me what he was planning to do in his speech at the World Missions Seminar. At that gathering, which would nearly fill the historic Boston Garden, my recollection is that he was to do a speech based on John 3. However, it was his plan to find a way to address an issue that he felt had been neglected in our movement—a concern for the poor and needy. Most people will remember little else Douglas said in that message, but his call for us to commit ourselves to the cause of the poor would become the basis for a new thrust in the Boston Movement.

I know I used this often as an example of how the Boston churches did not see themselves as perfect but as always in need of discovering fresh truth from the Scriptures. I had long felt that we in Churches of Christ had been greatly negligent in reaching out to the poor and was thankful, and am sure somewhat proud, that this need was going to be put on the front burner in our churches.

I believe the first efforts involved the collection of a LOVE Offering. However, in short order the organization known as HOPE *worldwide* was formed and was led by Bob and Pat Gempel. One of the upsides of the centralized leadership that existed in the movement was that something like HOPEww could be drawn up and implemented quickly once a need was seen. Almost immediately funds were made available and projects were begun.

I believe that God was at work, and the Gempels used their gifts to begin an organization that would have impact on thousands of lives around the world. The Gempels were able to take the funding from our churches and get many additional grants and gifts that enabled HOPEww to grow incredibly, attracting the attention of such notables as Colin Powell, Oprah Winfrey and

Senator Mary Landreau. From a remarkable AIDS clinic in South Africa, to new facilities for a leper colony in India, to a beautiful and modern hospital in Cambodia, to a group home for Romanian orphans to dozens of other projects in the U.S. and other countries, the needs of the many poor people were being met.

Each church in the movement was required to give a certain percentage to HOPEww. That money could come from the weekly contribution, or it could come from fund-raising the Christians did in the community. But in addition to fund-raising, HOPEww enlisted many disciples in hands-on efforts to provide the caring touch of Christ.

As a result, thousands of members of our churches have been in the inner cities, in soup kitchens, in food banks, in nursing homes and dozens of other places where needs are great. Some of the most sacrificial and unselfish service we have seen in our churches has come as a great number of men and women and teens showed the heart of Jesus to a hurting world.

In the new world of reevaluation, we are realizing that even with HOPEww things were not always done in the best way. While many of us gladly welcomed the opportunity to engage in this ministry, we have realized that some felt coerced, particularly in the area of fund-raising. In Boston, the leaders had decided not to take the funds for HOPEww out of the church's budget, but would ask members to raise the money from friends and family. This was not a bad idea, but to some it felt like an obligation and not a choice.

As the ICOC has become decentralized, the work of HOPEww has gone through a perilous time, and yet it is emerging, like DPI, as an organization with a future. As I write this, I am one of many desiring to help HOPEww remain viable.

For years I struggled to find a way to best help the poor. While there are other noble works that I could support, and do not believe HOPEww is the only valid way to help the poor, I have considered it a joy to be involved in these programs that have so directly made an impact on the welfare of others, combining concern for physical and spiritual needs.

My prayer is that my brothers and sisters in the ICOC will realize that what has been begun in HOPEww is more than worth carrying on, and that we will not allow mistakes in our ministries to cause us to throw out a precious baby with the bathwater. As we seek to build bridges with other groups, I pray that in this effort of taking care of people our churches and other Christians can work together and build greater bonds.

Handling Criticism

If you have followed me thus far, you know that this movement had its critics from the earliest days. You also know from the New Testament that it is no surprise that any biblical fellowship would receive criticism. From early on Jesus had his critics, as did his apostles, from within and without the religious structures. You certainly also know of Jesus' several promises that those who seriously follow him will suffer the same fate he suffered (2 Timothy 3:12, 1 Peter 4:12).

So in the early days of the movement, it was no surprise when those of us calling for serious discipleship found ourselves being criticized, usually first by religious leaders, then by parents of college students, then by administrators who were hearing from complaining parents and finally by members of the media. With Boston being a more high-profile city with nationally known universities, it was predictable that the dimensions of the criticism would grow.

Early in the 1980s a Crossroads-related church in the San Diego area had come under considerable media scrutiny, but in 1986, the famous *Boston Globe*, did a long story in its Sunday magazine titled "Come. All Ye Faithful." The teaser read: "In 1979 the Boston Church of Christ had 30 members. Today it holds services in the Boston Garden. Why is it so popular—and why so controversial?"

Six years later the reporters for *Time* magazine would come calling, and in their May 18, 1992, issue would run a story titled "Keepers of the Flock." This time the teaser read: "Boston spawns one of Protestantism's hottest churches, but critics call it a cult and accuse its leaders of dictatorship."

In October 1993, the ABC program 20/20 had a segment on the dangers of the Boston Church featuring John Stossel. Since some of us had been hearing accusations like those presented by the media for twenty years or more, we shrugged off most of what was presented as half-truths or outright slander. There were admissions by elders to the media that some discipling went too far and became too controlling, but on the whole we viewed such attacks as part of the cost of discipleship.

Of course as the Internet made its presence felt around 1993, there were many stories in that medium. Though our churches have undergone some drastic changes and addressed some abuses we were in denial about (which I will address shortly), to this day a search of the Web brings up a host of negative articles about the Boston Movement, the Boston Church, the L.A. Church and the International Churches of Christ.

Here is my perspective on all this. Some of the criticisms were no doubt legitimate. Many of them were not. We are responsible for repenting of the first. We must learn to rejoice in the second. As we strive to carry out the mission of Jesus, we will receive opposition. It should not surprise us. The elder who told me in 1980 that he had never been persecuted and "didn't want it to start now" had a serious misunderstanding of the message or else a rebellion against it. But this is tricky business. In 1998 in *The Prideful Soul's Guide to Humility* I wrote, "The humble man considers the words of his critics. He knows they may be wrong. But he recognizes that they can be right."[8]

Much earlier in the 1981 speech at the NCMS (found in Chapter Ten) I had said this:

> When opposition or insult comes, we need to examine our lives first to see if there is anything ungodly in us to justify the things being said. Sometimes we may find some truth in what the critic is saying. If so, we should deal with that, but all the while realizing that opposition will still come but now for the right reasons.

The tricky part is to have a heart that is pure enough to hear the right things that your critic says when you know that on many points he is wrong or that he doesn't see life through God's eyes at all. But we have to pray to do just that.

Shortly, I will speak of efforts I believe we need to make to connect with other believers, but one of my greatest fears is that as we do that we might be pulled back into a way of thinking that says "we must not rock the boat" or "we don't want the world to get upset with us." I have no desire to be persecuted, but you cannot follow Jesus and open your mouth and proclaim his message in this fallen world, and, as a general rule, be liked, honored and applauded. Can we be greater than our teacher? It strikes me that if nothing else, simply the practice of church discipline as taught by Jesus (Matthew 18:15–17) will incur the "tolerant" world's condemnation and probably get us branded as a cult.

We must acknowledge and correct abuses, but the positive news story about disciples of Jesus will always be the exception, no matter how many abuses and mistakes we correct. As the eminent scholar N.T. Wright observes:

> Those who follow Jesus are called to live by the rules of the new world rather than the old one; and the old one won't like it. Although the life of heaven is designed to bring healing to the life of earth, the powers that presently run this earth have carved it up to their own advantage, and they resent any suggestion of a different way.[9]

8. Thomas Jones and Michael Fontenot, *The Prideful Soul's Guide to Humility* (Spring Hill, TN: DPI, 1996), 177.

9. N.T. Wright, *Simply Christian* (New York: HarperSanFrancisco, 2006), 137–138.

I would pray that my brothers and sisters in other fellowships will be honestly willing to wrestle with this issue and ask why, in most cases, they are so free of opposition or criticism. This theme was so central to Jesus' message that it was one of the eight beatitudes. I do believe it is crucial to understand what a strong conviction we had about this in order to understand the way we reacted to criticisms and attacks.

The Teaching Ministry

One of my most encouraging experiences and one that I believe offers a great model for all churches came in my last three years in Boston. After the time of discipline and repentance in our churches, several leaders in the Northwest Region of the Boston Church decided that we needed to have a time for serious in-depth Bible study on Sunday mornings. We added an hour before the worship service for this.

In that region we were blessed with about seven or eight experienced teachers. Eventually we wanted to offer multiple classes but at the beginning—with unity a bit strained—we felt everyone needed to hear the same thing, so we decided to teach the Letter to the Colossians. Each Sunday two of us would take a portion of the text, but here is the unusual thing. We wanted to present a unified front and provide an example to the congregation of humility and an openness to discipling. So, at first, we all met together on Saturday mornings at 7:00 (often coming through the snow), so that the two that were going to teach would go over their material with the others and then get critique and feedback.

We had never had an experience like this. We would prepare our material and email it out to the others a couple of days in advance. In many cases men who had been teaching for many years would get so much input that they would end up completely reworking their lessons. At other times there was just some tweaking here and there, but the end product was always an improvement over the original.

Eventually, as we went on to teach on many other topics, we changed our plan so that the presenters would share their material on the Saturday a week before they would teach because getting the input just twenty-four hours before the lesson did not always offer enough time to do the revisions needed. The congregation was informed as to what we were doing, and speakers would often mention in a lesson that something they were using had been shared with them in our teachers' meeting. The church loved it. When they heard Tom Jones or Mike Hammonds or Fred Faller teach they knew they were hearing lessons that had been worked on by the entire group.

I had been teaching for thirty-five years, but had never been a part of a process like this that Wyndham Shaw called "developing community theology." While it is fair to say that not everyone started out thinking this was such a good idea, everyone ended up having a deep conviction that this dynamic was good and right. Today in Boston, Fred Faller and the other teachers there continue this process, and no one who has done it would want to do it any other way.

In September 2005 Sheila and I moved to the Nashville area to be near my parents. The Nashville Church had a number of capable speakers, and when I introduced this idea to them, they all were eager. From then until January 2007 the church did not have an evangelist, but five of us organized sermon series and then used this feedback dynamic to help sharpen each other. We let the church know what we were doing, and again the church loved it.

In 2007 when Frank Williams was added as our evangelist, not surprisingly he had never seen a dynamic like this (and understandably was a little cautious). He will tell you today that he loves it and recommends it to his friends in other places. He speaks at least two Sundays each month, and the rest of us still are in the rotation, and we are still giving and receiving input on our lessons both before and after we present them. By the way, one of the side benefits of this process is that it means no more "Saturday night specials," lessons thrown together late on Saturday and sometimes in the early hours of Sunday morning. For this, the church will thank you.

The day I revised this part of this book, I also presented my material for a Sunday sermon to the staff. I had what seemed to be a thorough and well-thought out outline addressing the idea of "In the World, but Not of It" in John 17. But, as always seems to happen, the group gave me some great feedback from some angles I would not have thought of. I can think of no reason that some process like this ought not to be going on in every church. Because it fits so well with humility, God always blesses it.

In many life situations we compare the upside and the downside of a decision or process. After seeing this practice work in two different churches with a variety of leaders, I can see absolutely no downside, only an upside. It is win/win. I would urge every person who preaches or teaches anywhere in the world to pull together a group for this purpose. A little more of self will have to die first, but you will be surprised at what will be raised up.

As a result of my conviction about this process I am handling the writing of this book the same way I do the presentation of a sermon or class. By the time you read this, it will have been read by more than thirty people who gave me input on it before it went to press. In this process, we know the presenter cannot take all the suggestions that are given, but the overall presentation is always better for having heard from others.

Pressure in the Ministry

You can see that for me the Boston years were, for the most part, a time when I was challenged, particularly by health issues, but, nevertheless, a time when I was most fulfilled. Yet, almost any reader of this book will know that not everything happening in Boston or in the worldwide movement was good. I will address that more fully in the next chapter, but I will make a few observations about the Boston Church here. Different people can give you different perspectives. I can only give you mine. In an odd or ironic sort of way, I suspect that the Boston Church and the movement it is part of were better and worse, more godly and more worldly than I will describe here. How someone who was, or is, in the movement will feel about that will depend on their own experiences and relationships.

When we arrived in Boston in 1987, the church had been through a truly remarkable eight years. Starting in the little white church building in Lexington, they had soon moved to renting the Arlington Baptist Church. From there they moved to the Boston Opera House, and from there to the historic Boston Garden. By the time we were there, most of the men and women who would be designated "world sector leaders" had already left Boston and were in place in what were being called pillar churches—Mexico City, Tokyo, Hong Kong, New York and London. However, other strong leaders had been brought in and it seemed growth continued for a time. Kip McKean, of course, was at the helm, and his fiery staff meetings kept the pressure on ministry leaders to bring in the results.

In 1989 Kip turned the leadership of Boston over to Tom Brown so Kip could travel more and supervise the work of churches around the world. During the year or so under Tom, growth continued, but I know that on at least one occasion Kip returned to Boston very unhappy with the results that he saw.

Tom would eventually lead the planting to Los Angeles, and Al Baird would be asked by Kip to take the lead in Boston. Al is a special man with a great heart for God and for people. He, however, was not the one needed to keep Boston moving the way Kip felt it should. I am not sure anybody was, especially in view of the fact that at the time Al assumed the lead evangelist role, seven church plantings were sent out, which included 120 leaders, a number of them from the full-time ministry staff of the Boston Church.

Boston was widely touted in those days as "the Jerusalem of the movement," (a moniker, like others, no doubt given it by Kip) and as such, it was Kip's feeling that it should continue to be a pace-setting congregation. He often would say that Boston might not continue to be the fastest growing or the largest church, but it should still be an example of great growth. While I do not believe that Kip ever thought that numerical growth was the only important factor, I am confident that it was for him the ultimate issue. The lack of it indicated lukewarmness and unfaithfulness to God.

Whatever Kip strongly believed made its way into the psyche of all those who were closely tied to him. When growth slowed, leaders felt compelled to call the church to deal with a lack of commitment, with cowardice and with selfishness. This would lead to what many would see as an addiction to a "push" mentality.

Seeing that Boston was not "turning," and Al did not seem to be the man who could turn it, Kip called his brother Randy in from Europe to lead the Boston Church and be the world sector leader for a new world sector composed of New England and Continental Europe. It is my judgment that Randy made some serious efforts to get Boston on a firm footing and to get the church back to some health that would lead to growth, but it seemed that his efforts did not really ever satisfy Kip.

While I know there were mistakes and methodology was used we would not consider today, Randy and Kay McKean did, from my perspective, a remarkable job of leading the plantings in Europe, and I give them much credit for the fact that we have twenty-eight churches there now still being faithful and reaching out in what may be the most "unopen" field in the world.

However, while the number of churches and disciples increased in Europe, Boston never really turned. I know that what Randy and Kay felt from Kip and the other world sector leaders was a sense of disappointment and probably something a good deal worse, and more and more as time went on. I am quite sure I don't appreciate the strain they must have been experiencing.

Unfortunately, the disapproval that Randy was feeling from those above him and from his peers, he passed on to other leaders in Boston, who in turn passed it on to those they led. Being on staff was something of a double-sided coin. On the one hand staff people were held up, honored and served in special ways. On the other hand they were put under great pressure to produce. I can remember talking fairly often to Boston evangelists who left staff meetings feeling discouragement from Randy's disapproval.

Randy would later confess and apologize to the whole Boston Church (before the flood of apologies that would come even later in the movement) that he had put too much pressure on the staff and had emphasized performance and numbers far too much. I have since learned that not only in Boston but in many churches, Tuesday was the least favorite day of the week for those in the ministry. Tuesday was the day of the dreaded staff meeting.

Month after month, year after year, Boston was not growing, and leaders were reminded often of what was happening in L.A. or even New York and Atlanta, and were told again and again that they just needed to work harder and call for greater commitment.

While I was writing and editing books with DPI with considerable fulfillment, most of our evangelists and women's ministry leaders were not enjoying such a good time. The same can be said for a good many non-staff members who experienced some of the sins, abuses and mistakes that will be much more fully examined in the next chapter. Not everyone felt the brunt of those, but some were seriously hurt. I am just thankful for those who kept trusting God and did not quit and have come through some of these times to what hopefully will be a brighter day where we start with an understanding of a gracious and forgiving God who gives us all approval we do not deserve.

The amazing thing to me is that even in such circumstances as I have described, God works. Many who are special brothers and sisters to me were reached out to and brought to Christ during these years. They were not converted to unhealthy patterns or "dysfunctionality" we had in the church; they were converted to Christ. Some who reached out to them may not have done so from the purest of motives, although I believe most Christians I know shared their faith from a good heart. But whatever the motives, Christ was preached (Philippians 1:15–18), people responded to Christ and lives were still being changed, and I can give you a fairly long list of those people. All credit for that goes to the grace of God and the power of the gospel.

Were some people brought to life in Christ because some evangelist was feeling the pressure to have a big "push" Sunday? Yes, probably on some occasions. Would most of us today recommend that approach to evangelism? No, because there is a much better way. But did God work even in our foolishness? Yes, because in some way that is the way he *has to work* most of the time.

Unhealthy practices cannot continue indefinitely. They can only be ignored for so long. Some of the stronger elders and teachers among the churches were addressing serious concerns out of the public eye, but almost no issue would be kept from the watching world after an evangelist in London released an open letter that would rock the movement.

If we just read the text carefully, we see that baptism is a union with Christ—a union with his death, with his burial and with his resurrection. That union is said to bring us to new life. Your baptism was vital. It united you with Christ in whom you find saving grace and the power of the Holy Spirit. How can we who have experienced such a union ever go on willfully in sin? We have died and have risen with Christ. Be thankful for what has happened to you. Make no apology about it. Preach it to others.

–From *Letters to New Disciples*, Chapter Fourteen, "Your Baptism"

A few days or a few weeks ago when you decided to follow Jesus Christ and be an imitator of his lifestyle, you made a commitment to love the poor, because Jesus loved the poor. For some of you this will represent a major change. Many people in first-world countries become disciples having never been involved with the poor and the needy. It will mean stepping out of your comfort zone. It will mean going to places you may seldom go. But a careful study of the Bible reveals that God has always had a heart for the poor and that he has always called his people to get involved in their lives.

–From *Letters to New Disciples*, Chapter Nineteen, "Remember the Poor"

13

Crisis and Reevaluation

In November 2001 Kip McKean was asked to take a sabbatical and no longer serve as missions evangelist or "leader of the movement" or as the lead evangelist for the Los Angeles Church. A year later these changes were made permanent. I will leave it to others more intimately involved to describe all that led to that action. Kip himself said in his resignation letter: "I am very, very sorry. My most significant sin is arrogance—thinking I am always right... I take full responsibility for how my sins have spiritually weakened and embittered many in our churches. I also take full responsibility for the spiritual condition of my family." As many would see it, he was not able to maintain this posture of humility.

I will offer this observation: This movement was built from its earliest days in Gainesville, Florida, on the conviction that for the church to advance there must be strong leadership. That is an idea that one can support biblically and was a needed word for the church of the 1960s and the church of today. However, there is another leadership theme in Scripture that was routinely overlooked (also from our earliest days), and that is what McIntosh and Rima call "the dark side of leadership."[1] From Abraham to David to Diotrephes (3 John 9) this is also an idea that has strong biblical support.

With a passion, Paul sought to drive home this lesson of the dark side of leadership to the leaders in Ephesus. Here is what he said:

> "Be on guard for yourselves and for all the flock, among which the Holy Spirit has made you overseers, to shepherd the church of God which He purchased with His own blood. I know that after my departure savage wolves will come in among you, not sparing the flock; and from among your own selves men will arise, speaking perverse things, to draw away the disciples after them. Therefore be on the alert, remembering that night and day for a period of three years I did not cease to admonish each one with tears." (Acts 20:28–31 NAS)

Knowing the dangers inherent in leadership, Paul told these men to first be on guard for themselves. "Take heed therefore unto yourselves" reads the KJV. Paul knew that the greatest danger the church had was right there among

---

1. Gary L. McIntosh and Samuel D. Rima, *Overcoming the Dark Side of Leadership: The Paradox of Personal Dysfunction* (Grand Rapids: Baker Books, 1998).

the leadership. "From among your own selves" a dark side would arise that would devastate the flock. But what is Paul's answer to this awful possibility? "Be on guard for yourselves." Every one of us who leads must have people in our lives who help us guard against the dark side. More specifically, we need people in our lives who will boldly call us all back to the cross—which is the only real corrective.

In 2001 DPI published a book entitled *Golden Rule Leadership.* In the book, the authors, Gordon Ferguson and Wyndham Shaw, addressed many of the problems in the leadership of the ICOC fellowship. Gordon wrote something I fear was too seldom heeded at the time (but it is not too late to implement):

> We [strong leaders] do not see ourselves as we are; we do not see ourselves as others see us. Our strong tendency is to think more highly of ourselves as leaders than we ought to think (Romans 12:3). Here is my strong suggestion for current leaders: *have other leaders under your charge read [this] book and then discuss each chapter together.* Begin by asking them to honestly evaluate your strengths and weaknesses in each area being discussed. Better yet, ask another mature leader into your group to lead the discussion, who as a neutral facilitator can draw out what people really think about your leadership. Those around you have learned to praise you, but most likely they have not learned to evaluate you. (I wonder why?) Without this kind of pointed evaluation, you are going to continue believing that you are further along than you are.[2]

I can hardly count the number of times I was inspired by Kip's ability to dream and communicate vision. I know that some of the ventures of faith in my life came from those moments of inspiration. I know there are many others who can say the same thing, but even more strongly than I. Sadly, I do not believe Kip (and some others) ever understood that the greatest of leaders also have a dark side that will either be taken to the cross or will destroy them and others. I pray that is a lesson he may yet learn and one that none of us will ever forget.

Whatever else his removal from leadership accomplished, it dispelled the idea or the possibility that the ICOC was a classic cult where the leader would never or could never be asked to give up his role because it was all built around him. In this case, the action with Kip opened the door to some major changes in our churches. Organizational and operational changes began to come immediately. It would take time for deeper changes to happen.

However, it is my opinion that the Boston Church, being led at the time

---

2. Gordon Ferguson and Wyndham Shaw, *Golden Rule Leadership* (Spring Hill, TN: DPI, 2001), 14-15.

by the overseeing team of Randy McKean, Gordon Ferguson, Wyndham Shaw and Dan Bathon, stepped out and set a crucial example that others were too slow to follow. On Sunday morning September 15, 2002, with the whole church gathered in Lowell, Massachusetts, each of these four men explained mistakes that they were convinced they had made, and then each specifically confessed sins and asked for forgiveness (see Appendix Three).

This time was followed by a series of "town meetings" in which the overseeing group met with various regions to answer more specific questions. Had that happened in more churches (and it did in a few), I believe some of the unfortunate events of 2003 that I will describe shortly, might never have taken place. I do know there was resistance among many leaders to clearly and publicly take ownership for errors the way Boston leaders had done. It would not be long before they would have little choice.

Six months after the Boston leaders had confessed, repented and started making specific changes, Henry Kriete, an evangelist in London and writer of an excellent book that DPI published,[3] in February 2003 released an open letter, at first to leaders, that described in great detail what he believed were four systemic sins in the ICOC movement. Those were (1) our corrupted hierarchy, (2) our shameful arrogance, (3) our obsession with numbers and (4) our seduction by mammon.[4]

Within days of its release, electronic copies of the letter were finding their way on to computers throughout the world. His words resonated with thousands. When I first read his letter, I saw that I was one of a number of leaders receiving it by email, and it appeared that his plan was to limit the distribution to this group. As it turned out, he passed the letter on to someone else who began the wide distribution of it. A fellowship of churches that had already begun to make some changes was now rocked by Henry's letter.

The book I mentioned earlier written by Gordon and Wyndham (*Golden Rule Leadership*) had attempted to address some of these issues. The book was enthusiastically received by some, ignored by most, and actually banned by some leaders in their churches (in the form of telling their book tables they could not sell it). One evangelist in Boston may have been right when he later put it this way: "God was calling our leadership to repentance by his kindness through *Golden Rule Leadership*. When leaders at high levels didn't listen to it, God sent Henry."

There was turmoil in many places. Congregational meetings and open forums were held. Some turned ugly. Resignations took place by the dozens.

---

3. Henry Kriete, *Worship the King* (Spring Hill, TN: DPI, 2000).

4. See Matthew 6:24 KJV which says: "You cannot love God and mammon." NIV renders it "You cannot love God and money."

Some churches were hit much harder than others. In London, for example, where Henry was at the time of his letter, chaos reigned. The church eventually broke into a number of smaller groups with almost no one left in a supported ministry leadership role. Some of the most painful meetings took place in the New York City Church where raw emotion poured out, with wrath directed toward evangelists and elders.

Some leaders publicly expressed thanks for the letter. The Chicago Church posted it on their Web site and asked that all members read it. Some, however, still blame Henry for the turmoil that followed. While we may question the judgment he used at the beginning, and as the reaction got rolling, I believe it is a mistake to think that Henry is to blame for what was happening in our churches. The things he mentioned had been going on for years, and not unknown to many leaders. They were bound to have consequences. Some leaders were trying to address the problems. Others were turning a blind eye.

I have heard it said that our churches stopped growing after Henry's letter, but growth had stopped many places long before his letter. I have heard it said that Christians stopped having one-another relationships as a result of his letter, but I had observed severe problems in this area long before his letter. I don't doubt there was more disorder after his letter, but my view is that it was only a matter of time before many of these things would have emerged. Others, of course, are free to disagree.

In my view, Henry's open letter articulated things that many had been feeling for some time but had not expressed, and thus it resonated quickly with thousands, like the small child's declaration in "The Emperor's New Clothes." While efforts like *Golden Rule Leadership* were addressing some issues, it is my belief that certain problems would have been ignored much longer if it had not been for his letter. Its circulation forced a kind of complete transparency that was still missing.

Certainly a harmful effect of the letter is that it painted all leaders with a broad brush, or at least that it is the way it was taken. Thus many good-hearted leaders not guilty of financial or leadership excesses found themselves virtually under siege. Some left the ministry. Others humbly stayed in through the difficulty and may just now be regaining the confidence to lead. In their lives we see the collateral damage that came from what may have been needed action.

There were many others who were not on paid staff but provided leadership and were also accused of being controlling. While there were cases where this was likely true, there were many other cases where it was an unfair depiction. Some who had poured themselves out to teach and shepherd others were unappreciated by some of the very people they had helped and were lumped in with others who needed to change. I have the highest respect for those, who like Jesus, endured mischaracterizations, sought to learn from our common mistakes and persevered in spite of pain.

In most every church, some remarkable apology letters were written. The magnitude of this was unprecedented in my reading of church history (see examples and summaries in Appendix Four), but that did not end the unrest. In April 2003, when some wondered if this movement could survive in any form, I wrote a piece that was posted on the ICOC supported Web site in which I attempted to give my perspective on the events we had witnessed and the serious questions now being raised. I am including it below, as it still well represents my thinking and deals with issues that some readers will not have heard addressed.

Closer Than Ever?

As men and women in our churches are processing all the revelations, confessions and apologies that we have seen in the last two months, and as many are revisiting the history of the last twenty years in an effort to make sense of it all, one thing I am hearing is that some may leave us and pursue their relationship with God some other way. It would not be surprising if disappointing revelations or a new awareness of mistakes resulted in decisions by some to leave. However, if this is a thought you have had, I am hoping that what I share with you here will at least cause you push the pause button. With such a major choice before you, I am writing to give you another perspective to consider. I am writing to ask you to take another look before you leap.

As those who have led us are confessing that they created a hierarchical system of discipling that was unbiblical and repressive, it can cause us to wonder what in the world we have been a part of for the last ten or fifteen or twenty years. As we hear leaders who were once held up to us admit that they managed a system that led to compulsory giving, we can feel manipulated and duped. Then as we hear that the money that was given was not always spent wisely and that spiritual leaders in some cases adopted the financial values of our culture, we just get plain mad. As we hear major figures admit that their leadership led to the creation of two churches—one for leaders with certain privileges and a certain arrogance—and then another for everybody else, we can feel as if we have been abused and devalued. We can hardly appreciate the honesty of the people when their very confessions make us realize more than before that we were so disrespected. When we hear apologies for the use of statistics and results to motivate us, we can wonder if this really had anything to do with God or if it was just about men's egos.

It is of little wonder that some of us are finding it hard to just forgive and move on. It is not surprising that some are wondering if they can stay with our churches, given the embarrassment, hurt and anger they now feel. Like a woman who has a repentant husband with a long history of abuse, we now don't know if we dare trust again. We consider giving up on organized religion altogether or going somewhere else without a history of hurt or perhaps just beginning our own efforts to be the church, since we are not sure we want to be overseen by any leaders.

It seems to me that all of these feelings, struggles and thoughts are easy to understand. Trauma affects some more than others (as we are seeing on the battlefields of Iraq), but it affects us all. What we have gotten in touch with as a church in recent months has been traumatic, and a few apology letters (even though heartfelt) and a few Scriptures and a few prayers (though much needed) will not make resolution quick or simple. I say this because if you are honestly wrestling with where your spiritual life is going to be lived out or even if it is something you aren't sure you want to pursue, I want you to know I understand what would lead you to such a point. However, since you have invested a great deal in this movement toward Jesus that we are a part of, I just want to give you something else to consider before you make a move.

As we face some of the painful things we may have repressed for some time or some of the new revelations that make us angry, I think there are several questions that we must wrestle with. First, was God involved in this at all? Second, was any good really done? Third, is there anything here that is redeemable? Fourth, is there any reason that staying with this movement would be the best choice?

Was God Involved in This?

With all these questions, we are struggling with the age-old issue of how God uses flawed human beings to accomplish his divine purposes. It is right to stir people with the message that we can all be a part of something that is from God and something that makes an eternal difference in people's lives. But then we can feel such disappointment when we see failures in people who proclaimed these lofty ideas to us. Man's sin has a way of obliterating God's glory, and so we ask whether God was involved in this at all?

This is where biblical perspective is badly needed. Two thousand years ago Jesus came, born of a woman, born under the Jewish law. He was God incarnate. He was the fulfillment of a plan that had been unfolding for hundreds of years. God was in Christ. In Jesus, God was working. But our Bibles don't begin with Matthew or Mark or Luke or John. There are thirty-nine books in our canon of Scripture that were written before the birth of Jesus. The clear message of Scripture was that God was working in all those years that led up to Jesus, but what was that history about? Do we find there story after story of righteous men and women who went from victory to victory? Do we find those who overcame all the temptations of the lower nature and always used money, power and influence in godly ways? Do we find a steady succession of leaders who led the nation of Israel to more and more righteous ends so that they finally produced a pristine temple and glorious people who were able to give the Son of God a hero's welcome?

That's not what we find in the Bible. From the stories in Genesis to the story of Jesus, God was at work. Early on, he had a chosen people. He had a nation that was uniquely his. From generation to generation he was patiently working out a plan, so that in "the fullness of time" (Galatians 4:4 KJV), he might send forth his Son. However, when you read through the Old Testament, you are struck not by the glory of Israel or the consistent faithfulness of her leaders, but by the flaws, the sin, the arrogance, the selfishness of both the people and the leaders. Are there heroes in the Old Testament? Absolutely, and Hebrews 11 describes many of them. But even these heroes like Noah, Abraham, Moses and Gideon were flawed and could easily have written their own letters of apology.

In 1 Samuel 4:21, the daughter-in-law of Eli the priest gives birth to a son, and the Scripture says, "She called the boy Ichabod, saying, 'The glory has departed from Israel....'" (Ichabod meant "no glory.") A second century BC reader of the Jewish Scriptures could have wondered if perhaps the whole nation shouldn't have been named Icabod. From Adam and Eve's sin in Genesis to the shameful practice described in Malachi of offering God their leftovers and discards (Malachi 1:8), these were often a people of "no glory." But was God still at work? He was. Had God given up on them? He had not.

In 1 Corinthians 10 Paul reasons that in some terrible times described in the Old Testament God was working to not only teach the people of that day, but to lay the groundwork for something more important. And then he makes this astounding statement:

> These things happened to them as examples and were written down as
> warnings for us, on whom the fulfillment of the ages has come. (1
> Corinthians 10:11)

If we only looked at Israel's failures and at God's discipline of them, we might just say, "Ichabod—no glory." But Paul says God was at work so that something might be clear to us "on whom the fulfillment of the ages has come."

It seems to me that there is a powerful truth here. As God works with his flawed and sinful people, what is happening at the moment may not be pretty, but the God who can work in all things for good has his eye not just on the present moment, but on other things that he wants to fulfill. How can we be sure then that some of the experiences we have had for the last twenty (or in some cases thirty) years are not leading to something more important?

According to Scripture, what sacrifices does God most value? Is it not "a broken spirit, a broken and contrite heart" (Psalm 51:17)? Right now in our churches, we are seeing dozens, if not hundreds, of leaders at many levels with broken and contrite hearts. Like David in that same Psalm, they are saying, "For I know my transgressions, and my sin is always before me" (Psalm 51:3). Is it not possible that God has brought us all this way to show the world what brokenness and repentance look like on a massive scale? Maybe we thought God wanted to show the world our impressive statistics and our growth charts, when all along he wanted to show others what humility and dependence on him really looks like.

After writing the last paragraph I went with a friend to pray at a favorite spot by the river near my home. He has been a disciple for more than twenty years, has never been a staff member, but deeply loves the church. He prayed that in this current climate, we would really demonstrate forgiveness and learn the freedom of forgiveness. As he prayed, this thought came to me: Since God loves to show forgiveness, since that is what he was doing dramatically in Christ, could it be that God has brought us all this way, not only to show the world what brokenness and repentance looks like on a grand scale, but to show the world (and the church) what massive forgiveness looks like? If so, how tragic it would be if we missed our opportunity.

Was Any Good Really Done?

The second question is this: As we look at what has happened in the last two or three decades of our movement, was any good done? For some people this is a no-brainer, but for others who are very focused on the pain and the problems, this can be a serious question. In the midst of some somber revelations, admissions and apologies, we can almost feel that there was nothing but error; and this is not a good feeling. It is particularly troublesome if one feels that way and then considers how much time or effort or money he or she has given to what now seems to be a failed cause. Others have addressed this question in various articles and letters that I have seen circulated on the Internet or posted on Web sites. I will just add a few of my own comments.

Once again a biblical perspective is helpful. On his "second missionary journey" Paul planted the church in Corinth, staying with them for a year and a half (Acts 18:11). Knowing Paul, we can be confident that during those eighteen months he was active doing the same things he had done up the road in Thessalonica. To that church he wrote: "We loved you so much that we were delighted to share with you not only the gospel of God but our lives as well, because you had become so dear to us" (1 Thessalonians 2:8). And a few verses later: "For you know that we dealt with each of you as a father deals with his own children, encouraging, comforting and urging you to live lives worthy of God, who calls you into his kingdom and glory" (1 Thessalonians 2:11–12). This was just the way Paul was, and we can be sure he was this way with every church. Later he would write to the Corinthians and remind them of the attitude he had while among them:

> Though I am free and belong to no man, I make myself a slave to everyone, to win as many as possible. To the Jews I became like a Jew, to win the Jews. To those under the law I became like one under the law (though I myself am not under the law), so as to win those under the law. To those not having the law I became like one not having the law (though I am not free from God's law but am under Christ's law), so as to win those not having the law. To the weak I became weak, to win the weak. I have become all things to all men so that by all possible means I might save some. I do all this for the sake of the gospel, that I may share in its blessings. (1 Corinthians 9:19–23)

I think we would have to agree that the Corinthians had sacrificial and servant leadership. They had great training from one of the best. And yet, some months after Paul left, he learned that the church had developed a litany of problems. There was division, there were lawsuits among brothers, there was the toleration of immorality, there were disputes over who had the greater gifts, a mockery was being made of the Lord's Supper, and there were some who even denied the resurrection of Jesus. Quite a mess. Was any good done in Corinth? Listen to these words:

> Do you not know that the wicked will not inherit the kingdom of God? Do not be deceived: Neither the sexually immoral nor idolaters nor adulterers nor male prostitutes nor homosexual offenders nor thieves nor the greedy

nor drunkards nor slanderers nor swindlers will inherit the kingdom of God. *And that is what some of you were. But you were washed, you were sanc - tified, you were justified in the name of the Lord Jesus Christ and by the Spirit of our God.* (1 Corinthians 6:9–11, emphasis added)

The church had some serious problems to deal with, and yet there were still people in that church who had been brought out of immorality, idolatry, prostitution, crime, drunkenness and the like. They had been washed, sanctified and justified. The fact that some in the church were behaving reprehensibly didn't undo the changes God had worked in these people's lives. Was Corinth a mess at the time of this writing? It was. Had eternal good still been done in that church? It had. Was the church at Corinth still enriched with spiritual gifts? Paul says that very thing (1 Corinthians 1:5–7). Were many in that church still in fellowship with Jesus Christ? Paul reminds them that they were (1 Corinthians 1:9).

The night before I wrote this, my wife and I met with a woman who has only been a disciple for a little over a year. As we counseled her about some issues in her life, I shared with her the story of our family's decision to move to Boston in 1987. I shared how it was a decision that required my faith and my level of surrender to go to a deeper point. I went on to share how God had blessed that decision. As I shared with her, I felt a great deal of emotion and gratitude welling up in me. I thought of the way God had cared for me during these years, how he had taught me much about dealing with a chronic debilitating illness, how he had helped me through a major depression, how he allowed us to help others find him.

I thought of a family who had been in our home just a few weeks earlier and how God had completely transformed them so that now they are not only a healthy family, but have recently taken in two foster children to give them a loving home. I thought of another couple who also were with us that night—how their marriage has been healed through the deep involvement of disciples after a devastating wound. Has any good been done? I believe the answer to that is clear.

Is it good that there are people in more than 150 countries who today are saying "Jesus is Lord"? Is it good that people who once worshiped the gods of money, success, sex, pleasure, popularity and power have now been washed and sanctified and justified in the name of the Lord Jesus? Is it good that most of our churches have a racial blend that would amaze the world? Is it good that there are hundreds of projects to serve the poor and the elderly that did not exist fifteen years ago? Without a doubt, there are things in our churches that need to change and must change. Without a doubt, we strayed from the biblical path in some serious ways. But has good been done? Without question a vast amount of good has been done. Through these jars of clay God's transcendent power has worked.

Is There Anything That Is Redeemable?

The third question is this: As we look at the challenges we find ourselves in today, as we look at a structure that seems to have come unglued in just a few months, is there anything here that is redeemable? Once again, I know that some people will quickly say, "Sure," but others are at such a place that they aren't confident at all or they have profound doubts. When it has been universally agreed that our movement is wracked with systemic sins, one has to wonder what can be salvaged.

If the good I described above is really there—and I am convinced it is—then there is so much to build on. Our churches are still full of people who have great hearts and want to find out what pleases God. As an elder, during the last two weeks, I have been involved in four family forums with four sectors in the church in Boston where we openly discussed any issue that anyone wanted to bring up. On Sunday morning I told the congregation that one of the things that impressed me in these forums was just how much people really care about the church. I have no doubt that what I saw here in my little corner of the world can be seen in hundreds of other places.

One of the decisions that most of us in a leadership role have made is that we are going to make sure that the Bible is studied in depth. We have repented of our humanistic ways of trying to build the church in some other fashion. The announcements about this decision have been received with great enthusiasm. People are eager to study what the Bible teaches about leadership and what the Bible teaches about spiritual gifts that are given to everyone in the body. They are just hungry for God's word. Is there anything redeemable when you have great numbers of people eager to study the Scriptures? Is there anything you can build on when people stop trying "to figure it out" and start listening to God who already has it figured out?

The transformation in our thinking has caused dozens of leaders to see that every member of the body is important and that we must find ways to lead inclusively. Can much more be done once we return to the spirit of Acts 15:22? ("Then the apostles and elders, *with the whole church*, decided to choose some of their own men and send them to Antioch with Paul and Barnabas," emphasis added.) Will we be a healthier church when every member knows that what he or she has to offer is valued and that efforts will be made to ensure that everyone's voice will be heard?

Earlier I noted the number of leaders who are showing a broken and contrite heart. Does God think a movement of people is redeemable when this becomes the dominant posture of its leaders? It seems to me that those are the very people God says are redeemable. If what we have been through has stripped us of our arrogance and our self-righteousness and has brought us to a deep conviction that "God opposes the proud, but gives grace to the humble," then we are not only redeemable, but we are in the best position we have ever been in. If we have been truly humbled—as I believe we have been—then that only means the cross of Christ can take a place in our lives that is greater than it has ever had. When this becomes true, we are truly connected to the wisdom and the power of God (1 Corinthians 1:24). That sounds like we have a future!

Is Staying Really the Best Choice?

The final question is this: Is staying really the best choice? At the present time some are wrestling with this decision. Please hear me: I do not in any way stand in judgment of you as you try to deal with this. You may feel betrayed, disappointed and hurt. You may have heard, "Hurt me once; shame on you. Hurt me twice; shame on me," and then felt you have a responsibility not to remain in an unhealthy situation. This is a struggle that should be honored. I would just ask you to consider a few final thoughts.

Is it not possible that given what we have been through, we are closer than ever to being where God wants us to be? Where else can you go and find leaders who have been as humbled as our leaders have been? Where else can you go and find people who have looked as carefully as we have at what biblical leadership really means? Where else can you go and find the deep conviction we now have that finances need to be handled by those who have nothing to gain from them? Where can you go and find people who now feel stronger than we do about providing motivation based purely on love for God, love for people and gratitude for the cross? There may very well be places where people are ahead of us in all these areas. If it is true, I praise God and pray we can meet them and learn from them.

However, in the meantime I have to believe that we as a movement are closer to God's vision for us than we have ever been. How did we get here? Not by our performance; that's for sure! We got here only by his grace. Have we arrived? Not by a long shot. Have we understood that we will not in this world ever arrive? I believe we have.

I thank God that he connected me with the beginning roots of this movement thirty-five years ago and for the way he helped me reconnect with it some years later. I thank God for the way he has blessed us. I thank God for the way he loved us enough to discipline us. I thank God for the way he has humbled us and forgiven us. And I thank God he has not stopped believing that we are at least among his chosen people, his royal priesthood, his holy nation, his people who can declare the praises of him who called us out of darkness into his wonderful light (1 Peter 2:9).

I thank God we are closer than ever to being a church where "Amazing Grace" is not just a song but the theme of our lives. I pray we will all stay and grow together in the grace and knowledge of our Lord Jesus Christ.

Thomas Jones, April 2003

The year following Henry's letter was one that involved much reevaluation. It was a time of getting in touch with what is good that must be preserved and what is bad that must be done away with. The first was fairly easy. The second was been very painful. It was hard to hear stories I had not heard before and to see the devastating effects of some of the systemic sins Henry described. It was difficult for me to realize that in some ways I was living in a protected bubble in a corner of this movement, and that not everyone was enjoying the support and encouragement that I was.

It was painful to hear stories of faithful disciples who were excluded because they had questions and reservations that they could not in good conscience ignore. It was embarrassing and heartbreaking to face the fact that while I did not embrace or participate in some of the things being exposed, I had not made it clear to others outside our movement that I still respected their faith and honored their work. Beyond that, I had not given them free access to me so they could express their concerns and fears.

Over the years, I maintained some contact with other Christians outside our fellowship, but I did not with vigor advocate the idea that anywhere God has a son, I have a brother, and where he has a daughter, I have a sister. I did not make it clear in public settings that I believed he had many children outside our churches. I never for a moment believed that the kingdom of God was limited to our movement and never taught that to anybody. I spoke against that idea at times to certain leaders (most of whom also did not believe it), but like Barnabas in Galatians 2, I allowed the pressure of our church culture to keep me from fully embracing those who were as saved by grace as I. For this I am deeply sorrowful and along with others am now trying to show the fruit of repentance.

I would, however, like to return to the good that I believe has been done.

I elaborated on that in the piece above, but I want to add a few more thoughts. This is not done, I pray, to be defensive, but so that God might be praised for the way he has worked by his grace in spite of our sin.

The Boston Movement has been rightly criticized, I believe, for over-simplifying some fairly complex theological issues, and I would add that we have, as well, over-simplified the condition of those who remained in the "mainline" church. We can only ask for forgiveness and grace and pray that others will not now over-simplify what has gone on in our movement. It is all too easy to agree with the sensational headlines and tabloid shows, or to generalize from anecdotal accounts and say that this was a toxic faith that brought ruin and pain wherever it went. It is easy to paint with that broad brush, but it is simply not true, and time spent with any number of people who have seen their lives change as they have grown close to God and to others, and have poured out their lives for their neighbors, for students, for teens, for the poor and needy and the orphans will show that it is not true.

On the other hand, there was sin among us, and that sin did hurt people in major ways. I have mentioned earlier the pain suffered by Milton Jones in Seattle. At my meeting with him in 2004, I gave Milton a very preliminary copy of this book. In our time together, he admitted that it was hard to hear the good things that have happened in our churches because of the deep hurt he had felt. I think those of us in the ICOC must try very hard to understand that and realize Milton is not the only one who has to deal with that. Our sin sometimes masquerading as righteousness did damage, and three years later or ten years later we need to listen to those who still need to talk things through.

However, in the providence of a sovereign God, sin does not undo the good that his Spirit did in the hearts of humble, pure-hearted and sacrificial people who were never abusive, never hungry for power, never motivated by numbers and only wanted to find out what pleases the Lord. Our sin does not even undo the good that was done by some who had mixed motives and allowed themselves to be seduced by worldly thinking. As already noted, even those were used by God as they preached Christ (Philippians 1:16–18).

My desire is to hide from no sin that has been found among us and, with the help of God, hear from any wounded brother or sister who needs understanding, encouragement and support. But, I also cannot and will not deny the good things God has done in many lives, and I will work and pray to maintain the things that were right that led to those good changes.

To paraphrase Philip Yancey: God has chosen to risk humiliation and embarrassment by putting himself into us who are jars of clay, into us who are sometimes emotionally fragile, into us who can be prideful and self-deceived, into us who will always make some mistake if given enough time.[5] In 1995 I referred to this concept and then added this at the end of the book *Glory in the Church*:

> The fellowship of which I am part is no more perfect than I am; we are a work in progress. But I see God and his glory shining through. I routinely see some things I would see in the world only rarely. I often see other things I would never see in the world at all; they are produced only by the power of God. There is glory in the church![6]

In the churches of the ICOC fellowship I have seen what can be seen in other Christian fellowships. I have seen the human and I have seen the divine. We can make no excuse for sin, but we must rejoice in what God's grace accomplishes in spite of us.

Nothing tells us more about life than this death. No event shows us more the character of God. No speech ever spoke so clearly about the values we all need. What happened when Jesus of Nazareth went to that hill outside the city gates will never in this world be fully understood. No scholar, preacher or poet can really take us to its depths. No one can fully fathom the mysteries that are here, but the closer we can get to it all, the better we will be. God wants a mighty movement in our day that will advance against darkness on every continent. But he will bless no movement that is not centered on the cross of Jesus Christ.

–From *Letters to New Disciples*, Chapter Twenty-Three, "At the Foot of the Cross"

---

5. Philip Yancey, *Disappointment with God* (New York: Harper Paperbacks, 1988), 274–275.

6. Thomas Jones and Sheila Jones, eds., *Glory in the Church* (Spring Hill, TN: DPI, 1996), 143.

14

Recommitment and Renewal

As I write this final chapter, it is now four years since a tsunami of change hit our churches (and when I use that term in this chapter I will be referring to the congregations of the International Churches of Christ). For some time we have been ready to move on. As I see it, moving forward must include: (1) never forgetting the mistakes that were made, (2) holding on tightly to the things we did that were right, and (3) being open to new possibilities.

Please do not think that I present the following analysis in these three areas as in any sense final. Hardly a month goes by during which we don't learn something else from looking backward or looking afresh at Scripture that helps us understand how to better go forward. However, I believe we will be served well by continuing to think carefully about these three matters.

Hard Lessons

Among those lessons we learned or sins that were exposed and renounced, I would include the following:

1. We have seen the damage caused by authoritarian and harsh leadership, and we have learned that leadership can have a dark side to which none of us is immune.
2. We have been convicted of the arrogance involved in identifying our group with the universal kingdom of God on earth.
3. We have seen how ugly things become when leaders forget that they are first and foremost servants and that no man is ordained to lord it over others.
4. We have seen the ugliness of favoritism and the need to respect every member of the body of Christ, helping every person feel valued and useful. We must no longer neglect the weak to concentrate on the strong. We must not label people and pass those labels on to other leaders, so a person feels trapped and unable to get out of "the box."
5. We have learned that motivating with numbers or pressure or performance expectations may produce short term results but also the ungodly fruit of competition and pride, as well as a culture of fear and people-pleasing.

6. Related to this, we have seen the damage done by a hierarchical system of discipling (which I believe was developed in good faith) that has people thinking about their position and competing to rise in the ranks to be closer to the top leader. We have seen the error in telling people they had the authority in discipling relationships that Scripture only gives to congregational leaders, and how the result was a high level of unbiblical control over others' lives.

7. We have seen that it is crucial for the church to have financial integrity, but that this will not happen without openness, transparency and disclosure.

8. We have learned the harm it brings when we cause people to give under compulsion, but the grace that comes in cheerful giving. For example, giving for missions is highly commendable, but when it is presented as a requirement, induced with pressure and not done from free will, the result is often bitterness or at least an absence of joy.

9. We have seen that our churches must be taught the Bible in an in-depth way and that frothy motivational or entertaining messages are not enough.[1]

10. We have also seen that Scripture can be wrenched from its context and used and abused to defend some grand scheme of men when we need to read Scripture contextually with all its balance and healthiness, letting Scripture determine our agendas.

11. We have learned that the gospel is not the gospel of discipleship or of total commitment, but the gospel of God's grace, with discipleship and commitment being the responses to that gospel.

12. We have learned the foolishness of "spin" and the use of the wrong type of historical revisionism where we rewrite history to make ourselves look better than we were or to enhance the stature of certain leaders. In a famous movie line, one character tells another "You can't handle the truth!" What God has shown in both Old and New Testaments is that his work (with Israel and with the church) can handle the truth. There is no need for spin.

The mistakes and sins described here are not pleasant to remember. Some will wish that I had not talked as much about them. But we must never forget. God in his mercy has forgiven us, but we must never forget the damage these things bring, and we must be determined not to go there again.

Financial experts tell us that in the wake of the 1929 stock market crash

---

1. In Appendix Fifteen where I describe what you will find in the culture of the International Churches of Christ today, I share more about an increased emphasis on scholarly study.

and events such as Black Friday in 1987, we have become pretty good at fix-ing things after the fact so that we don't make the same mistakes again, but we are not so good at anticipating what the next big problem may be. In our churches we must be sure that we at least get the first part of that. We must look carefully at what has happened and fix what we did wrong so that we do not repeat the same mistakes.

Many Right Things

At the same time, we must never forget the good things that we learned and practiced, that were and are in line with biblical principles. Not only must we remember these but we must be deeply committed to them going forward. Though I referred to some of these already, let me summarize with this list:

1. The conviction that the Scriptures are inspired by God and absolute-ly sufficient as our standard.
2. The centrality of the cross of Jesus in the conversion process.
3. The need for personal sin to be faced in order for there to be true repentance.
4. The value of studying the Bible personally with people carefully before they make a decision for Christ.
5. The absolute necessity to make Jesus Lord (and take up the cross) as we put faith in him as savior and are baptized into him.
6. Involvement in each other's lives according to the principles of the dozens of "one another" passages in the New Testament.
7. Specifically, the need to have people in our lives to whom we confess our sins and with whom we are open about our lives. (But that should be a mutual thing, not a one-way street.)
8. The need for every member of the body to be a disciple of Jesus with a disciple's (learner's) heart and disciple's commitment.
9. The concern every believer is to have for reaching the lost (while not forgetting that different people have different gifts).
10. The need for a world vision and a realization that Jesus calls us all to his passion to reach the entire world.
11. The need for strong leadership (which we now know must also be humble leadership).
12. The biblical call to be submissive to leaders and respectful of those over us in the Lord.
13. The need for pure dating relationships and for a strong stand against sexual immorality.

14. The biblical principle for Christians to marry only Christians.

15. The need to take the time to build strong marriages and families.

16. The practice of showing concern for the poor and needy.

17. The effect that unity, love and zeal have on the guests who come to our meetings and particularly the effect of our multi-racial congregations.

18. The importance of powerful worship services, with open sharing of lives, zealous singing and convicting biblical preaching.

19. A realization that the practice of biblical discipleship will still bring opposition from religious and non-religious sources no matter how much like Jesus we become.

20. The power of unity among congregations. (We must keep this even when it is not mandated by some hierarchical structure.)

21. The need to train and raise up leaders.

22. The need to plant other churches who plant still more churches.

23. The need for and blessing of generosity and of "seeking first the kingdom of God and his righteousness."

24. The importance of church discipline and a willingness to deal with sin in the church.

25. The importance of addressing the heart not just behavior.

26. The need for a strong women's ministry with women teaching women.

It should be evident by now that I have no illusions about our churches being perfect. However, a commitment to these things has been very much a part of the church culture in which I have lived for at least the last twenty-five years. Not one of these things must be abandoned or compromised. By the grace of God, our family of churches has seen that all these can and must be a part of our life together.

Four years ago as we went through a painful trauma and needed discipline, I wrote down some dangers I thought we faced, knowing the way the pendulum can swing. This is what I put down on my handheld PDA, where they still are today:

Dangers We Now Face

1. That we will stop calling people to a radical commitment ("deny yourself and take up your cross daily"—Luke 9:23).

2. That we will stop preaching that it is a narrow way (Matthew 7 says that it is).

3. That we will accept little involvement in each others lives. (Romans

12:5, 10 teach that we belong to one another and must be devoted to one another.)

4. That bringing others to Christ will stop being a priority. (The Great Commission is still there in Matthew 28.)

5. That we will become fearful of criticism and take a negative view of all persecution. (Jesus promised in Matthew 5 and other places that it would most certainly come.)

6. That we will become fearful of confrontation and no longer bring each other loving admonishment. (Colossians 1 and 3 call us to that very thing. Love demands it.)

7. That we will have a fear of strong leadership or strong preaching. (There can be no biblical religion without prophetic proclamation.)

8. That the grace of God will become, for some, a license to sin. (Romans 6 says we cannot go on sinning expecting that grace will abound. Galatians 5 says we must not use our freedom to indulge the sinful nature.)

Let me say just a bit more about concern for number four above. When we believe that we are the only group that is saved, there is in that belief a potent motivation to evangelize and particularly to get people into our group. As long as some of us felt that way, we stayed engaged in evangelism and felt bad if we were not. Once we openly acknowledged that people can biblically get to Christ without going through us, some of us decided that the call to spread the word was no longer so essential. Using some very faulty reasoning or relying on some misleading emotions, we stopped making the sharing of our faith a priority.

Maybe we were just glad to take a break from evangelism often motivated by guilt. But is the cross of Christ not enough motivation? Is there not something wrong if we have to rely on a sectarian spirit or the pressure of a ministry to share with people the good news?

For a time, I felt my fears might be realized, but now four years later, I am still concerned but not as much. I see tendencies in all these directions among some individuals and some churches, but I see many others who are so focused on Jesus and the Scriptures that they are guarding against giving in to any of these temptations.

More Things to Learn

While there are bad mistakes we want to avoid and sin to which we do not want to return, and there are many good things we want to practice all the more, there are also some things I would hope we could still learn. I would include these things:

1. *That we would keep studying the link between grace, faith and discipleship (commitment), until we see what a grand connection there is between these great concepts.*

I have written about this in Chapter Seven of my book *Strong in the Grace*. Given our history of preaching a performance model (wittingly or unwittingly), I find the roots of that approach still deep within us, and I fear some will underestimate that and what an ungodly model it is. Paul was a champion of grace, so much so that he was accused of giving people a license to sin. That charge was absurd, but his emphasis on grace led some to make it. We must become fearless champions of grace. But I think some of us are afraid to go there. We are concerned about the results. We must give up that fear. When properly understood there is nothing about salvation by grace through faith that undermines the call to serious discipleship. In *Strong in the Grace* I put it this way:

> In two of his great letters that deal with justification by grace through faith, Paul describes our response to grace in ways that line up completely with what Jesus taught about being a disciple. To the Galatians, Paul said, "I have been crucified with Christ and I no longer live, but Christ lives in me. The life I live in the body, I live by faith in the Son of God, who loved me and gave himself for me" (Galatians 2:20). The Greek here literally says "I have been co-crucified with Christ." Putting faith in Jesus means denying yourself and taking up the cross. It means dying to all efforts at self-justification and all efforts to control your own life. To live by faith in the Son of God means to say "I no longer live, but Christ lives in me." Later on to the Galatians Paul will say, "Those who belong to Christ Jesus have crucified the sinful nature with its passions and desires" (Galatians 5:24). Those who have trusted in the grace of Christ will continue to talk about taking up the cross and will continue to get on it.

Later I added this:

> Having written in many ways about the grace of God in the first eleven chapters of Romans, Paul begins chapter 12 with these words: "Therefore, I urge you, brothers, in view of God's mercy, *to offer your bodies as living sacrifices,* holy and pleasing to God—this is your spiritual act of worship" (Romans 12:1, emphasis added). What is the only appropriate response to the grace of God? It is to offer yourself completely to God—putting your whole self on the altar. Is this not the same as Jesus' message: "In the same way, any of you who does not give up everything he has cannot be my disciple" (Luke 14:33)? Both passages are for us today.

It is my conviction that the only way we can be theologically sound is to have our message firmly rooted in the grace of God. I am not convinced that every person of influence in our churches is as firmly grounded there as we need to be. As we are strong in the grace, we can boldly preach the life of discipleship and commitment and obedience.[2]

2. *That we would learn much more about the value and power of team leadership.*

Throughout the history of this movement this has not been one of its strengths. But evangelists, elders, teachers and deacons are all biblical roles and all are needed to work in concert with the others. Everything about the spirit of the New Testament cries out for this kind of leadership and not that type where any one person calls all the shots and has all the power.

As I write this, I have just finished watching the NCAA Championship Game for this year. After the game, the winning coach (and yes, again he was a Florida Gator) paid tribute to his players and the way no one individual goes for the glory but how they play as a team. We have different gifts, just as those athletes I watched have different gifts. The tall center and forwards needed those speedy guards, and vice versa. The long range sharp shooter needed the quick hands of the ball hawking defense. We all bring something different to the table, and we are all needed. It is no different in the church. Team leadership and biblical humility are a perfect fit and bring the healthiest results.

One-man-on-top leadership is almost a part of the spiritual DNA in this movement. It will take effort and a lot of honest communication and correction to change it.

3. *That we would learn new ways of encouraging and supporting life-changing relationships among our people.*

This I believe needs to be done without the requirement of assigning people to one another, although I do not find this to clash with Scripture if this is what local leadership decided was best as long as they do not put one person in authority over another. While I am aware that everyone's experience was not mine, some of the best things that happened to me in the last twenty years happened because I had prayer partners or discipleship partners. In our old system those were usually worked out in some leaders meeting, and I was told who I would be with. I was in some of those meetings myself trying to figure out who we would put with certain other people.

---

2. A most useful book in helping us see this biblical connection is Gordon Ferguson's *Romans: The Heart Set Free* (Spring Hill, TN: DPI, 2001), in my mind a largely undiscovered resource.

Though I would not want to return to that method, two aspects of these relationships often caused good things to happen: (1) That relationship became a consistent one where we usually met once a week to share our lives, confess our sins, look at Scripture and pray. (I realize that in most relationships with our "over/under" mentality, confession often was offered in only one direction, but this was not my experience. (2) I gave my heart to the relationship with the faith that God would work—and he did. Today I see too many people unconnected, but desperately needing those kinds of relationships for the sake of their purity, for the sake of their marriages, for the sake of their ministries, and for the sake of their salvation.

My prayer is that we will learn ways to foster those relationships throughout the church in ways that do not involve lording it over others. We must foster a true "one another" spirit where both people feel responsible for each other, even in those cases where one obviously needs to mentor the other. At the same time, we need to be on guard for relationships where there is an unhealthy dependence or "co-dependence," but the centrality of strong, consistent relationships with God at the center could not be clearer in Scripture. If you don't have relationships like this, I urge you to be part of the solution. Pray. Take action. Make them happen.[3]

4. *That we would learn or remember that our renewal or reform movement began with a focus on campus ministry. That we would commit ourselves to a return to those priorities and efforts that brought so many college students into the kingdom.*

Yes, it is a different day. We now have a history of reaching college students and upsetting a lot of parents and college administrators in the process (and, by the way, I know of no way a counter-cultural message like Jesus' will not do that no matter how careful we are to avoid abuses). In 1973 there had not been articles written in campus papers about our efforts, and I know of no examples where we had been banned from campuses. There was no World Wide Web to retain dozens of articles opposed to what we were doing or what we had done wrong.

Even if it might be harder to reach students today, they along with our teens will be needed to keep our churches alive and zealous. And besides, there is still no time in life when it is easier to spend time with people than the college years when most are still free of demanding job schedules and family

---

3. In the summer of 2007 DPI released a 4-CD set titled *Relationships: At the Center of the Target* in which I discuss the biblical basis for making relationships such a priority and look at how Scripture says those relationships should be. As the title implies I find this a crucial topic for all concerned about New Testament spirituality.

responsibilities. I know that a few years ago, renewed efforts were made in the ICOC fellowship to focus once again on the campus, but somehow in a system that was "nigh unto passing away" it never got much traction. That seems to be changing now.

The National Campus Ministers Seminar, which was such a vital annual meeting in the developmental years of the ICOC, just celebrated its fiftieth anniversary in Churches of Christ. They surprisingly gave an achievement award to Jim Bevis who had been one of the lead planners in the CE Seminar in Dallas in '68. A seminar in campus ministry was held in the summer of 2007 at Harding College, which is affiliated with Churches of Christ. This event was planned by some zealous campus ministers to revive the interest in campus ministry that was seen in the '60s and '70s and focus on what had worked most effectively in recent years.

The ICOC has its own International Campus Ministry Conference which has been growing in attendance and influence, so the campus has not been forgotten, but I hope going forward an even greater priority will be given to it and that we share in this with other "fellowships" so we might mutually encourage each other's faith and efforts. That leads to my last point.

5. *That we would learn to build better relationships with other Christians out-side our lines, so we might learn from them, and pass on to them the things we have learned.*

There are others out there who want to honor Christ with their lives, and even those who teach the same response to the gospel as do we. They want to help reach the world for him. It is crucial and right that we respect their faith. Some of them have told me "We want to learn from you." I am speaking particularly about those who share with us a common heritage in the Restoration Movement, including those in Churches of Christ (acappella) and those in Independent Christian Churches.

A year or so after Henry's letter, some efforts were made at reconnecting with the mainline Churches of Christ. Four leaders from the ICOC shared the podium with four leaders from the mainline group at the Annual Bible Lectureship at Abilene Christian University.

Since I knew well everyone on the program except the moderator, I was intensely interested in this event. Of course, in my role with DPI I had often worked with the four men from the ICOC: Al Baird, Gordon Ferguson, Mike Taliaferro and Gregg Marutzky. But I also personally knew all the panelists representing the Churches of Christ and three of them I knew very well. Terry Smith and John Wilson were both men I had worked with in Memphis and

Springfield respectively. Jack Reese completed his Ph.D. at the University of Iowa not far from Kirksville, Missouri. We had known each other from Springfield and Mid-America Seminar days, but we connected several times when I was in Kirksville and he was in Iowa. Tom Brown had grown close to Jack when he attended ACU for his master's degree, and Jack and I were drawn closer by our friendship with Tom. Jim Woodruff was a long-time friend and co-worker of Terry's in both Searcy, Arkansas, and Burlington, Massachusetts, and I had been in his home.

I was not able to attend the forum but found myself getting quite emotional as Sheila gave daily reports to me from Abilene. I still thank God that all these brothers were open to this meeting. The repentance, confession, humility and love expressed by brothers on both "sides" at the forum had to be viewed as a positive step forward. The following year that event was repeated on a smaller scale.

Jack Reese, dean of the college of biblical studies at ACU and a prime mover in these events, was invited to speak at several conferences sponsored by the ICOC fellowship. (I consider his book, *The Body Broken*, to be must reading for all of us concerned about the unity of all God's people.)[4] Dr. Tom Olbricht has spoken at several events hosted by the Boston Church, and the elders from the Boston Church have attended several events for leaders hosted by mainline churches. The Chicago Church brought a professor from Harding Graduate School in to teach. However, at the time of this writing, efforts to communicate and reconcile do not seem to be gaining momentum.

In my judgment there are several factors contributing to this. On the mainline side I believe there are at least three issues: (1) pain caused by the elitism and judgmentalism of ICOC members, (2) a continuing suspicion that the ICOC will return to some of its problematic ways and (3) their preoccupation with resolving their identity crisis, as referred to in the March 2007 issue of the *Christian Chronicle*. Those of us in the ICOC can help with the first with a willingness to do more listening to the effect our posture had on others, with the second by the way we live and speak, and with the third by praying for those in other churches.

If we in the ICOC are to help others overcome their fears about us, I would suggest we start by watching the way we talk. One example would be for us to no longer use the word "disciple" as a shibboleth or code for someone who is part of an ICOC church, as in "Is he a disciple?" Almost without exception, when I hear that, it is like the phrase from my childhood, "Is he a member of the church?" The former almost always means is he a part of our

---

4. Jack Reese, *The Body Broken* (Abilene, TX: Leafwood Press, 2006).

ICOC fellowship. The latter meant is he a member of the Church of Christ, as opposed to the Baptist Church, etc. It is so right to talk about being a disciple but any word can be used in a sectarian way.

The word "believer" is used in Acts interchangeably with "disciple." In fact "believer" is used just as often in the non-gospels as is "disciple." Amazingly to me, the word "disciple" does not appear in the New Testament in Romans through Revelation.

In the last chapter of *Strong in the Grace,* I present my case that we need to keep talking about being disciples, but we must not act like people can only be Christians (and disciples) if they use the word the way we do or if they verbalized that in baptism they were becoming a "disciple," or if they have gone through a series of studies just like we use. By that test no one in the Book of Acts would be a Christian and probably nobody in the first century church. This is just one example, but I believe we need to seek to eliminate any stumbling blocks that we can without compromising the message.

As for the concerns, on the ICOC side, I see primarily a fear that any significant reconnection with the mainline group would result in a return to the kind of lethargy I have described above. I believe others in our churches fear the same dangers I do (beginning on page 141), and they believe that increased relationships with either of the large groups would likely lead toward those conditions. As leaders in our fellowship of churches see leaders from the Churches of Christ and the Christian Churches speaking out boldly, calling people to the cross, to godly relationships and to the mission of Jesus, I believe many will be more open to reconnecting. In a recent conference I attended I heard such from both groups.

I see two common challenges that we all have: we are busy and we are naturally not humble. We are busy trying to keep our own churches healthy and growing. I understand all it takes just to keep a church functioning on a week-to-week basis, particularly one that takes the whole mission of Jesus seriously. It is so much simpler to just do our own thing than to build some bridges that may require not only time but emotional energy. It is hard enough just to keep relationships in our own congregations reconciled and united. It can seem like Mission Impossible to bring together people who may never have known each other. But to paraphrase the words of C.S. Lewis found in *Mere Christianity:* "If something has to be done, there is no sense talking about whether or not it can be done." Building the unity of all God's people is something that must be done, and with God's help it can be done.

A recent unity document affirmed thus far by more than 70% of the ICOC congregations contains the nineteenth century Restoration Movement slogan

"We are not the only Christians, but we are Christians only." Once we make such a statement, we are saying we are in the same family with others not in our circle, and once we acknowledge we are in the same family, there are obligations and responsibilities that follow. It would be most hollow for us to use a slogan from a unity movement and not pursue unity. If this is not one of our concerns, repentance is clearly needed.

Unfortunately, we are more than busy. We are all naturally prideful. We defend our way and our methods and our theology. We are reluctant to give others credit. The only hope for any kind of godly unity is that we crucify that pride and learn humility from Jesus. Almost daily meditation on Paul's words in Ephesians 4 will be needed:

> As a prisoner for the Lord, then, I urge you to live a life worthy of the calling you have received. Be completely humble and gentle; be patient, bearing with one another in love. Make every effort to keep the unity of the Spirit through the bond of peace. (Ephesians 4:1–3)

If we are not willing to pray that we will have this kind of mind and heart, there is little chance of us connecting in ways that help us and change us all. But with such a heart, mountains of division can be moved. (For more on this see Appendix Sixteen: The Power of Humility.)

There are some of my friends who feel pursing relationships with other groups is a misplaced emphasis and not one that holds much promise. While they could be right, I believe that Jesus' prayer in John 17 demands that we make no premature judgment about this matter, and Ephesians 4 would admonish us to "make every effort." In my mind there is just no question what Jesus and the New Testament writers would call us to do.

In the last chapter I wrote that "in the churches of the ICOC fellowship I have seen what can be seen in other Christian fellowships. I have seen the human and I have seen the divine." Especially with the COC and ICOC, I am afraid that those in each group are quick to see the human in the other group and not so quick to see the divine. In fact, we have been quick to doubt that the divine could possibly be in the other. It seems to me that people in each group have certain issues that we key in on and then reason, "Since they think this way or since they do that, I can't possibly affirm their faith." I see that tendency in myself. This must change in order for us to have connection and unity.

We need to do some serious study of Romans 14 and understand why Paul would say to people thinking very much like we do:

> You, then, why do you judge your brother? Or why do you look down on your brother? For we will all stand before God's judgment seat. It is written:

> "'As surely as I live,' says the Lord,
> 'every knee will bow before me;
>   every tongue will confess to God.'"
>
> So then, each of us will give an account of himself to God.
>   Therefore let us stop passing judgment on one another. Instead, make up your mind not to put any stumbling block or obstacle in your brother's way. (Romans 14:10–13)

God is at work in us all, and our flesh is at work in us all. The Spirit is in us all, but none of us has arrived. We must extend the grace to others that we want extended to us. Paul goes on to say just a few verses later in Romans 15:7: "Accept one another, then, just as Christ accepted you, in order to bring praise to God." With help from God I believe we can develop relationships in which we can challenge each other, call each other higher, and help each other with our blindspots while still respecting each other's faith.

As a result of my recent efforts to communicate with other believers, my observation is that those of us in the ICOC have more trouble respecting the faith of others than our brothers and sisters in other fellowships do. In the last twenty years it seems others have been moving away from a spirit of judgmentalism, when only recently have we renounced an attitude of exclusivism. Both ugly qualities are often still in our DNA. I suspect we fear that letting go of them will mean we will become doctrinally flabby and functionally lethargic. This is why we need to study and embrace Romans 14.

It is a huge world. It seems that such a small number of us are serious about being followers of Jesus. We need to be united with everyone who is committed wholeheartedly to Christ so that together we might have the greatest possible impact.

In the last two years my wife and I have made several efforts to broaden our relationships. In the months before this book was released we attended two meetings that brought together people from the Restoration (or Stone-Campbell) Movement. I have particularly been heartened by my conversations with those from the Christian Churches included but not limited to those involved in leading their Stadia church planting efforts. (See www.stadia.cc.)

I appreciate the efforts of my friend Dr. Douglas Jacoby (www.douglasjacoby.com) who planned an International Teachers Seminar in 2006 to focus entirely on the question of "Who Is My Brother?" with the goal of opening up communication with those in Christian Churches and Churches of Christ. Speakers were from all three groups.

Such a coming together will have its challenges. It is easier for us to stay in our comfort zones, to keep doing things the way we have always done them, to keep having in the same speakers, to keep singing our same songs, to keep practicing evangelism and fellowship the way we have done it, to keep interpreting the difficult passages the way we have decided is best, and also to keep some of our dysfunctional family dynamics just as they have been. But I would propose that there are strong biblical reasons for us to reject the "religion as usual" approach.

I am resolved to pursue new connections while staying committed to and being united with our ICOC fellowship and my local congregation and its growth. I believe we can see significant movement in this area because I believe it is God's will. I realize that changing views takes time and effort. Almost every church in the ICOC fellowship included in its apology letter some statement about wanting to correct the impression that we think we are the only Christians. I am suggesting we put some action behind those statements, reach out to our brothers and sisters and see what God does. If it gets a little messy or a little hard, I pray we will not give up. If there can be a radical openness to the Spirit and a willingness to take some risks, I believe we can do much more when there are connections than where there is isolation.

There have already been a few cases where brothers and sisters from different streams of Christ's church have spoken at each other's events. I pray it will happen more often. There is so much we can learn from each other. It can only be the enemy that wants to keep us apart.

As I write about such things, I want to pledge to anyone thinking with me about this that I will do more than just talk about this need. I have my own fears, as I have already mentioned, but this strikes me as crucial if we are serious about getting the gospel to our warming planet of almost seven billion people that may be about to go through any number of global catastrophes. We just cannot afford the luxury of doing our own thing without connecting and partnering in every possible way with others with whom we have so much in common.

As this book was being finished, Sheila and I drove eleven hours to meet Gregg Marutzky and speak together at Restoration Forum XXV, one of the meetings I mentioned earlier. It was well worth the effort. We spent time with deeply committed brothers and sisters that we all look forward to being with again.

Those of us in the ICOC inherited a culture of isolationism from the Churches of Christ of the late nineteenth and twentieth centuries. We may have rejected other things from their posture, but we accepted this one fully. We bought the car, took it home and have driven it most every day. Some leaders in the Boston Movement decided it was just a lot easier to call all the radical disciples together and leave the others behind. It was decided that it was more efficient and effective in building to be isolated from other believers. I understand why it was done. I gave my tacit approval. But while we may make some new mistakes, I do not want to have any part in making that one again.

"What would Jesus do?" is still a good question. If he came today, can you see him fellowshipping only with those in "our" group? As plans were made to plant churches and train ministers, can you see him only working with "us" and avoiding or ignoring those across town who also get up every morning to surrender to him as Lord? We are talking here about the Jesus who respected the faith of a "heathen" Roman centurion and that of a Canaanite woman from the region of Tyre and Sidon, and the Jesus who used a Samaritan woman with a bad reputation to draw a whole town full of her people toward him. None of those people were in "the right church." Or try to imagine what Jesus would have thought if Peter led one church and John led another in the same city, and they acted like the other didn't exist because they had some differences of opinion?

God willing, I will be just past sixty years old by the time this book comes out. Special friends of mine, who were younger than I, have already gone on to that eternal city. They are no longer searching. People generally live longer these days, but there are no guarantees, especially for someone with MS. However, I pray that God will allow me to live long enough to see groups of believers who once ignored each other, coming together with humble hearts to respect each other's faith and learn from each other what God has been teaching them. The ultimate goal is unity so that the world may know of Jesus.

I urge you to join me in this prayer and then ask what God would have you do. See Appendix Seven for some ideas about how we can act.

Going Forward

Jones family 2007 (Amy married Ryan Black in 1999)

The spirit I saw in the movement that began in 1968 at one life-changing seminar is not dead. There are signs of life, revival and renewal in many places. We now live in the Nashville area, and the church here has just been through a remarkable time beginning with Ed Anton's seminar on repentance which led to a Solemn Assembly, a day of corporate repentance, the likes of which I had not seen.

We certainly have not arrived, but, praise God, we feel we are again on our way to better places. We have our challenges, but we are seeing a gleam in many eyes again as we focus on being the salt, light and leaven God has called us to be. Best of all, we are seeing people confess Jesus as Lord, put faith in him and be united with him in baptism.

We hear encouraging news from many places. *Disciples Today* Web site (www.disciplestoday.net) lists 350 congregations outside North America and 145 in the U.S. and Canada in the ICOC fellowship. It is quite inspiring to go to this site and just look at the list. It would be interesting to know whether in the history of mission work any group has ever planted churches in most every country in the world in a twenty-five year period and at the end of that period seen virtually every church led by nationals. Remarkably, that is the case with this movement. To God and his grace be all the glory.

Sitting in that seminar in Boulder, Colorado, in 1978, I started believing this could happen. I am not sure I saw it happening in twenty-five years or happening the way it did. We can only thank God that he put treasure in jars of clay and did amazing things. In spite of mistakes and sins, "Jesus is Lord" is still on the lips and in the hearts of people around the world in countries most of us had never heard of in 1978.

For example, there are ICOC churches with seventy-five Christians in Kazakhstan, nineteen in the strange and amazingly isolated country of Turkmenistan and seventy-six in the tiny country of Togo. Indeed, God is a gracious and faithful God. Most of them know nothing about the Boston or Crossroads controversies. They just want to follow Jesus and are thankful someone brought them the good news.

In Appendix Five you can find just a sample of events from 2007 going on in our churches—all indicators of churches that are beginning to dream and thrive again. In Appendix Six you will find a much more personal report on just one small group Bible study in the Boston Church written by my long-time friend Jack Frederick. He knew nothing of the things I was writing, but emailed this to me just as I was finishing this book. It seemed most appropriate to include it, for I believe it describes the spirit returning to our churches. If you have any doubts what God can do with us, you need to read this.

As I write this about the ICOC fellowship, I want to encourage us to rejoice in and hold up growth and victories outside our fellowship, as well, and be thankful when Jesus is recognized as Lord and obeyed in whatever group it might be.

Over the years I would often flinch when leaders in our churches would refer to our movement as "The Modern Day Movement of God." Eventually, I believe God dealt with the hubris involved in that declaration. While I do not believe what we were doing was ever "the" (as in one and only) movement, I do believe it was "a" movement of God, and it was one I can say I have been most blessed to be a part of. I would not like to see what I would be like, what my marriage and family would be like, and what our relationships with others would be like, were it not for what God has taught me and done with me in this movement.

As I anticipate living the last portion of my life, I look forward to continuing toward my ultimate goal with hundreds of disciples in this movement who have been the greatest of friends and partners in the gospel, but perhaps I look even more forward to those God will add to our number through conversions and through times of reconciliation.

From now until your life ends, you will face things that will be difficult. You will have a "bad" day or a "bad" week. But nothing that happens will change God's eternal nature, his tireless work and his unconditional love for you. You will always have good reasons to "rejoice in the Lord" (Philippians 4:4). You have a source of joy that the world knows nothing about. Turn the handle and let it flow.

–From *Letters to New Disciples*, Chapter Sixteen,
"Living with Joy and Gratitude"

Epilogue

Let God Do His New Thing

For he was looking forward to the city with foundations, whose architect and builder is God.

Hebrews 11:10

For here we do not have an enduring city, but we are looking for the city that is to come.

Hebrews 13:14

Growing up in Sheffield, Alabama (pop. 15,000), with no greater ambition than to make a decent living, find a nice girl to settle down with and keep up my golf and tennis games, I would never have imagined what an adventure God would have in store for me. It would have seemed unbelievable that I would ever leave my comfort zone in the northwest corner of my state. But God in his grace interrupted my life. He presented me with some hard choices and then somehow gave me the courage to make them. I heard the call to obey, but I did not know where I was going. I only knew that faith said "go." Many of you know exactly what I am describing. It is also true of you.

Now I look back and marvel. I marvel at the places I have gone, at the events I have witnessed, at the people who have become my friends, at the things God has allowed me to do. Growing up in the segregated South in the days of Jim Crow segregation laws, it would have seemed like ridiculous fiction to talk of Sheila and me being in Johannesburg, South Africa, with 1500 brothers and sisters from many races or, for that matter, to one day move to Birmingham, Alabama, the home of Bull Connor, the notorious director of public safety in Martin Luther King's day, to start an interracial church. But both happened.

As a high school student who knew two other people from a foreign country, it would have stretched my credulity to think that I would have good friends from Europe, Asia, Africa, the Middle East and Australia.

As a child of the Deep South, Nashville and Memphis seemed like northern locations. Boston seemed like a foreign country. But we would spend eighteen years there. And it was very hard to leave.

As one who grew up in a very traditional, legalistic and uninspiring church where the most interesting thing was some occasional awkward and funny baptism experience, I could not possibly have envisioned assembling with 16,000 excited Christians in the legendary Madison Square Garden in New York City, where we might have believed that some day we could have a church of maybe 200. And yet on a Sunday morning in 1996 I sat on the third row and turned around during a song to behold the crowd. It was the most Christians I had ever seen in one building. They had come just from the New York and New England churches. As I looked at the joy on the faces, as I felt the vibrations of celebration, as I watched the clapping hands and swaying bodies in the dim corners of this famous place, I stood in awe.

Here is an understatement: Interesting things happen when you take those first steps toward Jesus and start on the road to the city whose builder and maker is God. For me and many others it has been quite a ride, and it isn't over yet.

Of all the things I have learned about this journey, maybe one of the most important is that we do not travel alone. This book has been about a move-ment—a group of people who chose to travel together—because God said that's the way to go. Like other groups, we have at times lost our way and wan-dered off into some places that are not good. We have even at times treated some other travelers with something less than kindness and respect. For sure we just ignored some going in the same direction as we were. At times we may have resembled a traveling circus more than a traveling church. But because we travel *toward* God and *for* God and with *faith in* God, we have been loved and disciplined and forgiven and given hope and promises by God. And with the different ups and downs, because of God, we can say, it has been good to be together. And we can say it will be good to finally get there and be togeth-er forever.

In the Bible we find various images used to describe us who journey together—church, family, body, kingdom, nation, priesthood. To Jeremiah God gave another image. We are a pot. Hear his words:

> This is the word that came to Jeremiah from the Lord: "Go down to the pot-ter's house, and there I will give you my message." So I went down to the pot-ter's house, and I saw him working at the wheel. But the pot he was shaping from the clay was marred in his hands; so the potter formed it into another pot, shaping it as seemed best to him.
>
> Then the word of the Lord came to me: "O house of Israel, can I not do with you as this potter does?" declares the Lord. "Like clay in the hand of the pot-ter, so are you in my hand, O house of Israel. (Jeremiah 18:1–6)

When I read these verses I think of the song "Have Thine Own Way." That hymn is a personal expression of our desire to be shaped and molded by God.

> Mold me and make me after Thy will,
> While I am waiting, yielded and still.

While that is a great thought for all of us, in the book of Jeremiah God was not talking about what he would do with an individual. He was talking about the nation, the group, the corporate body. We who travel together must be willing to let God be the potter and mold us and make us (collectively) "as it seems best to him."

My fellow travelers and I have been committed to some right things. We have witnessed some incredible events. Perhaps we started feeling invincible. But it is not surprising that we too have become marred even while in his hands. I think the church—given enough time—always becomes marred in his hands. We have a way of fouling things up or getting off track. It certainly didn't take churches in Corinth or Galatia or Thessalonica long to become marred in his hands. But God can always take that marred pot and shape it as it seems best to him.

Our calling is to be very open to letting him do that and not demand that the pot look like something we have predetermined. We know some basic things God wants. I listed twenty-six of them back in Chapter Fourteen. They will not change. We are in search of a city, but we are not nomads and wanderers. God has given us some clear directions. However, there may be some new and different ways he wants to shape us so we can accomplish these things and our prayer should be that we as a church or a movement in the church would be like clay in the potter's hands, not telling him how it should be done, but open to what seems best to him.

Is there any reason to believe that the creative God who made our elegant universe, has grown dull in his "old age"? Is there any reason to believe he is out of "new" ideas? Not according to Isaiah, who gives us this word from God:

> "Forget the former things;
>   do not dwell on the past.
> See, I am doing a new thing!
>   Now it springs up; do you not perceive it?
> I am making a way in the desert
>   and streams in the wasteland." (Isaiah 43:18–19)

After reading Jeremiah's metaphor from the potter's house, let's return with Isaiah back to the image of traveling, as through a desert. As we journey on, we must be guided by the word of God, but never bound by tradition. We must be committed to the Scriptures, and, at the same time, always open to the Spirit. He may be showing us some new way to apply the Scriptures or some new paradigm for ministry or some new way for us to be inspired and refreshed. The saddest places in the world seem to me to be those churches from my childhood that are just like they were fifty years ago and not expecting anything new. God says "I am doing a new thing!" I am convinced he started something in the late 1960s that was as new as it was needed. Is there any reason to believe he has tired of new things or that his nature has changed so he has become stodgy and unimaginative? I don't think so.

We have decided to follow Jesus, and we are not going to turn back. But the pot that has been marred must be open to being molded into something new. To use the images of both prophets, we may have no idea what the new pot will look like and we may have no idea where a new route may lead us, but we must move forward with a total openness *to God doing it all his way*. I believe that is where all this started forty years ago, and I am convinced that is the key to finding what should come next. I urge you, then, to pray together with others, "Mold us and make us, O God, and do your new thing among us." Maybe we do understand only backward, but we can certainly pray our way forward.

> "Behold, I am coming soon! My reward is with me, and I will give to everyone according to what he has done. I am the Alpha and the Omega, the First and the Last, the Beginning and the End.
> "Blessed are those who wash their robes, that they may have the right to the tree of life and may go through the gates into the city." (Revelation 22:12–14)

From the pre-readers of this book we have learned that the things shared here often prompt people to make comments about their own memories of the times and events this book describes. If you would like to read the thoughts of others and add your own, visit our Web site:

www.insearchofacity.net

Appendixes

Meeting at Crossroads Church – November 10–11, 1975

Copy from the Crossroads Church Bulletin, November 16, 1975

CROSSROADS MEETING

In meetings initiated by Parker Henderson and held on November 10 & 11, 1975 at Crossroads Church of Christ in Gainesville, Florida, an understanding was reached on the seven charges that were made and circulated about the Crossroads Church and its teachings. The charges and answers given are stated below:

1. CHARGE: Baptism is a miracle in the same sense in which the resurrection of Christ was a miracle.
   ANSWER: The use of the word "miracle" was an unfortunate choice of words. Baptism is not a miracle in the commonly understood or Biblical use of the term "miracle". However, baptism involves not only the action of man, but also of God. Baptism involves "faith in the working of God who raised Christ from the dead". God acts in baptism in that it is God who forgives our sin.

2. CHARGE: That since baptism is a miracle, that miracles have not ceased and are prevalent in the lives of men today.
   ANSWER: Miracles have ceased and do not exist in the lives of men today.

3. CHARGE: That the Holy Spirit leads and/or directs Christians today separate from and independent of the Word of God.
   ANSWER: We do not endorse such teaching. The Holy Spirit does not in any way lead or direct Christians today separate and apart from the Word of God.

4. CHARGE: That the only reason that women are forbidden to lead in prayers in the public worship service where men are present is tradition and is not forbidden by the Scriptures.
   ANSWER: The Bible does not authorize women to lead the public services in singing, prayer or preaching.

5. CHARGE: That women are allowed to lead in the prayers in the devotionals and "soul talks" where men are present.
   ANSWER: In the spirit of Romans 14, since this practice has become a source of controversy and division in the brotherhood, we will forego this practice in all congregational activities such as devotionals and "soul talks" and the practice thereof will not be advocated.

6. CHARGE: That there is no Biblical distinction between works that save and works that do not save.
   ANSWER: We do not believe that there are works that merit salvation, but we do believe that man must comply by faith to the conditions of salvation such as the conditions which James in Chapter 2 calls "works".

7. CHARGE: That Christian fellowship must be extended to all persons who have been "baptized for the remission of sins."
   ANSWER: Christian fellowship must be extended only to persons who obey Jesus in becoming Christians and who live the Christian life.

Page 2 - Meeting at Crossroads Church, November 10, 11, 1975

The elders and minister of the Crossroads Church stated that it is
their desire to have men on their seminars and other programs who
hold to God's Word without compromise. Questions have been raised
about some of their speakers in years past. Some have been eliminated;
others are being investigated. They desire to use the utmost care in
the selection of their seminar speakers in the future and plan to do
everything humanly possible to avoid using any man who teaches false
doctrine. They cannot guarantee, of course, that everyone will agree
on the selections or the conclusions reached in their investigations.

The elders and minister have stated that they will weigh carefully all
speaking invitations, but do not consider the appearance on a seminar
or a lectureship as an endorsement of the other speakers on the program.
Their desire is to speak where the most good can be accomplished where
they are able to freely speak their convictions. They will endeavor
to use extreme caution in participating in any program that would lead to
any wrong impression concerning their basic doctrinal positions.

We believe that all parties should now make every effort to mend fences,
correct misunderstandings and seek reconciliation and that this reconciliation should be made as public as the charges and differences have been.

In brotherly love,

Rogers L. Bartley   William H. Fugerer

R. H. Whitehead   Van Land

Chuck Lucas   Bob Martin

Parker Henderson   Ernest Underwood

J. D. Bales   Archie Luper

Barney Colson   Ira Y. Rice, Jr.

Richard Rogers   B. C. Carr

Appendix Two
A Strange New Sect

Reprinted from Fall 1979 issue of Campus Journal

The Middle East at the time of Jesus knew nothing of newspapers or modern electronic journalism. There was no Jerusalem Tribune to carry the story of the crucifixion of Jesus, and there were no investigative reporters around who could dig into the story of the new movement that began following Jesus' resurrection. However, we recently found ourselves wondering what kind of report an "unbiased" journalist might have filed had such media existed at the time. Utilizing some accounts in the Book of Acts and Jesus' own predictions that his followers would be slandered, we have put together the following possible story. This is certainly not presented as an accurate picture of the early church (for that we refer any reader to the Book of Acts). It is presented as a possible way the early Christians might have been viewed by the "secular press." We believe such reflections have value for today's situation.

—The Editor

I arrived in Jerusalem about 3:00 in the afternoon after a dusty trip from Caesarea. I had come to this center of Jewish life to investigate reports of a new and aggressive religious sect which was often referred to as the "Way." Religion is part of the daily life of these people in Judea, but this new movement was generating an unusual amount of attention.

Many consider the Way to be the actual community of God on earth. Others think it is a weird, horrifying example of brainwashing and mind control, and it has been branded by many in Jerusalem as a dangerous sect. Things started rather quickly a few years ago at a Pentecostal festival when around three thousand were immersed into water to initiate them into the movement. At first the citizens in Jerusalem responded favorably to the love and concern shown by the members, but it wasn't long before the mood began to shift.

The members of the sect pledge their allegiance to Jesus of Nazareth, a rather enigmatic figure who was executed by crucifixion about 50 days before the aforementioned Pentecost. The followers of the Way claim this Jesus was resurrected after three days, and they are obsessed with following his teachings to the letter. Among his commands, apparently there is a call for his disciples to carry his message to every person on earth, and most of the problems in Jerusalem come from the over-zealous way they seek to be obedient at this point.

They are not content to just conduct their rituals, but they insist on going door to door as well as into the public places to make converts. People are often badgered into joining the movement with talk of sin, righteousness and judgment. They have filled Jerusalem with their teaching with an effort to make every citizen feel guilt because of the death of their leader. Every rabbi, shop owner, innkeeper and beggar in Jerusalem knows of the movement, and opinions are strongly negative toward the leaders including a certain Peter and John.

The religious leaders are especially alarmed by this strange brand of Judaism, and they have denounced it often, as they previously denounced the Nazarene who started it all. They cite the break-up of traditional Jewish family bonds as sufficient evidence that the new movement is demonic and deserving of contempt. The Nazarene apparently did teach that his disciples must hate parents and other relatives in order to be in his "kingdom." And Jerusalem abounds with stories of fathers and sons who no longer live in harmony. The members of the Way talk of peace, but their teaching brings a sword that slashes away at family relationships.

From all reports, discipline in the community is harsh, even barbaric, at times. According to reliable sources, the members of the movement some months ago were all selling possessions and property to help fill the depleted treasury. It is likely that reluctant members were coerced into liquidating their assets.

One man and his wife reportedly balked at such moves and fell out with the leadership. Details are sketchy, but it is known that the couple died in the midst of the controversy. Members of the sect claim they fell dead as an act of God, but family members of the two deceased persons are asking for an official investigation. The incident apparently left the entire movement in the grip of fear and the leaders more able to control the followers than ever.

The government in Jerusalem is outspoken in its criticism of the Way. Sect leaders have been jailed on several occasions and ordered not to speak this controversial message again, but they have consistently refused to tone down their efforts to proselytize others in the city. Had it not been for a certain respected member of the Sanhedrin, this Peter and John would most likely have been executed some time ago, and many government officials are now convinced that harm could have been avoided if these executions had been carried out.

Just a few weeks ago one of the "lesser lights" in the movement was executed by stoning, and his death seems to have opened the flood gates of hostility toward the sect. As one shop owner told me, "We've had all of this fanatical junk we can take." We talked with one woman whose son joined the movement near its inception. Tears rolled down her face as she spoke. "I love my son and don't want him harmed, but this thing is so horrible that I hope they get it out of Judea whatever the cost. I have five other children, and I'm scared to death that they will be contaminated by this sect that talks about nothing but crucifixion."

There are some signs that the action of the government and the religious community is working. Many sect members have left Jerusalem since the stoning, but that may be bad news for other parts of the empire. Already reports are coming in from as far away as Syrian Antioch that the carriers of this so-called "good news" are preaching their message there.

One aggressive Jewish leader, Saul of Tarsus, spoke to us of his intention to travel even to foreign cities to stop the movement. He plans to leave this week for Damascus. According to long-time Jerusalem watchers, such action is unusual and shows the seriousness with which Jews are taking the movement, even at a time when they seem to have stifled it in Jerusalem.

No one can say at this point what will become of the Way. Its members are usually very committed, highly disciplined, and concerned about obeying everything the Nazarene taught. It does not appear they will be easily persuaded to alter their convictions or methods. If Jerusalem is an accurate barometer, however, public opinion will probably be against them wherever they go. With men like Saul working to arouse opposition to the sect, we feel reasonably confident in predicting a rough future for it especially if it tries to move into such areas as Asia, Achaia, or Rome. But to quote one gentleman whose wife and daughter joined the movement, "These people are definitely weird, but I wouldn't be surprised if they turned the world upside down before they are through. I'm not saying that would be good, you understand. I am just saying it might happen."

—Tom Jones, *Campus Journal* editor

Appendix Three

Boston Church Apologies and Repentance

Boston Congregation Meeting, September 15, 2002

Six months before Henry Kriete's letter and well before a spate of apologies were offered by leaders throughout the ICOC fellowship, the overseeing team of the Boston Church—Randy McKean, Gordon Ferguson, Wyndham Shaw and Dan Bathon— confessed and apologized to the church in two large meetings in Lowell, Massachusetts. There were no recordings made of the event, but one Boston disciple, Becky Dodge, made careful notes to give to friends. The leadership of the church would later ask her permission to print these notes on the church's Web site where they remained for many months. These are her unedited notes as they appeared on the site. The very specific confessions of the four men are found at the end of these notes.

Randy McKean: Introduction: God Is In Control

Randy McKean opened the morning with the above topic, reminding us that the challenges will always come — at all stages in life and in different ways. He defined a leader as "just men with more responsibility, with our own foibles and sin, striving to do right by God." Our allegiance is first and foremost to God and not to man.

Daniel 4:23-37 Nebuchadnezzar had to learn that God is in control. The bible gives us the good and the bad, the mighty and the fallen. God's agenda is being fulfilled. We are a movement of God, moving into all the nations. We are presently reaping the results of weaknesses of leaders. God is working to get us where he wants us to be. "I deeply love the Boston Church," and he read Phil 1:3-7 to describe his feelings for Boston. He believes Boston is a church honored in heaven for what we have done; it is <u>astounding</u> (his emphasis) what the church has done over the years. Remember — God is still in control.

Wyndham Shaw: Taking Personal Responsibility As Your Leaders

I've been here 15 years, turned 50 this year, a grandchild due in February. He mentioned a song by a group "5 For Fighters" or something like that, who sing a song about the challenge of Superman to be ordinary and extraordinary at the same time. Same struggle as a Christian. Leaders can feel they need to be perfect. They (as we are) are sinners in need of grace who need to turn to God to find the power. The legacy of our movement is disciples who accept the high expectations of Jesus and who carry out the message by the grace of God. No matter how long the race, where it takes us, we must take responsibility to finish the race. Take responsibility for my sins. Produce God's holiness in our changes and repentance.

People brought in to Boston at different times and for different reasons. I want to repent and reaffirm a current vision. The Overseers Group (McKeans, Shaws, Fergusons, and Bathons) minister to Boston and Europe and manage a $20 million budget.

1. The Overseers Group has done a lot of fasting and repenting.

2. They want people to feel respected. The lack of growth is indicative of how God is disciplining us. He's pointing us in a new direction; midcourse changes are needed to run the race because many of us are in midlife. Five WSL's have fallen in their roles in the last few years (he mentioned Kip and Doug Arthur here, but no details). With no growth in 3 years, they want to determine how the leaders failed so that we can grow again.

Not a time for panic or disillusionment but faith, hope and love. God is not shaken by the sins of his people nor is he impressed by the past. God wants broken and contrite hearts to persevere in running the race. 2 Peter 5:5-7 Be clothed with humility — not one time, but at all times. God gives grace to the humble. Goal today is to be clothed with humility. Repentance is shown in deeds. No "magic plan." Will have town meetings over the next several weeks to allow disciples to ask questions and to provide input. Boston is the genesis of and crucible for leadership dynamics — all the thrills and spills! Overall, God is pleased, but is calling us to a new stage — an older, stronger church after growing pains. As leaders, we will repent, not a one time step, nor will it prevent us from revisiting the past.

Gordon Ferguson: Restoration for God

"I am grateful for this day. I've been longing for it to come." Been here 15 years, have a son with two boys and a daughter with a daughter and a son on the way.

1. *God's plan is for restoration* — Church here is pure gold. You've been through more than anyone else. You deserve our heart and today we give it to you. Changes come secondary to trying to restore what God wants. Jeremiah 6:16-19 A prophet who cried often, out of conviction for his own and others sins. "Ancient paths" are the will of God almighty, which is to restore the bible. Challenge is staying with God's will. Cycle of good, leading to bad, leading to discipline, repentance and then blessing. God desires our church to be amazing yet sin blocks it. Genesis (Adam and Eve), Noah, Abraham, Judges, the pattern repeats itself. It was the same in the New Testament — In Acts 2, the church was great, everyone helped each other, shared everything, the gospel

was spread in 30 years. Then dark times began. Paul, in 1 Timothy 4:1-3, had to write a very sad passage. People will invent things in the name of religion. 2 Timothy 4:1-5 — challenge was people were going to leave the word of God. Restoration has a simple answer — go back to the Word. It's a never-ending process for sinful human beings.

2. *Restoration is an ongoing process. In the early church, apostasy soon set in. They* were "unified" in the Dark Ages (Catholicism) but not based on the word. In the Reformation period, men said something is drastically wrong, mostly based on the lives of the leaders. Luther and Calvin said, "we need some scripture/bible." This led to the Protestant movement, because they were protesting against the Catholic church. They didn't restore the bible so by the 1700's they had over 150 faiths within Protestantism. Then they realized, we don't just need to reform, we need to restore God's word. Let's leave our denominations, backgrounds, preconceived ideas and let's restudy baptism, communion, etc. They tried to unify based on the bible, which eventually led to the formation of the Church of Christ in the early 1800's.

As late as 1960 it was the fastest growing church but it became more doctrinally focused—like the Pharisees and the Sadducees, less evangelistic fervor. Many understood the Great Commission, and in the late 1960's, as the country was going through a lot of change and students were questioning things on their campuses, many began to find students listening and rejecting the status quo. The Crossroads church of Christ was formed, but it was basically a fiery campus group inside a dead church. Some were sent out to campuses, and then it became a church within a church. One can't put new wine into old wineskins, and so Kip came to Boston in 1979 to start a church where ALL would be disciples and therefore the whole church would be unified. Many miracles since then, and we remain in awe in spite of the failures. There are challenging times across the movement. Philippians 1:7 (can't read my own writing) — Many are wrestling with leaders across the movement. Change is hard but need to make changes for God. Growth doesn't come through easy change, i.e. not by sitting on the back porch and gazing out to the horizon.

Matthew 16:24-26 Some things won't change
Matthew 22: 34-40
Matthew 28:18-20
Ephesians 4:4-6

3. *Restoration must be specific.* What's been done has been good and right but sometimes misguided. Strong preaching (Titus 2:15) and insistence on

submission to authority (Hebrews 13:7) have been part of the church. But we went too far on some things, as in submission. To the leaders — need to humble out and let others lead you. Sometimes advice went too far. Advice isn't law or "thus sayeth the law." The more it's based on the bible the better it will be. But Randy addressed this in the past — advice is advice. The "one man leader" of a congregation — as a church grows in size and age it needs a team to meet all needs (thus the overseers group). Discipling (I preached on this in 1981, called it the "missing ingredient" as I was not yet here) — we need others in our lives. There's been too much of an "over/under" method. We need to be friends, mentors. As we grow, see it as spiritual friends who need each other. Can (in a wrong way) depend on a discipler to "fix" me. Need group discipling, where we volunteer to be open and initiate.

In the body, Gordon's greatest regret is that so many feel like second class citizens. There has been too much clergy/laity and God is taking care of that (a little humor since we've had so many layoffs, there's hardly anyone left!). Some who didn't make staff felt like they "never made it." And when some moved here to go into the full time ministry and weren't appointed, that was especially hard. Some moved here to go on mission teams, and then weren't picked. And when Boston leaders said, "We sent out our best," where did that leave everyone else?? I now prefer to say that we sent the best and kept the best. Our relationship with God is not based on performance, but on being his sons and daughters.

Heart/Motivation/Personal Choice — There is a difference between commitment and conforming and conviction. Mistakes were made in finances and evangelism, where people were pushed to do what they didn't think was best for themselves. Even with good results, it's not good for the people. The leaders pushed the disciples too far. "If you were pushed past where your heart was and got hurt, I'm sorry. Please participate with us. It's always right to get more of a body feel."

Need to restore humble leaders and repentance.

(Now each leader got up and confessed their sin, apologized to the congregation, and asked for forgiveness.)

Personal Statements

Randy McKean

We are a restoration movement but also a reactionary movement (against a lack of lordship). I failed to emphasize some things for fear of going back to wrong things, and so we weren't "restored" properly. We are a remnant movement, had to start all over again, but it has some lacking in it because of that (he specifically mentioned the lack of wisdom from not having older disciples who had "been there" to guide us). We primarily began with youth and small numbers and not much age/experience/maturity to get us to where we are now. Now have age, size and distance to deal with. Have done a poor job of dealing with the age of our membership. In the bible, the way of continual restoration is through repentance. Hosea 6:1-3, 14:1-2.

In regard to the staff, I put too much pressure on them, too much emphasis on performance and numbers leading to bad motivation and practices. That was passed on to us. I am deeply sorry. I made the staff feel not trusted, respected, and probably, not even liked. I am sorry for my part in this dynamic.

I have failed to appreciate the aging and maturity process in the church and not had input from others. I have failed to ask enough input and therefore people felt unneeded, unimportant, and not valued, and they have lost heart, leading to a fear of speaking up. I made people feel they could never do enough. I've been more concerned for me than for you.

I have failed to effectively speak up and deal with motivations that weren't best and so allowed a wrong emphasis to be there. I even felt faithless and hopeless at times that changes could be made through me. It's the sin of cowardice and being fearful of consequences.

I am going to be a better listener, seek input, emphasize that everyone is needed and important, and that people feel that at their emotional centers. I want you to feel valued. I am going to empathize and emotionally feel for others (Kay has been trying to help me with that for years, so have the elders). I am going to trust myself less and others more, while remaining full of compassion and conviction. Not just words on paper but my heart.

Wyndham Shaw

My depth of prayer life and bible study has not increased to match the load that I have been asked to carry. Being an elder is all about caring about the people. I am committed to making a difference. I've been pushing people to baptize because of what it meant to my image and my performance.

I've not pushed myself after becoming a HOPE leader and since being appointed an elder. I've not had a personal ministry and have justified this by all of the "crisis management" that I do. But my example cannot be as one who manages crises, but that of a disciple. I've allowed staff roles to develop into a clergy mentality, which has led to a congregation within a congregation. We've been dependent on a system — an example being how you would be studying with someone and then we jump in and take the study from you so that someone could be converted faster. We are committed to returning the ministry to the people.

I've accepted too many tasks and not been available to people. I need to do what's important. Leviticus 5:1.

I've allowed conflict to remain at the kingdom level (ie, outside our world sector) and within our world sector. I have repented and spoken to everyone at this point. And I will uphold righteousness. I've laid guilt trips on people for leaving Boston, based on how it would reflect on me. People have not felt my acceptance because of that. I am repenting of wanting to be spoken well of rather than speaking up. I can be sentimental and cowardly.

Dan Bathon

I've had an opportunity to influence world sector leadership. In not speaking up, I've been cowardly. Ezekiel 3:17 re: kingdom and leadership practices. Feels leaders didn't balance 1 Corinthians 1:19 (seeking and building the kingdom) with the equally important teachings of loving one another, being kind, compassionate, and not burdensome, 1 John 5:7. I made commands burdensome to staff and people. I needed to say "This is not right...."

I saw conflict between top leaders and I didn't call for resolution quickly. Matthew 5:25. So I am responsible for the damage. Financial Gifts — I failed to warn strongly about the risks of the stock market. And so people put their hope in riches and not in God, the opposite of 1 Timothy 6:17. And so the layoffs came (he was crying here) and so many staff couples who worked hard for so many years left. And their lives and dreams were disrupted. My many jobs kept me from being diligent.

I need to be a better shepherd. Leadership dynamic — A leader is called by God. We need leadership and God's hand in bringing it about and taking it out. I put personality of leadership over principles of God. I call this our family of God yet created an environment where people were afraid to speak up. I failed in the areas of evangelism, prayer, and bible study. This is the most displeasing to God. Heb 12:11, Rev 3:19.

Gordon Ferguson

In my ministry leading days I have a performance mentality. And if you are not aware of it, then God and I are certainly aware of it. It became much too big a deal. Because of how I was raised, I was/am an insecure person who tries to impress and motivate others in wrong ways. When I first came to Boston, I got discipled on my tongue — insensitive at best and harshness at its worst. Matthew 6:33 — I wanted to look good and make the kingdom successful. Here he gave an example of his insensitivity: where Dave Malutinok's wife's grandmother was sick and BYND was coming up. She wanted to be with her dying grandmother, but Gordon said, It's BYND, you need to be here. He started crying over this. Fortunately, Randy set me straight, he said.

I failed to protect you when I saw things and didn't fight for change. No courage or conviction.

In Matthew 28, Jesus said to teach them to obey, need to follow through. I said the right things for a number of years, but saw things and didn't fight for change.

As a disciple, there were times when my spirituality wasn't enough. I carried the load, but not spiritually.

Evangelism failures. Elders talk about their load and it makes the people feel like their load is too great. Then you feel too burdened to be evangelistic, and that's not right.

Know that your leaders are sinners, but they're repenting. We're all works in progress.

Reactions: In the Golden Rule of Leadership, there was one chapter that should have been included which was not at the beginning. It goes out now as an insert. It's called the Golden Rule Followship. We can react in ways that are not best (to this message):

Three Reactions that wouldn't be good:

1. Those who are right can say "I told you so."
2. Those who have been wrong can have a defensive pride.
3. Those who have been wronged are prone to bitterness.

One thing I have learned over time — Most Christians expect to be mistreated by the world, and they usually respond ok to that. The biggest test is when they're wronged by those in the church and the challenge is to respond in a Christ-like way. Those we love we hurt the most. Once we've apologized, we usually feel ok. But some need to work through all the details.

Closing — Chip Mitchell —Rejoicing!

Need to rejoice over brokenness. Acts 3;13-20. Broken heart—But God brings refreshing from a clean slate. Brought on (1) by God, who chooses to accept our apologies and forgive and by (2) the changes I make. As God's mercy compels us, so we can compel others by our choices. Changes like going from prideful to humble, selfish to sacrificial, critical to grateful, grumpy to happy, harshness to compassion, ill-willed to kind. Will only be momentary unless we have a connection to God. Psalm 33:18-22. When leaders fail, I still have God, who will not fail me.

Repentance Letter, March 16, 2003

After the release of the Kriete letter, the Boston Overseeing Team decided to move the leadership of the congregation to the seven men who were serving as elders either for the whole church or in the regions. The following letter was written by the Overseeing Team as they gave over the oversight of the church to the elders.

March 16, 2003

> But if we walk in the light, as he is in the light, we have fellowship with one another, and the blood of Jesus, his Son, purifies us from all sin.
> If we claim to be without sin, we deceive ourselves and the truth is not in us. If we confess our sins, he is faithful and just and will forgive us our sins and purify us from all unrighteousness. If we claim we have not sinned, we make him out to be a liar and his word has no place in our lives. (1 John 1:7–10)

Brothers and Sisters in the Boston Church,

Let those of us on the overseeing team (Gordon Ferguson, Wyndham Shaw, Randy McKean and Dan Bathon) say at the outset that we deeply regret all failures of our leadership, and deeply appreciate all gestures of grace and forgiveness on your part. We also want to say that trying to communicate our feelings through a written document is very challenging, and we ask you to listen carefully for our hearts as you read. Around the globe those in our fellowship of churches are in a major time of transition, re-examining many practices and many are coming to God in humility seeking renewal and change. We rejoice in all repentance, public and private, and want to stay in this mode ourselves, as God continues to show us our sins and weaknesses.

Many letters, articles and apologies have been published recently, which have served to motivate and inspire us to keep taking our own repentance deeper. We have much agreement with what these other apologies state. Certainly we agree that the abuses are systemic and present to one degree or another in about every church. However, they are present to different degrees in various ministries in those churches, depending on the specific leader. But we all guilty to some extent, and the higher up in the system of leadership we are, the greater the responsibility before God. This explains why this letter comes from the overseeing team.

Areas where we are convicted that we have shared in these systemic sins include, but are not limited to, the following: harsh and/or arrogant leadership; authoritarian discipling relationships; sinful motivation through the use of statistics and insensitive accountability; fostering financial giving under a sense of compulsion; and the misuse and misapplication of Scripture. The remainder of this letter will provide further details of our sin and repentance in these and other areas, along with an update on what we have done to put past repentance into action with needed changes.

We realize that there are a number of people who have moved from Boston or who have left the Boston Church over many years and it is our hope that this letter will be made available to them either through the Internet or in some other fashion. If you know some of these people, we would appreciate any efforts you can make to see that this letter is sent to them.

In September 2002 the leaders in the Boston Church who made up the overseeing team came before the entire congregation in Lowell, Massachusetts, to confess our sins, apologize, share our repentance and ask for your forgiveness. Included was confession about making some feel like second-class citizens, not valuing those who are older and more mature, motivating with a concern for numbers and performance, not listening enough, not including non-staff people in important decisions, and doing things to perpetuate a clergy/laity system. We want to say clearly that we are deeply sorry about the way our sins and failures may have affected you and your family, your schedule and most of all your faith.

We realize that the things that we said in that meeting were not made available on the Internet in as timely a fashion as they could have been, and we are sorry for that oversight. For some time now, notes of that meeting have been posted on the Boston Church Web site, and they will remain there for several more weeks to allow anyone who has not read them to have that opportunity.

Since that meeting the leaders in Boston have initiated a series of changes that hopefully demonstrate our ongoing repentance. It now seems good to give the church an update on some of those things. We also want to share with you other areas that have since been identified where additional repentance and changes need to be made.

In the months after that September meeting, a series of town meetings were held where the floor was open for questions and concerns to be expressed. A great deal of input was received from you in those meetings, and we all became more deeply aware of the needs and concerns of the congregation. We invited, and continue to invite, anyone who feels hurt by individual leaders to come and share those hurts and sins with the leaders who caused the pain. We welcome the opportunity to hear the specifics about what you have been made to feel, and to resolve those things with you.

After the input from the town meetings, changes were made to encourage the development of leadership teams in every region of the church, where paid staff and qualified non-staff leaders would work side by side to provide direction. At this writing, significant progress has been made in that area, with most regions now having such teams in place or working toward that end.

Additionally, the decision has been made to broaden the base of leadership for the entire Boston Church based on biblically identified roles. The group that we have known as the overseeing team recently met with the all of the elders and evangelists in the church and with other "leaders among the brothers" (Acts 15:22). This last group is composed of staff and non-staff people of influence within their regions. The goal of this group will be to help develop a collective leadership, which will represent a fresh biblical vision of how to provide leadership for the entire congregation. This group is working to find the best way to insure inclusive and efficient leadership. This letter is from the overseeing team, but at the end of it you will find the names of those in this working group (as well as a statement of their support of the things written here).

At this time we would like to address several additional issues with the congregation.

1. **Ongoing repentance (2 Corinthians 7:10-11).** We need to clearly say that though we began a process of repentance and change at least as early as last September, we do not believe we have fully dealt with the things that need to be addressed. One of our fellow leaders in another church recently remarked that repentance is not a destination but a direction. We are repenting. No one is saying we have made it through. We do not say, "It is over." It will be over when God says it is over, and we pray for the humility to keep seeing anything that is not in line with God's will. Repentance and restoration must be an ongoing process for all churches and all Christians. We invite your additional input to help us see areas where more repentance or change is needed.

2. **Leadership example (1 Peter 5:1-3, 1 Timothy 4:12).** We see in Scripture that one of the primary roles of a leader is to be an example. We wish to apologize for our failure to be consistent examples of sacrificial and servant leadership. We believe that in some cases wrong leadership styles may have contributed to people leaving the congregation and, where this is has happened, we are deeply sorry. We would invite you to share with us specifically any ways that our leadership may have hurt you or ways in which you see that it did contribute to someone's decision to leave our fellowship. Those of us in

the overseeing team wish to express our apology also to the staff for the way in which our actions or inaction have hurt them and we ask for their forgiveness. Another weakness in our example has been in calling others to seek help with their lives, while not always seeking such input ourselves. We wish to pledge to let everyone see our progress (1 Timothy 4:15) in loving God, loving one another, loving the lost, loving the poor, and in getting help in all these areas.

3. **Financial accountability (2 Corinthians 8:20-21).** We apologize for having a financial process that has not been more open to non-staff evaluation and review, and want to express our intention to make major changes in this area. One of the first changes we want to communicate is our decision to reconstitute the Board of Directors of the Boston Church of Christ, so that there will be more non-staff people serving on the board than staff members. The new board will represent a broad cross section of the congregation, and will have broader authority to deal with financial issues and questions than in the past.

    Additionally, we recognize that there needs to be a careful review of staff compensation. Some policy changes related to our expense reimbursement for ministry staff have already been approved, but we see this as only a beginning. The Boston Church has been following the salary model that is currently used in all U.S.-based churches in the International Churches of Christ, but it is evident to us that we must review the approach being taken. A resolution to form a task force consisting of one non-staff representative from each region was passed by the Boston Church board Monday night. This task force will represent a cross section of the church, and will work (with some staff consultation) on what is fair compensation for staff members. As a part of this examination of staff compensation, we see the need to carefully examine the role of ministry staff women who have significant responsibilities with their children and their homes. We need a model that recognizes and fairly compensates our women leaders for their work, while, in some cases, not expecting that they can or should maintain the same ministry responsibilities as their husbands. Overall, we recognize a need to have a salary structure that will be commended by the congregation.

    Also in regard to finances we want to apologize to you for the fact that money was not always spent wisely. Once money is given, it is no longer yours, but neither is it ours – it is God's. At times we took a more conservative approach than other churches, particularly with the salary model, increasing salaries less than what we could have according to rules in place at the time. However, there were times when other expenditures were in excess of what was appropriate and needed. At times, we allowed the financial culture of the late '90s to influence our decisions more than biblical principles, and for this we are very sorry. Going forward the church will always have non-staff people as a part of the process of determining what is best in the management of finances. To adapt 2 Corinthians 8:20-21: "We want to avoid any criticism of the way we administer [your] liberal gift[s]. For we [will take] pains to do what is right, not only in the eyes of the Lord but also in the eyes of men."

4. **Biblical roles (Ephesians 4:11-16)**. In our ongoing effort to review our work in a spirit of repentance and restoration, the decision has been made to no longer use the terms "region leader" or "region elder." Going forward we will have evangelists and elders who serve in regions, but may also serve in wider roles when the needs arise. Leadership in our regions will be provided by leadership teams composed of some combination of elders, evangelists, deacons, and teachers or other leaders who are commended by the disciples. We are also assessing the women's ministry role to make any changes that need to be made in it. Much in-depth study is currently being done to biblically define leadership roles.

5. **The one body (Ephesians 4:1-7)**. Recent widely-circulated letters and articles from various disciples have addressed the need for our churches to correct either impressions given, or teaching done, on the idea of the one church. We are happy to join with other congregations in saying that while we clearly believe there is one church (Ephesians 4:1-7, 1 Corinthians 12:13) and believe the biblical teaching about how one enters the church (Luke 14:25-33, Acts 2:38, Romans 6:1-4, Galatians 3:26-27), it would be arrogant of us to think that we can draw the boundaries for that church and dogmatically say who is in it and who is not. That is something only God can do, and we repent of having arrogantly assumed his role in some of our statements, studies or implications. God will make these determinations on an individual basis by the truth found in his Word (John 12:48). We intend for there to be more clear teaching on this in the future. We understand that

from time to time we may need to come back to the congregation to more correctly teach on other subjects where there has been inadequate or incorrect teaching.

6. **Biblical study (2 Timothy 2:15).** We recognize that we have not placed the priority on the careful study of the Bible that is needed. Our church schedules and our various efforts to grow the church have often reflected a humanistic attitude. We have not given a high priority to in-depth biblical teaching, which is so vital to our faith and to our ability to build the kind of church that God desires. For this we are sorry and pledge ourselves to make the necessary changes so that our ministry is based on this type of study of the Scriptures.

7. **Brotherhood unity (1 Peter 2:17).** We recognize that God's family includes disciples in other congregations throughout the world and that we are responsible for seeking unity with them. Recent events and the changing face of the church have certainly strained relationships both within congregations and between congregations. We are grateful for the unity that we have with our sister congregations throughout New England and Europe and will continue to work to keep those bonds strong. We want to pledge ourselves to work for unity not only in New England and Europe but throughout the world. This is clearly God's will (John 17) and it will take a collective effort to defeat the forces of darkness and to bring Jesus to those who are yet lost. The transition from a dictated unity to a true unity, a forged unity, will take great love and perseverance by all of God's children. We want to make clear our desire to "love the brotherhood of believers" (1 Peter 2:17).

8. **Continued openness (Psalm 139:23-24).** Finally, we want to once again say that on these or other matters we wish to receive ongoing input from you, the members of the congregation. Please understand that we are inviting you to continue speaking the truth in love to us. Primarily we would urge you to carefully study the Bible so that you might help us all find more biblical solutions to the challenges we face. Serious prayer and Bible study are vital needs at this hour. We understand that we are all a work in progress, but we want to make that progress.

God has done great things among our fellowship of churches. In the last twenty-four years we have seen miracles in our own lives and miracles around the world. As God always does, he has put his treasure in jars of clay and used us in spite of our weaknesses. As people grateful for his love, grace, and forgiveness, we want to keep changing and keep growing. We want to get rid of anything that keeps us from valuing one another, trusting one another, and loving one another deeply. "In every way [we want to] make the teaching about God our Savior attractive" (Titus 2:10), because we know God "wants all men to be saved and to come to a knowledge of the truth" (1 Timothy 2:4).

As leaders, we understand our responsibility not only to help the church make the changes that will best glorify God and advance the gospel, but we understand the need to continually examine our own lives and receive help from God and others to make the changes we personally need to make. As we strive to be examples in that area, we call on each of you to do the same, so that with one heart and one mind we make Jesus known in our world and bring many more to the foot of the cross.

May his grace be with you all.
Gordon Ferguson, Wyndham Shaw, Randy McKean, Dan Bathon

We the brothers referred to on page 2 have worked with the overseeing team to give our advice and input concerning this letter. We wish to commend it to the church and wholeheartedly express our desire to be a part of the ongoing repentance and restoration described here.

Elders:
Jack Frederick
Tom Jones
Tracy Larr
Clarence Webster

Evangelists:
Phil Arsenault
Brad Bynum
David Cedano
Sal DiFusco
Rich Fisher
Frank Hines
Brian Homet
Kevin Miller
Hector Morales
Jim Lenahen
John McGuirk
Chip Mitchell

Robin Rodriguez
Brian Scanlon
Sajjan Sharma
Roy Stagg
Jim Valente
Mike VanAuken
Andy Yeatman

Teacher
Kelly Petre

Other leaders:
Mark Buchholz
Ken Lowey
Dave Malutinok
David McAnulty
Ken Ostrowski

Source: Boston Church of Christ Web Site
www.bostoncoc.org

Appendix Four
Items Contained in Other Apology Letters

In the days following the release in February 2003 of Henry Kriete's open letter, titled "Honest to God," the leaders of most churches in the International Churches of Christ wrote an apology letter to their members or held some kind of any open meeting in which apologies and new commitments were given.

One of the most comprehensive letters came from the Los Angeles Church, the largest church in International Churches of Christ, and contained detailed comments on the following points:

1) Arrogance in the staff — Matthew 20:25–28
2) Weakening other churches — Philippians 2:3–4
3) Giving Through Compulsion — 2 Corinthians 9: 6–8
4) Authoritarian discipling — Ephesians 5:21
5) Improper Teaching of the One True Church — Ephesians 4:1–7;
   1 Corinthians 12:13
6) Not Emphasizing the Greatest Commandments — Matthew 22:37–40
7) Not Fulfilling the Role of the Elders — 1 Peter 5:1–4
8) Abusive Accountability — Ephesians 2:8–10
9) Not Teaching the Bible in Depth — Hebrews 5:11–6:3
10) Discouraging Older Disciples — Ephesians 4:11–16

Other sins confessed and apologies offered in the letters of other churches included the following:

- Selfish ambition among leaders
- Not correcting errors in First Principles material for non-Christians
- Motivating through numbers and statistics
- Favoritism (toward ministry leaders) — One church for leaders; one for members
- Misuse of the idea of "falling away"
- Culture of fear and control
- Works-oriented culture
- Legalistic dating rules
- Failure to use Biblical leadership, favoring one man rule
- Wrong teaching about bearing fruit
- Cowardice in standing up to what they knew was wrong
- Harshness (several)
- Lack of care with finances. Not enough accountability in place. Lack of openness with the membership

Appendix Five

Sample of Events in ICOC Churches — 2007

Thanks to the Disciples Today Web site led by Roger and Marcia Lamb for this information.

Single Parents Beach Week
4/7/2007 - 4/14/2007
Outer Banks, North Carolina USA
Richmond Church of Christ

Church Builders Workshop
4/9/2007 - 4/11/2007
Reston, Virginia USA
Baltimore Church of Christ

"Look Beyond" Campus Retreat
4/13/2007 - 4/15/2007
The Grand Canyon, Arizona USA
Los Angeles Church of Christ

2007 International Youth Ministers
  Conference
4/19/2007 - 4/22/2007
Boston, Massachusetts USA
Boston Church of Christ

2007 Spring Singles Retreat
4/27/2007 - 4/29/2007
Thousand Oaks Ranch, Texas USA
DFW Church of Christ

35th Anniversary Reunion
5/18/2007 - 5/20/2007
Davie, Florida USA
South Florida Church of Christ

HOPE *worldwide* Global Summit
5/19/2007 - 5/20/2007
Dulles Hyatt, Virginia USA
HOPE worldwide

Summer Teen and Campus Internships
6/1/2007 - 8/15/2007
St. Louis, Missouri USA
Greater St. Louis Church

Summer Campus Internships
6/1/2007 - 8/29/2007
San Antonio, Texas USA
San Antonio Intl Church of Christ

HOPEww Gulf Coast Reclamation
6/2/2007 - 7/14/2007
New Orleans, Louisiana USA
HOPEww Gulf Coast

The Swamp Family Camp
6/6/2007 - 6/9/2007
Athens, Georgia USA
Atlanta Church of Christ

HOPE Youth Corps
6/6/2007 - 8/14/2007
Kenya, Brazil, India, Jamaica, USA
HOPE *worldwide*

Central American Conference
6/7/2007 - 6/10/2007
San Pedro Sula, Honduras
International Church of Christ in San
  Pedro Sula

The Swamp Camp Sessions
6/10/2007 - 7/28/2007
Athens, Georgia USA
Atlanta Church of Christ

Midwest Youth Camps "The Mission"
6/17/2007 - 8/4/2007
Illinois, Minnesota USA
Chicago Church of Christ

R Camp
6/17/2007 - 7/28/2007
Camp ArthuReeta in Schwenksville,
  Pennsylvania USA
ACR Churches

Asian Christian Jubilee "Believe!"
6/21/2007 - 6/24/2007
Manila, Philippines
Metro Manila Christian Church

International Apologetics Conference
6/22/2007 - 6/24/2007
Irvine, California USA

JoBurg Church 21st Anniversary
  Celebration
6/24/2007 - 6/29/2007
Johannesburg, South Africa
JoBurg Church of Christ

2007 International Campus Ministry
  Conference
7/5/2007 - 7/8/2007
Boston, Massachusetts USA
Boston Church of Christ

UK Mother & Daughter Weekend
7/6/2007 - 7/8/2007
High Wycombe, England
London Churches

London churchwide service
7/15/2007 - 7/15/2007
London, England
London Churches

Jerusalem Mission Trip
7/15/2007 - 8/14/2007
Jerusalem, Israel
Jerusalem Church of Christ

Florida Discipleship Conference "Start
  the Fire"
7/19/2007 - 7/22/2007
Orlando, Florida USA
Florida Churches

West African Leadership Conference
7/20/2007 - 7/22/2007
Lagos, Nigeria
International Churches of Christ Nigeria

African Mission Leadership Conference
7/23/2007 - 7/25/2007
Abuja, Nigeria
International Churches of Christ Nigeria

West Coast Singles Conference
7/27/2007 - 7/29/2007
Rancho Mirage, California USA
Los Angeles Church of Christ

Volunteer Interns — All Ages
7/29/2007 - 8/11/2007
San Antonio, Texas USA
San Antonio Church of Christ

Christian Unity Summit
8/4/2007 - 8/5/2007
Omaha, Nebraska USA
Omaha Church of Christ

UK Teen and Preteen Camps
8/12/2007 - 8/19/2007
Oxford, England
UK Churches

Inchree 2007 Week of Fellowship
8/23/2007 - 8/30/2007
Scottish Highlands, Scotland
Glasgow Church of Christ

London Churchwide Service
10/7/2007 - 10/7/2007
London, England
London Churches

2007 International Leadership
  Conference
10/7/2007 - 10/9/2007
Anaheim, California USA
Los Angeles Church of Christ

Spiritual Adventure Tour for Singles 28
  Years and Older
10/7/2007 - 10/16/2007
Cape Town, South Africa
Cape Town Church of Christ

Mid-South Discipleship Conference
10/26/2007 – 10/28/2007
Nashville, Tennessee
Mid-South Churches

Mexico City Church 20th Anniversary
10/28/2007 - 10/28/2007
Mexico City, Mexico
Iglesia de Cristo en Mexico A.R.

Biblical Study Tour & Intl. Teachers
  Conference
11/3/2007 - 11/9/2007
Ephesus, Turkey
Douglas Jacoby

London Churchwide Christmas Carol
  Service
12/16/2007 - 12/16/2007
London, England
London Churches

Appendix Six
One Bible Talk

Author's note: Jack Frederick is an engineer with the Raytheon Corporation. His family and ours spent much time together in the Boston Church over eighteen years, and he and I served as elders together for ten years. Not aware that I was working on this book, he sent me this piece he had written about a small group he is involved in. I include it as an appendix as an example of the kind of heart and spirit I believe you find in many churches in the ICOC fellowship.

Our Bible Talk is a special family devoted to God and to loving one another (Acts 2:42, John 13:34-35). At this point some of your minds are shutting down, going to sleep, because you think "My Bible Talk is so NOT like that!" I ask God to open your eyes as he did Elisha's servant to what God sees (2 Kings 6:17). Our Bible Talk has consistently been blessed with 3-4 baptisms each year. I believe your Bible Talk, (I hope you do have a Bible Talk) has the same gifts from God mine does.

Now some more good news...I don't lead my Bible Talk, I'm just part of it. That's good news for me and for the group that doesn't have to listen to me!

- My Bible Talk leader, many of the Bible Talk members, and I work 50+ hour-a-week jobs.
- Others carry different loads.
- Many of us are "older." The average age is 46.
- The average years in Christ is 14.
- Our Bible Talk leader is 66 years old, his wife just turned 60. She is youthful, he's just old! (Sorry Milton.) They have no full-time ministry experience, and they have five grown children and six grandchildren. Some of their kids are disciples and some not. I'm not far behind them in age, with three children and two grandkids.
- In our group we have three women whose husbands are not disciples and rarely come to anything with them, some are antagonistic.
- There are housewives, blue collar folks, engineers, doctors, immigrants, unemployed, etc. Divorcees; one a brother, the other a sister.
- Two members have severe emotional disorders, one a Vietnam Veteran with emotional and health problems from the war and homelessness.
- One brother is a 60 year-old flute maker from Peru, another a green card lottery winner from Ghana with a wife and eight children back in Ghana.
- One brother is a biker replete with tattoos.

- There's a Finn married to a Brazilian, two young Cambodian couples, a Thai sister married to a prison maintenance guy.

How about some charity here…do you feel bad for me yet? Are you fired up!!! Are you asking, what's so special about this group? Do you suddenly feel like your Bible Talk is full of "sharp" people?

Thus far this year we've been blessed with four baptisms…in one month. We have four additional studies right now and lots of visitors coming to church, Bible Talk, parties, etc. One couple was baptized in June, wed in July and initiated a campus ministry in September where the sister works. We don't talk much about evangelism but we do it. Our Bible Talk leader loves the poor and helps us focus on helping the poor and needy. Just now he is on a flight to Phnom Penh, Cambodia, where they go each fall to volunteer in the Sihanouk Hospital for HOPE. He and his wife are generous by example. They are good BT leaders but their strength is devotion to prayer and trust in God.

For our weekly DP time, time as discipleship partners (is it OK to say that?) he and I meet for an early morning prayer walk. We meet in a big cinema parking lot and walk fast to get cardio-exercise…we're older and he's a cardiologist. In fact he's also the head of medicine for his HMO, practicing plus managing fifty physicians, nurses and admin folks. Back to DP time, for fifteen minutes we talk about prayer needs for ourselves or for others, we share good news, or confess our sins. God hears our conversation, but then we focus on praying these things to God, asking him to deal with our requests and needs, and bless us. After 45–60 minutes we are tired but refreshed, ready to go about our day and our week. Often I've been up till 2:00 or 4:00 am the night before, tired but deeply in need of this inspiring time. I've never said "I wish I'd stayed in bed" or "I wish I hadn't done that this morning." We love and encourage one another. The same is true of the people in our Bible Talk…they love one another and love doing things together and for one another. I think that God blesses us because of our prayers and because we love one another (John 13:34-35). This has produced a great love for one another. If you read this and learn how to "crank my Bible Talk," you missed the boat. This is written to encourage you to totally depend on God through prayer and your friendships with the other 3000 Jesus-es around you (ref to *Upside Down*, circa 1987).

I'm thinking you would all like to know more about this incredible BT group. If you are still in the "how do I crank this" then initiate retro rockets, relax and chill…this would be a time to stop where you are and pray. Even better, stop and pray with someone…if it's a co-worker that's double good for you...you get to be humble, reach out and publicly acknowledge your faith.

I'll share things about our group you can imitate. I'll try to keep it family so it's not dry, boring and self-help-ish. Don't try to make these an equation or formula lest you squeeze the life out of this helpful input. Rather, absorb it into your life. Rub it on your head and let it run down upon your beard (Psalm 133).

Prayer: Did I mention that Milton & Debbie taught us to believe in prayer, to depend on it, not to depend on our ability? That will be on the test...you might want to remember it. Depending on prayer is enabled through living long and experiencing many failures of your own power and intellect. Milton has failed, I've failed, you've failed, therefore we can learn to build great loving BTs & Family Groups like Milton's. That's the transitive property of God which says "we are all hopeless without God, but through God we can do all things."

Complement & Compliment: Milton & Debbie are my best friends but they were not given more gifts and talents than the rest of us. They love to study the Bible with people, they are evangelistic and hospitable, but Milton is not a very fun person. He was an engineer before he became a physician...this killer combination yields a guy who likes to read dry medical journals and plot data on graphs. Engineers can tend toward nerdiness. I'm an engineer, too, but I received a transplant of the "fun" chromosome. Milton is structured and evangelistic and structured. I'm nurturing and am no friend to structure, so we need one another (1 Corinthians 12, Romans 12). I won't be as hard on the rest of the group but we are all different and needed. One sister is a grandmother who brings her four grandchildren to church each week, all under 5 years of age. Many of our baptisms have come from her quiet sharing with co-workers. She is a CR graduate, a recovering alcoholic. Linny is Cambodian. At 21 years old she was a Buddhist who came to America to marry a husband she'd never met. Her English was not good, and she knew nothing of Jesus when she came with her sister-in-law. Her husband watched her and after some months asked her to read the Bible to him each morning. In a few months he was buried with Jesus and is a great servant and joy. Van & Anny are in their 20s. They didn't get the message that we no longer focus on evangelism...they bring 5-10 people to church each week.

Know One Another: I could go on to identify each person's gift and quirks, but suffice it to say God brings us together in our differences because we need one another to be whole. Because we love one another we not only tolerate one another's differences & gifts, we value them…rejoice in them! Commit yourselves to KNOW one another. Jesus says eternal life is to know (Greek, *gnosis*) God, then Paul ups the ante when he prays for the disciples to really know God (Greek, *epi-gnosis*). We should seek to know God as we know our best friends, the way you know what they really like. In our Bible Talk group we benefit greatly from getting to know one another, really knowing, understanding and caring. As with our kids, seek to find what others like, what they enjoy. Do these things with people in your group.

Remember The Poor: We get busy doing good things, we learn to crank the ministry but we miss the simple value of helping the poor, which is so important to God (Matthew 23:23). We've learned how much we need to help the poor. During a time of confusion and apathy the churches lost their compass in planning activities to help the poor. During this time the Drakes led our BT to begin a Thanksgiving Day walk to raise money for the poor…they planned this walk in their upscale neighborhood. The upscale neighbors gave money. Milton says if we help the poor we will be evangelistic.

Go Into All Nations: We are concerned about needs in our Bible Talk and in our community, but we also care about those in other nations (Matthew 28:18-20). We pray for them, we give financially and we go into all nations. Every year the Drakes go to Cambodia to serve in the hospital. While there last year they drove six hours roundtrip to visit Linny's parents. Linny had been a Christian 2 months. Her parents live in a village and speak no English. The Drakes traveled fifteen thousand miles to visit the parents of a young disciple (and work in the hospital). A few months ago I took a trip to visit the churches across Europe. I've been discipling a brother in Dublin for the past year at his request, and I had made the time to speak with most of the disciples in Dublin on the phone.

After a year I agreed to visit. Remember the fifty-hour-a-week job? I took vacation, just like Milton does, to go visit the disciples I don't know. I visited ten churches in ten cities in five nations in ten days. I slept an average of four hours a day, some of that on planes. I paid my own expenses (with the money God gave me through my job) except what some in the Bible Talk contributed. I had one agenda: to communicate how much our Bible Talk loves the disciples across Europe. In effect our Bible Talk visited the disciples across Europe. We took books on prayer to each church. We shared what God was doing in our Bible Talk. We spoke of how we love one another and urged them to love one another. We shared that six people were studying the bible in our Bible Talk of 25 people. Two people were baptized into Christ while I was in

Europe, two more upon my return to America (these two started a campus ministry in September!). The churches in all these nations were moved by our Bible Talk's love for them and by the living example of a loving and fruitful Bible Talk, those who love and disciple one another and who take the good news to those around them.

There are more simple things we can share to help you build a great Bible Talk / Family Group…write to us or just come and see it for yourself. I pray that you will be blessed as we have by God! I hope you have a family like ours!

……………………..

Update note from Jack April 2007: I wrote this on the flight from Boston to Virginia Beach Conference in October 2006, a one hour flight. I didn't have to think, I simply wrote from the heart. By year's end we saw two more baptisms. We split the Bible Talk into three groups, one of which eventually re-merged with the original to meet specific needs. Now in April 2007 the two Bible Talks are growing. The Drakes' group has six new people studying the Bible and the Lorees' new planting has six additional people studying the Bible. We still depend on prayer. We continue discipling relationships. We face challenges in life and in our faith but we press on trusting God. I don't remember what it was like to be in a Bible Talk that didn't have so many studies. I don't remember what it was like to "not be in a Bible Talk." I didn't mention that I also serve as one of six elders in the Boston Church, one of three non-staff elders. Being a part of an active, faith-filled Bible Talk doesn't add to my load, it lightens my burdens. It's not about me. It's not about us. It's not about how much we know or what gifts and talents we've been given. It's about Jesus! He doesn't need us; he can make the rocks sing (Luke19:40). He can make Legion preach (Mark 5:20). Our Bible Talk is not impressive, Jesus is impressive! Are you so dull you think he can't do this and more with a Bible Talk you're in? I don't intend to make this sound easy. It's not easy, but it is simple. Jesus was about simple. His responses to the teachers and rulers of his day were simple. This ain't rocket science, the New Testament was written in koine Greek, the language of the common people (koine = common). We are all very common in Jesus' eyes…he was impressed with the common (Luke 21:2). He was never impressed with titles, the rich, the mighty or the erudite. Do you need help to learn, understand and apply the things I wrote about in your life? Spend more time with kids, learn to think simple like they do. That's Jesus' recommendation: I didn't think it up (Matthew 18:2–4).

I love you and I hope sharing what God is doing with common people like us (like you) will encourage the rest of you common people to do likewise. Pray for us and we will pray for you.

Appendix Seven
Ideas for Reaching Out to Other Believers

1. Pray as Jesus did in John 17.
2. When you think of the church in your city, pray to see it as God sees it. When you think of "loving the brotherhood," ask how God sees the brotherhood.
3. Visit www.Connect4Change.net and participate in a new effort to meet disciples from other fellowships in the Restoration Movement, work on understanding, and share lessons we are learning and methods we are using to make a difference.
4. When you meet someone from a Christian Church, a Church of Christ, or some other fellowship, set up meal together. Do some of the following:
   A. Share your spiritual journeys.
   B. Watch out for judgmentalism (i.e. "sounds different from us").
   C. Pray together.
   D. Look for common ground. Things everyone can feel great about doing together.
   E. Study together how you do evangelism.
   F. Ask them to read this book and then discuss the list of 26 things in Chapter Fourteen.
   G. Work to get elders and ministers connected to plan some efforts to bring people together.
   H. Ask them to read the notes from the speech: "If the World Hates You" (Chapter Ten) and discuss the thoughts you both have.
5. At conferences and other events, advocate for inviting speakers who have a strong biblical message but are outside your "tribe."

Appendix Eight
Your Baptism
Reprinted from Letters to New Disciples

Dear new ones,

In this letter I am going to write to you about your baptism into Christ. This is a very biblical thing to do. When Peter and Paul wrote letters to young disciples, they frequently took them back to their baptisms and reminded them of all that happened at that point in their lives.

Baptism, sadly, is a controversial subject in the religious world. I say "sadly," because there was no controversy at all about it in the early church. One gets the idea that there was complete unity about its purpose and its meaning. Because it is controversial today, I am going to be extra careful in this chapter. I am not worried about offending someone. I have counted the cost of including this section. I already know that this book would sell many more copies in religious bookstores if I would just leave out this chapter. No, it is not fear that motivates me. Instead, I am going to be very careful because I want it to be clear that everything I am saying here is connected directly to what the Bible says. I do not want anyone to be able to say that something was pulled out of context or distorted. I also want you to be able to share with others with the greatest of confidence what your baptism meant and what theirs can mean. I do not want you to ever feel apologetic for clear biblical teaching on this subject.

Christians baptize others who want to become disciples because Jesus commanded it. Once again we turn to Matthew 28:

> Then Jesus came to them and said, "All authority in heaven and on earth has been given to me. Therefore go and make disciples of all nations, baptizing them in the name of the Father and of the Son and of the Holy Spirit, and teaching them to obey everything I have commanded you. And surely I am with you always, to the very end of the age." (Matthew 28:18–20)

The mission is to go and teach people to become disciples. When people decide they want to accept that calling, they are to be baptized, and then they are to be discipled to Jesus—that is, taught to obey everything he commanded.

Some time ago, someone who was a disciple came into your life. In some way, that disciple asked if he or she could teach you what following Jesus is all about. After a short time or maybe a long time, you agreed. You heard Jesus' message and after some amount of time, you decided you needed him and his saving grace; and you said, "I want to be his disciple." Immediately, arrangements were made for you to be baptized.

Peter's sermon in Acts 2 details for us what was being accomplished in your baptism. Speaking to the huge crowd gathered for the festival of Pentecost, Peter first told them about Jesus and how they had crucified him. Then we read these words:

> When the people heard this, they were cut to the heart and said to Peter and the other apostles, "Brothers, what shall we do?" Peter replied, "Repent and be baptized, every one of you, in the name of Jesus Christ for the forgiveness of your sins. And you will receive the gift of the Holy Spirit." (Acts 2:37–38)

Here we have an apostle of Christ, who had been given the keys to the kingdom of heaven (Matthew 16:19), on inauguration day for the church of Christ. He is telling the people who were cut to the heart what they must do and what would be done for them when they did it. He tells them to repent (to turn their minds and go in a new direction toward God) and to be baptized. He further explained what baptism accomplishes. He said it is "for the forgiveness of sins" and is followed by the gift of the Holy Spirit. I probably do not need to say that all this is very important. What can be more important than being forgiven of sin and receiving the gift of God's Spirit? Why would anyone want to teach anything different from what the leading apostle taught on the day when a whole new era began? Would God have allowed error in the definitive, for-all-time statement about how to become a Christian and how to become part of his church? Our all-powerful God had orchestrated this plan for centuries. Would he have blown it right when it was clearly culminating? I think we would all have to respond with a resounding "No!"

In response to God's clear message and direction through Peter, three thousand people were baptized that day in the area of the temple. (And as one who recently visited that spot, I can tell you that there were plenty of water pools there to accomplish that task.) But I want to remind you also that Peter promised that the same results of baptism in the name of Jesus would be for "all those that the Lord our God will call." That means you. That means a friend you are sharing with.

This same Peter and his fellow apostles then taught others this message, who passed it on to still others. Jesus' plan (in Matthew 28) began to work. One such person who learned this message was Philip, who became an evangelist. Through some Spirit-led decisions, he ended up sharing the good news with a man from Ethiopia. We could write much about this incident, but I include it here for one reason: We have been seeing what baptism is inwardly:

A decision to repent and follow Jesus as Lord. But this passage makes it clear what baptism is outwardly:

> As they traveled along the road, they came to some water and the eunuch said, "Look, here is water. Why shouldn't I be baptized?" And he gave orders to stop the chariot. Then both Philip and the eunuch went down into the water and Philip baptized him. (Acts 8:36–38)

I include this because some people today teach that baptism is only a spiritual experience, not a literal or a physical one. Obviously, this is not the case. We are talking here about immersion (from the Greek word *baptidzo* which means to "dip, plunge or immerse") in water. The picture is hard to misunderstand. Two grown men walked down into the water and one immersed the other. The one who was baptized then went on his way rejoicing (v. 39). He had found the Messiah. His sins had been forgiven. He had received the promised Holy Spirit. I trust that brings back memories for you.

So we have the command of Jesus; then we have the examples in the book of Acts (there are many more that we could look it), and now we come to the comments made to newer Christians in the letters of Paul and Peter.

First, we will look at Paul's statement in Romans 6. He has just been talking about how salvation is by grace, but he does not want anyone to think that means a license to sin. He says,

> What shall we say, then? Shall we go on sinning so that grace may increase? By no means! We died to sin; how can we live in it any longer? Or don't you know that all of us who were baptized into Christ Jesus were baptized into his death? We were therefore buried with him through baptism into death in order that, just as Christ was raised from the dead through the glory of the Father, we too may live a new life. (Romans 6:1–4)

Paul's purpose was not to write a treatise on baptism. His purpose was to convince them that they should not continue in sin. To do this, he reminded them of their baptisms because what happened there needed to have a cataclysmic effect on sin in their lives. So what happens in baptism, according to Paul? (1) The disciple died to sin. (2) The disciple was baptized into the death of Christ. (3) The disciple was buried with Christ through baptism. (4) The disciple was raised out of baptism to live a new life.

In the next two verses Paul added an exclamation mark to what he had already said:

> If we have been united with him like this in his death, we will certainly also be united with him in his resurrection. For we know that our old self was crucified with him so that the body of sin might be done away with, that we should no longer be slaves to sin.... (Romans 6:5–6)

If we just read the text carefully, we see that baptism is a union with Christ—a union with his death, with his burial and with his resurrection. That union is said to bring us to new life. Your baptism was vital. It united you with Christ in whom you find saving grace and the power of the Holy Spirit. How can we who have experienced such a union ever go on willfully in sin? We have died and have risen with Christ.

Be thankful for what has happened to you. Make no apology about it. Preach it to others.

© Discipleship Publications International
5016 Spedale Court #331, Spring Hill, TN 37174

Appendix Nine

Down in the River to Pray

Revisioning Baptism as God's Transforming Work
A Review by Thomas A. Jones

Those of us in the ICOC fellowship are rightfully reexamining many things. Coming as we do from a heritage in the American Restoration (Stone-Campbell) Movement, we have long been careful students of the New Testament teaching on baptism and have seen our emphasis on it as one of key teachings that distinguish us from the evangelical world. If there is anything we don't feel we need to adjust, it would probably be our teaching on the role baptism plays in our coming to Christ. While I believe there is much truth in that, we must realize that on any subject, we have more to learn.

In their work, John Mark Hicks and Greg Taylor write with a conviction that believers from various traditions all stand to gain from reexamining their theology of baptism. Those in our fellowship will find much in their work that reinforces what we have taught, but we will also find things that will challenge us to rethink some of our assumptions and conclusions.

Hicks and Taylor are from the American Restoration background, but they write with an irenic spirit not always typical of works on baptism from this movement. Beginning with the New Testament teaching and with the conviction that it determines what is normative, they then examine the historical development of baptismal theology. While believing that many of those developments were not healthy, they show respect for the faith and heart of those who came to different conclusions. When this is combined with their emphasis on the fact that the central issue is not baptism but faith in the grace of God that comes through Christ, the result is a book that prayerfully will open some productive dialogue with people of various traditions.

Hicks and Taylor argue for a "high view" of baptism. They see it as a key element in the conversion narratives of the New Testament. They are concerned that baptism is more important than people in most traditions have believed—including our own—but not for the reasons some might suppose. At the same time, they would help us not to make more of baptism than the Scriptures would teach and help us put baptism in a larger context of God's gracious plan to transform his people.

If their conclusions are valid, or at least if they are raising some of the right questions, there is an inevitable tension to be confronted. We must learn how to maintain a high view of baptism and still relate graciously to those committed believers who don't share our theology. We must work out how to hold to the role of baptism in the conversion process while, at the same time, seeing that God's grace covers a variety of defects in our theology, performance and character.

For example, many of us hold dear the text where Paul says, "Watch your life and doctrine closely. Persevere in them, because if you do, you will save both yourself and your hearers" (1 Timothy 4:16). We hear the call to be committed to both right life and right doctrine, and yet none of us believes we will ever have the perfect life. As we strive to live to please God, we rely on his grace to save us in spite of times we fall. In the same way should not all strive for the right doctrine and want to teach faithfully what the word teaches, while at the same time acknowledging our theology will sometimes fall short just as do our lives? Ultimately everyone will be saved by faith and an obedient heart, not by perfection in either life or doctrine.

As Reuel Lemmons, esteemed editor of the *Firm Foundation*, once wrote: "We want to do Bible things in Bible ways and have a thus saith the Lord for every rule of faith and practice. But that produces a fear-dominated sense of law-keeping that almost does away with grace entirely. We become almost gnostic in our emphasis upon salvation by knowledge rather than by faith."[1]

How we resolve these matters will have impact on our evangelism and on our relationship with other believers with whom we often share many fundamental convictions, but differ at this point. To work this though will mean we must not label those who take a different view from ourselves or "write off" someone who wrestles to keep a high (and biblical) view of baptism but also a loyalty to the "weightier" issue of justification by grace through faith.

My personal view is that no one of us is wise enough to tackle this issue on our own (regardless of our intellect and skill), since we all bring a bit of bias and emotion to the subject. Instead I believe a view that is most faithful to God and most edifying to the Body of Christ will emerge in honest dialogue and open exchange of ideas in a safe and God-focused environment.

I would recommend this book, but encourage you to process its material in a safe fellowship that will raise a variety of questions. In the meantime, we should have no reluctance to proclaim the gospel of God's grace and to teach that the proper response to it is faith in that grace that expresses itself in repentance and baptism.

John Mark Hicks and Greg Taylor, *Down in the River to Pray: Revisioning Baptism as God's Transforming Work* (Abilene, TX: Leafwood Press, 2004.)

---

1. Reuel Lemmons, "Revisiting our Isolation Theology," Internet article found at http://www.geocities.com/nucmanchh/isolation_theology.htm.

Appendix Ten

Dealing with Depression

An Opportunity to Change

Reprinted from A Man in All Seasons

Thomas Jones

My own views about depression have been shaped by personal experience as well as by study of the Scriptures. When I was only thirty and striving to be a disciple, I had a month long bout with depression that I would later realize was fairly mild. However, God used it to get my attention. As I searched for answers, I found sin being exposed in my life, and as I dealt with it, I found the depression being relieved. I came out of that experience with a renewed zeal for life and ministry and some of my most productive years followed. My conclusion was that depression was primarily a spiritually based problem that could be dealt with by godly sorrow, confession and repentance. This, along with a number of other issues, brought me into sharp conflict with a clinical psychologist and several leaders in the traditional church where I was serving as campus minister at the time.

Seven years later, I again found myself battling a more serious depression. Given my earlier experience, I was convinced it must be caused by a heart that had wandered from God. However, my many efforts to find a spiritual component in the depression only resulted in the condition growing worse. Eventually I moved and became part of the Boston Church where I made the effort to get open about every possible thing with such friends as Wyndham Shaw and Gordon Ferguson.

During this time, I continued to serve, to share my faith and to lead in various situations. I expressed to these brothers my great reluctance to use medication to deal with the depression, but we all finally came to the conclusion that the problem was so debilitating that I needed to be open to pharmacological help. After a long struggle with the whole idea of medication, interestingly enough, it turned out that I had bad side effects to three different drugs that I tried and could not continue them. Having finally decided to get some medical help, my depression deepened when that door also was closed.

It was about this time that I prayed a rather radical prayer that showed the depths of struggle. The depression was so deep and my thinking so tortured, that I remember exactly where I was when I prayed, "God, kill me, or God, change me!" The depression was profound and I felt a strong desire to die, but since I would never take my own life, I was quite open to God doing it for me and doing it quickly. But what I wanted more was to change.

It was shortly after I had prayed this prayer a number of times that certain things began to come together for me that would eventually form the basis for my book *Mind Change*. The things I learned saved my life and changed me. *I am thankful God chose this option rather than the other!*

Over the last seven years depression has continued to be a factor in my life from time to time. I have never become completely free of it. (This may have something to do with the fact that I also have multiple sclerosis, a progressive illness that regularly gives one new losses to deal with.) But by the grace of God, I have gained a perspective on it that has enabled me to respond to depression and has enabled God to use it in my life. Though my thinking is still in process, my own experience and the considerable time I have spent with other people who are dealing with depression have led me to several insights, conclusions and convictions.

1. Depression is a complex phenomenon that can have several, oftentimes overlapping, causes. (1) Some depression seems to be spiritually based, caused by real guilt over sin that has not been dealt with. (2) Some depression seems to be based in unresolved issues, particularly unresolved relationships and wounds from the past. (3) Some depression is what is normally called "reactive," that is, a reaction to loss, failure or disappointment. (4) Some depression seems to arise in those who have an "accused personality" and a natural tendency to think negatively. (5) Some depression seems to have no connection to these causes and comes on those who have many normal reasons to feel good about their lives. (A forty-one year old disciple who fits this description came to me recently when he was extremely and mysteriously depressed.) Interestingly enough, this last type is often the most difficult and leaves the individual with the greatest sense of hopelessness and inability to function normally. This would seem to be what the psychologists call an "endogenous" depression that has roots not in external circumstances, but apparently in a chemical/medical issue. *Most often, depression seems to involve several of these components.*

2. It takes careful listening, great patience, considerable time and much prayer to determine what the root of the problem is. I have learned to approach each person who has these issues with a great deal of humility. To discover what they need is often like untangling a mass of cords, cables and phone lines like those under my desk that keep all my electronic devices running.

3. If the depression is medically based or significantly contributed to by a chemical imbalance, telling the person that they just need to repent or just to be more of a servant may actually deepen the depression. They try to do that, but when they still feel very depressed, the downward cycle just speeds up. "I must be a horrible or really messed-up person because I do what is right and just get worse." I can remember that after going out to give and serve, I would come home to deal with very black and tortured thoughts about who I was and how I had done so poorly.

4. Some people get a great deal of help from medication. In many cases, it enables people to think clearly and not be tormented by the dark and twisted thoughts. I know several people who are now doing very well in their walk with God and their service in the kingdom and are very grateful for the freedom that the medication has given them to think more normally. Being free from the constant temptation to die and being able to get excited about what God can do has been a great blessing. Those who have bipolar disorder (manic-depressive disorder) unquestionably are helped by medication, and going off of their medications can have disastrous consequences. To those who ask what people did who lived before we had these medications, I can only say that God is faithful to all those who turn to him. However, now that we have medications, it seems only right to use them, but always in connection with efforts to think spiritually.

5. Even in the most severe depression, we are still free to choose. We are not victims. Yes, depression is tough. Yes, it brings maybe the greatest of temptations. I have often told people that with MS and depression, there is no question about which is the most difficult. Yes, there is the temptation to disbelieve all God's promises, the temptation to give up, the temptation to wallow in self-pity, the temptation to doubt that you can make any difference, and even the temptation to take one's own life. But even in the face of all that, we can choose to believe. "Against all hope, Abraham, in hope believed" (Romans 4:18). I believe that this is the most powerful lesson that I have learned. We can always say, "Yes, I feel all these things, *but God…*" For me, this became the secret to overcoming.

6. When depressed people sin, sin must be dealt with biblically. "But I was depressed" is never an excuse. There is only one way to deal with any sin: godly sorrow, confession and repentance. However, it is not, in

most cases, biblical to tell the depressed person that his depression is sin. Thinking this way just caused my depression to grow deeper and more powerful. It was those friends and spiritual advisors who convinced me that I could still be faithful even while dealing with depression that helped me to overcome in it.

7. I would never recommend medication without spiritual counseling. As the medication helps a person to think more normally, he needs to train his thinking to focus on spiritual solutions and spiritual perspectives. "Train yourself to be godly. For physical training is of some value, but godliness has value for all things, holding promise for both the present life and the life to come" (1 Timothy 4:7b-8). Seeing medication as *the* answer keeps us from learning all God is trying to teach us.

8. Whatever the causes, God can use depression. Our goal should not be the elimination of depression from the world. A world in which everyone is "fixed" by Prozac or some new generation of anti-depressants would not be a better world. Most people are so much better off *after* facing depression and dealing with it spiritually. Depression, like nothing else I know of, can lead us to see our need for God. Depression is one of the "all things" of Romans 8:28 in which God works for good. A spiritual leader I know recently said, "I'm amazed at how the goal of Americans seems to be ease, painlessness and staying 'up' and 'happy' at all times." In a seminar I led two years ago ("Finding God in Pain and Problems") I pointed out that the problem with most people facing physical or emotional pain is that they want to find relief far more than they want to find God.

From personal experience, I know a good deal about depression, but there is much about it that remains a mystery to me. It always humbles me, whether I see it in myself or in someone else. Wherever I find it, it causes me to pray and seek God. Ultimately, he is the answer to all our needs.

> No, in all these things we are more than conquerors through him who loved us. For I am convinced that neither death nor life, neither angels nor demons, neither the present nor the future, nor any powers, neither height nor depth, nor anything else in all creation, will be able to separate us from the love of God that is in Christ Jesus our Lord. (Romans 8:37–39)

Addendum: For a most interesting and fresh perspective on depression see *Lincoln's Melancholy: How Depression Challenged a President and Fueled His Greatness* Joshua Wolf Shenk (New York: Houghton Mifflin, 2005).

Lincoln's Melancholy tells—for the first time—the full story of Lincoln's life-long depression, how he managed it, and how it came to fuel his epic work. Drawing on seven years of research, this book shows how the science and literature on depression offer insight into Lincoln's journey, and how Lincoln's story challenges and enriches our understanding of depression.

Appendix Eleven
Understanding Multiple Sclerosis

What is multiple sclerosis?

Multiple sclerosis is a chronic, unpredictable disease of the central nervous system (the brain, optic nerves and spinal cord). It is thought to be an autoimmune disorder. This means the immune system incorrectly attacks the person's healthy tissue.

MS can cause blurred vision, loss of balance, poor coordination, slurred speech, tremors, numbness, extreme fatigue, problems with memory and concentration, paralysis, blindness and more. These problems may be permanent or may come and go.

Most people are diagnosed between the ages of 20 and 50, although individuals as young as 2 and as old as 75 have developed it. MS is not considered a fatal disease as the vast majority of people with it live a normal lifespan. But they may struggle to live as productively as they desire, often facing increasing limitations.

Who gets MS?

Anyone may develop MS but there are some patterns. Twice as many women as men have MS. Studies suggest that genetic factors make certain individuals more susceptible than others, but there is no evidence that MS is directly inherited. It occurs more commonly among people with northern European ancestry. People of African, Asian, and Hispanic backgrounds are also diagnosed with MS, however, the incidence is much lower.

What are the typical symptoms of MS?

Symptoms of MS are unpredictable, vary from person to person, and from time to time in the same person. For example: One person may experience abnormal fatigue and episodes of numbness and tingling. Another could have loss of balance and muscle coordination making walking difficult. Still another could have slurred speech, tremors, stiffness and bladder problems. Sometimes major symptoms disappear completely, and the person regains lost functions. In severe MS, people have symptoms on a permanent basis including partial or complete paralysis and difficulties with vision, cognition, speech, and elimination.

What causes the symptoms?

MS symptoms result when an immune-system attack affects myelin, the protective insulation surrounding nerve fibers of the central nervous system (the brain and spinal cord). Myelin is destroyed and replaced by scars of hardened "sclerotic" tissue. Some underlying nerve fibers are permanently severed. The damage appears in multiple places within the central nervous system. Myelin is often compared to insulating material around an electrical wire; loss of myelin interferes with the transmission of nerve signals.

Can MS be cured?

Not yet. There are now FDA-approved medications that have been shown to "modify" or slow down the underlying course of MS. In addition, many therapeutic and technological advances are helping people manage symptoms. Advances in treating and understanding MS are made every year, and progress in research to find a cure is very encouraging.

What medications and treatments are available?

The National Multiple Sclerosis Society recommends treatment with one of the FDA-approved "disease-modifying" drugs as soon as possible following a definite diagnosis of MS with active or relapsing disease. These drugs help to lessen the frequency and severity of MS attacks, reduce the accumulation of lesions (areas of damage) in the brain, and may slow the progression of disability.

What are the different types of MS?

In an effort to develop a common language for evaluating and researching MS, an international survey was conducted among scientists who specialize in MS research and patient care. Analysis of responses resulted in defining the following categories, which were introduced in 1996.

Relapsing-Remitting

Characteristics: People with this type of MS experience clearly defined flare-ups (also called relapses, attacks or exacerbations). These are episodes of acute worsening of neurological function. They are followed by partial or complete recovery periods (remissions) free of disease progression. Frequency: The most common form of MS at time of initial diagnosis.

Primary-Progressive

Characteristics: People with this type of MS experience a slow but nearly continuous worsening of their disease from the onset, with no distinct relapses or remissions. However, there are variations in rates of progression over time, occasional plateaus, and temporary minor improvements.

Frequency: Relatively rare.

Secondary-Progressive

Characteristics: People with this type of MS experience an initial period of relapsing-remitting MS, followed by a steadily worsening disease course with or without occasional flare-ups, minor recoveries (remissions), or plateaus.

Frequency: 50% of people with relapsing-remitting MS developed this form of the disease within 10 years of their initial diagnosis, before introduction of the "disease-modifying" drugs. Long-term data are not yet available to demonstrate if this is significantly delayed by treatment.

Progressive-Relapsing

Characteristics: People with this type of MS experience a steadily worsening disease from the onset but also have clear acute relapses (attacks or exacerbations), with or without recovery. In contrast to relapsing-remitting MS, the periods between relapses are characterized by continuing disease progression.

Frequency: Relatively rare.

Appendix Twelve
Ministering to Physically Challenged Disciples

This material was originally presented to a group in the Boston Church who were training to provide shepherding in the lives of small group members. It is presented here with thanks to God for all the lessons taught me by physically challenged disciples.

Realities

1. People have physical challenges. Sickness is a reality. Disabilities affect people physically and emotionally.
2. Chronic illness and other chronic physical challenges take an emotional and relational toll on those who have them and those who live with them.
3. Studies have resulted in estimates that about 30–35% of the adult population faces some on-going physical challenge (PC).
   This means two things:
      (1) We all have a substantial number of PC people to work with.
      (2) Being PC is still a minority status (with all the challenges that brings).
4. As people age, PCs increase and so as our movement ages and our church ages, we will have more PC issues to deal with, not less.
5. Illness can mask other problems or can be used deceitfully.
   • Psychosomatic illness does exist.
   • Some people do exaggerate illness or pain in order to manipulate others, to excuse themselves from activity or to avoid responsibility.
   • Some people have a real illness, but for various reasons don't really want to get well.

Working effectively with people always takes into consideration *all* of the realities.

Biblical Teaching

Not only must we take into consideration the realities; we must take into consideration biblical teaching ("the whole counsel of God") and the qualities of Christian character.
   (1) *Compassion is vital.*
      • It is found in God in abundance. (Psalm 103:13, Psalm 116:5)
      • It is not found in most of us naturally, but must be put on. (Colossians 3:12)

- Jesus was filled with it and demonstrated it right and left especially with the sick. (Matthew 15:32, Matthew 14:14, Matthew 20:34, Mark 1:41)

Typical passage:

> Filled with compassion, Jesus reached out his hand and touched the man. "I am willing," he said. "Be clean!" (Mark 1:41)

We are not ready to counsel the sick if we are not *filled with* compassion.

(2) *Wisdom and judgment are essential.*
- 1 Thessalonians 4:14 teaches "different strokes for different folks." (Some need support and affirmation; others need a challenge; many need a combination.)
- We should go in with compassion and a listening ear. (James 1:19, Proverbs 18:13)
  - A. This gives us the opportunity to get in touch with where people really are.
  - B. It gives them the opportunity to feel really understood. Nothing is more important in working with people than causing them to feel you hear them and understand them. This brings *emotional clearance*. Until this happens they cannot hear you. All your wonderful insight and excellent direction will fall on deaf ears.

My approach: assume the best with people. Operate on that assumption *until proven wrong*.

Once you have heard people and helped them feel understood, there is more you can do. There is truth you can speak. Two things will be true:

1. You will know much better *what* truth they need to hear.
2. They will be much more likely to hear you because you will have built trust.

What Does the Physically Challenged Disciple Need to Learn?

1. Realize that circumstances alter your life (*bios*) but that they don't end your life (*zoë*).
2. The principles of 2 Corinthians 1, 4, and 12; Philippians 4.
3. Your illness can become a vehicle through which God works in most unexpected ways.
4. It is great when people understand and are supportive. But realize two

things: (1) no one ever can fully understand and (2) you can still live well even if you are misunderstood. Disciples are always misunderstood people.

5. Sin is still your greatest challenge. Deal with sin biblically

6. Whatever the challenge, God is always greater.

7. Whatever happens, don't lose your sense of humor. Proverbs 17:22: "A cheerful heart is good medicine, but a crushed spirit dries up the bones." It is a gift of God. If you don't have one, buy one, get trained to have one. Do whatever it takes.

Recommended reading: *Mind Change, This Doesn't Feel Like Love, Power in Weakness, You Gotta Keep Dancing.*

Appendix Thirteen
Letter to Randy and Kay McKean

After the appearance of the Evangelization Proclamation (February 1994), I wrote the following letter to Randy and Kay McKean. A statement in this just released document represented a misuse of Scripture, as I saw it, and though it might have seemed harmless enough to some, it was becoming an example of declaring certain things to be biblical doctrines almost by fiat and then repeating them so often that everyone accepted them.

Feb. 15, 1994

Randy and Kay,

I am writing about a passage from the recently published "Evangelization Proclamation" issued by the world sector leaders. First, I want to say that I wholeheartedly support the call of this proclamation, and I thank God that I am part of a movement committed to getting the message of Jesus to the entire world. I thank God for the leadership he has raised up to help bring this about, for without such leadership there would be no hope of this goal being reached. I feel very blessed and privileged to be able to work with and to serve such leaders. I am behind the financial plan developed by our leaders and will do all I can to support this plan.

However, the one passage that I believe is biblically inaccurate is the following:

> "In the next few months the Bible doctrine from Acts 11:26 of Saved = Christian = Disciple was crystallized."

I spoke at length with Kip about this idea several years ago when he published his article "Restoration through Revolution" in *UpsideDown* magazine. I understand that Kip is making the point that churches should be composed only of disciples and I certainly agree with that, but it is not correct to say that there is in Acts 11:26 a Bible doctrine of "Saved = Christian = Disciple."

(1) Acts 11:26 is an historical footnote, nothing more and nothing less. It simply tells about something that happened. Disciples were called "Christians" and most everyone agrees that it was the non-believing world that gave them this name. It may very well be true that anyone who is a disciple is also saved and can also be called a Christian, but Acts 11 does not teach this and it is not right to say that it does.

If we can say Acts 11 teaches "Saved = Christian = Disciple" then we could say Acts 20:7-8 contains a Bible doctrine that communion should be taken in an upstairs room where there are many lamps. We recognize that the second is just an historical note, not a doctrinal statement. The first is no different. I am confident if people in other churches were to exegete a passage the way we have with Acts 11, we would be quick to point out the fallacy of their argument.

(2) The NT makes no effort to teach that Christian = Saved or that Disciple = Christian. There would seem to be a simple reason for this: *Every* reference in the NT to "Christian" is a reference to how the unbelievers referred to disciples. There is no effort in the NT to equate something unbelievers would say with the saved state of disciples. Simply put: the word "Christian" was used very differently at the time the NT was written than now.

Why make so much noise about this point? Doesn't the Bible teach that one has to be a disciple to be saved and that the term Christian is a valid one for a disciple to accept even from the world? I asked myself these questions before writing and thought long and hard about them, but here are my concerns:

(1) Our movement is built solidly on the idea that the Word of God is our guide, but can only build what God wants if we "handle correctly the Word of Truth." The statement I am referring to is becoming one that appears each time there is a carefully worded record of our position and commitment. *But this statement is not true.* No matter how harmless it may seem to some people, it should bother us that a statement about the Bible that is not true has become almost a cornerstone of our movement.

(2) We must guard against something we see over and over in the world, namely the idea that if something is repeated often enough everyone accepts it as true. Our enemies do stories on us as a cult and then quote their own stories. They repeat something long enough and loud enough until everyone regards it as true. I'm afraid this is what has happened with this statement. It has been repeated over and over and it amazes me how so many otherwise thoughtful people now repeat it as if it were true. But Acts 11:26 does not teach that Disciple = Christian = Saved. All it teaches is that disciples of Jesus were called

Christians by non-believers for the first time in the city of Antioch. Nothing more and nothing less. This passage doesn't even teach that the disciples liked the name Christian or adopted it. We later learn that they did, but this passage doesn't teach that.

As a movement, we like to keep things simple. We like to draw very clear lines and make things very black and white. But this desire must be governed and restrained by the Word of God and the correct handling of the Word of God. It is never right to try to make something clearer than God made it. And certainly it is never right to say some passage in the Bible teaches something when it does not teach it (even when it is a general truth taught elsewhere).

I remain open to being shown something I may be overlooking here, but if the concerns I have expressed are valid, I would urge you to discuss them with others who signed the proclamation so that nothing will diminish the integrity and credibility of our movement.

There was a time years ago when I probably considered this "your movement" or "their movement" but I do now understand that it is "my movement." It is a movement that I love. It has been a movement that has blessed me and my family. I would not want to be anywhere else. I need this movement and I need its leaders. I just want us to be faithful to God and his word in every way.

I look forward to your thoughts.

With the greatest respect and appreciation for your diligent work,
Tom Jones

Verses:
ACTS 11:26 and when he found him, he brought him to Antioch. So for a whole year Barnabas and Saul met with the church and taught great numbers of people. The disciples were called Christians first at Antioch.

ACTS 26:28 Then Agrippa said to Paul, "Do you think that in such a short time you can persuade me to be a Christian?"

1PETER 4:16 However, if you suffer as a Christian, do not be ashamed, but praise God that you bear that name.

Appendix Fourteen
A Brief Primer on the Restoration Movement

I wrote this book primarily for those with roots in what is sometimes called the Restoration Movement in America, although I hope it gets into the hands of others from other traditions. As I finished the book it occurred to me that a brief description of the Restoration Movement might be helpful to some readers not familiar with it. Of course, in our day most readers will have access to the Internet and a quick search in an online encyclopedia like Wikipedia will bring up more information than I will be able to give here.

Stone and Campbell

This movement traces its beginnings to the early part of the nineteenth century and began during what is called The Great Awakening in the United States. At first there were several smaller movements in places from New England to South Carolina, from Pennsylvania to Kentucky. Unaware of each other and with their own distinctive emphasis, they all had in common a desire to return to a simpler practice of New Testament faith without all the doctrines and organizational encumbrances that had come to characterize the various denominations. A desire for Christian unity was also in the forefront of their thinking.

Eventually these groups learned of each other's efforts and coalesced around two main leaders—Barton W. Stone from Kentucky and Alexander Campbell, a native of Ireland and a descendent of Scotch and Huguenot ancestors, who lived in the U.S. first in Pennsylvania and eventually in Virginia and West Virginia. Both men believed in letting the Scriptures serve as the only sure guide to life and doctrine and felt that the various and often conflicting creeds should be discarded. Both had a desire to see greater unity among those who were believers. They shared a desire to leave denominational structures and forms.

Campbell was more the intellectual, and Stone was more a man of the heart. Campbell was more the logician and Stone more the evangelist. When Campbell made a trip to Kentucky, Stone, who was older and had been working for restoration (or reform) longer, heard him speak and would later write:

> I heard him often in public and in private. I was pleased with his manner and matter. I saw no distinctive feature between the doctrine he preached and that which we had preached for many years, except on baptism for remission of sins. Even this I had once received and taught, as

before stated, but had strangely let it go from my mind, till Bro. Campbell revived it afresh.

In 1824 the two men met to discuss what they might do together. They concluded that their differences were minor in nature. It would take until 1833 for the two groups to more formally unite. Various slogans were used to help others understand the goals of the movement: "No creed but Christ," "Christians only, but not the only Christians," "In matters of faith, unity; in matters of opinion, liberty; in all things, charity (love)." Some have mistakenly thought that this slogan had its origins in the Restoration Movement, but it was really an adaptation of a slogan that had been around for at least two hundred years usually phrased, "In essentials, unity; in non-essentials, liberty; in all things, charity."

The union of Stone and Campbell gave the new movement a healthy balance. In the words of one writer:

> Thus these two independent streams of reform influence flowed together, each supplementing the other and both significant of the desire of the age for liberty and union in the truth.[1]

Walter Scott

In the winter of 1822 Campbell met another man who would become a key leader in the movement. Walter Scott was only twenty-five, but within a year he would begin having great influence as an evangelist. In temperament he seemed to be something of a combination of Stone and Campbell. Scott was convinced that they key idea in the Scriptures was found in Peter's confession that Jesus is the Christ. This same Peter was given the keys to the kingdom, and as such he clearly described the way one should respond to the gospel when he preached the first post-resurrection sermon on Pentecost.

It was Scott who introduced the famous five-finger exercise that led to hundreds if not thousands of conversions. One of his favorite methods was to come to a town and meet with school children. He would say, "Now lift up your left hand. Beginning with the thumb say with me, 'Faith, repentance, baptism, remission of sins, the gift of the Holy Spirit." This drill was repeated going faster with each repetition. Then he would tell the children to go home and do this for their parents and tell them that the man who taught this to them was going to be preaching that night and they were invited.

The new reform movement or restoration movement, as it would come to be called, spread like wildfire across Ohio, Indiana and Kentucky and eventually to many other states.

---

1. Allan B. Philputt, Internet article. www.mun.ca/rels/restmov/texts/wwarren/ccr/CCR15H5.HTM.

Unity Gives Way to Division

In various places, groups would be designated as Disciples of Christ, Church of Christ, or simply Christian Church, but though they might use different names, they were united in their basic plea and the message they taught about how to respond to the gospel. In a hundred years the movement grew from a handful to over a million believers.

In the years following the Civil War two distinct groups began to form in the movement. In the South most congregations used the name "Church of Christ" and with few exceptions had chosen to reject the use of instrumental music in worship. They saw this as an innovation not supported by Scripture. They felt the same way about the start of missionary societies which involved an organizational structure outside the local church. While these believers had a right to do as their consciences dictated, these churches increasingly became more and more legalistic, confrontational and exclusive. They often would not extend fellowship to those who did not conform to them on these issues. As is often true, there were some notable exceptions to this spirit (names like K.C. Moser, E.W. McMillian, G.C. Brewer, Batsell Barrett Baxter and Reuel Lemmons come to mind). Churches influenced by such men could be found but the dominant culture of Churches of Christ encouraged legalism, pettifogging, personal attacks and self-righteousness. An example of this legacy is found in Chapter Two of this book in the Open Forum at Freed-Hardeman College.

In the northern states most churches went by the name Christian Church or Disciples of Christ. While still committed to the restoration idea, to using the New Testament as their guide, and to the view that faith, repentance and baptism belonged together in responding to the gospel, they did not find in the Scriptures anything that would forbid the use of instruments in worship or that would prohibit churches from organizing to do mission work.

The Silence of the Scriptures

The two groups essentially divided over the silence of the Scriptures. "We speak where the Bible speaks and are silent where the Bible is silent," had long been a slogan in the movement. The southern churches understood that to mean that the church should not do anything unless it was authorized by Scripture. If the Bible was silent on an issue like instrumental music, then it was not authorized. The northern churches saw it as meaning that where the Bible has made some clear declaration then we speak that, but where the Bible is silent, we do not make a rule (as in this case, "You must not use instruments.").

More Fractures

After nearly forty years of contention, the Federal Census of 1906 recognized that the Churches of Christ (COC) and the Disciples of Christ were two separate bodies. What had long existed was given official status.

As the Churches of Christ went their own way and ended up with many more divisions within their ranks over a host of issues (located preachers, Sunday schools, number of communion cups, orphan homes, etc.). One estimate of a long-time observer is that they currently have twenty-six separate groups. The Disciples had their own challenge. Higher criticism of the Bible had become popular in European universities and seminaries in the latter part of the nineteenth century. By the early part of the twentieth century it was making its way into many American seminaries as well. The net effect was to undermine the authority and trustworthiness of the Bible. As this understanding (or misunderstanding) took root in various schools where Disciples' ministers were educated, it was not long before the idea of restoring the New Testament church was no longer part of the agenda in many churches.

Throughout this period there were those churches and leaders among the Disciples who never accepted this view, and eventually they formally separated from, as they saw it, "the Disciples of Christ denomination" and formed the North American Christian Convention, which was a loose association of independent churches still committed to the ideals of the Restoration and certainly the authority and inspiration of the Scriptures. Today that group still meets annually for their NACC conference, and they have recently been reaching out to the acapella Churches of Christ in efforts to bring reconciliation.

The twentieth century was characterized as a period of little or no contact between the now three distinct groups of the Restoration heritage (or Stone-Campbell Movement). The "Disciples of Christ" had chosen a view of the Bible that made their approach much more consistent with that of liberal mainline Protestant denominations. The Independent Christian Churches (ICC) would have probably been quite open to dialogue with the Churches of Christ, but the latter increasingly viewed the use of instrumental music as a salvation issue and wanted no part of fellowship with those in the Christian Churches, certainly doubting their status as Christians.

It is difficult to accurately track the growth of the Churches of Christ and the Independent Christian Churches during the twentieth century. Since both groups believed in no denominational structure, official records were not kept. At one time in the '60s it was said that the COC was the fastest growing religious group in the United States, but recent studies have brought that claim into question. At one time it was suggested membership in the COC had reached two million, but more careful examination concluded the number might be even under one million. Currently both "bodies" seem to each have about one million members.

From CE to Crossroads to Boston

It was during a period of stagnation in the 1960s when some in Churches of Christ were recognizing that growth had slowed and that a number of key biblical concepts were missing in the preaching and teaching of the church, that the Campus Evangelism Movement began. Seeds planted by this movement then grew into the Crossroads Movement and subsequently to the Boston Movement. The movement that would come to be known as the International Churches of Christ (ICOC) had its roots in the COC side of the Restoration Movement. Much of its own theology and practice would be a combination of teaching learned from the COC (some good, some not so good), teaching formed in reaction to perceived weaknesses in the COC, along with insights gained from fresh study of the Scriptures.

It has been nearly two hundred years since Alexander Campbell's father, Thomas Campbell, penned the Declaration and Address, a document often cited as one marking the beginning of the Restoration Movement. The Campbells' dream of unity among believers has been far from realized. Perhaps in our day, God is giving us a new opportunity to see it happen. This book was written, at least in part, in the hope that it might encourage others to continue to work to this end.

Renewed Calls for Unity

Beginning in the early 1980s efforts were made to start dialogue between the Independent Christian Churches and Churches of Christ. A publication titled *The One Body* was begun by Don DeWelt soliciting material from writers in both groups. Soon an annual Unity Forum was begun and continues to this day. At the 2006 North American Christian Convention held in Louisville, Kentucky, Christian Church organizers invited leaders from Churches of Christ to work with them on the program, and speakers and teachers included participants of both groups. For our own effort to encourage communication between the COC, the ICC and the ICOC please visit www.connect4change.net.

Appendix Fifteen
Today in the International Churches of Christ

Here are some of the things you will find in the church culture of the International Churches of Christ. Of course, there might be exceptions but this is the general experience.

1. A belief that the message of Jesus is radical both in the nature of the grace it brings and the commitment he calls for. All are called to die to mediocrity and to live surrendered lives.

2. The baptism of adults and teens that have carefully looked at Jesus, his grace and his call. It is understood that in baptism one is putting his/her faith in Christ, dying with Christ to an old life and being raised to a new life.

3. A majority of people in each congregation who do not have a background in the Churches of Christ or the Christian Churches. The majority of people are those who have been baptized into Christ in the last twenty-five years and did not have previous experience in another church from a Restoration background. This is great contrast to those in the average congregation of the Churches of Christ.

4. Racial and age diversity. Rarely will you find a congregation in the United States that is mostly white, black or Latino except in areas where the demographics of the area make diversity almost impossible. Many congregations have something approximating balance between whites and African-Americans or whites and Latinos. Older congregations (those twenty-five years and older) tend to have a healthy mix of young, old and in-between. Newer plantings may have a higher percentage younger people.

5. A continuing emphasis on reaching the lost, now almost always without the unhealthy emphasis on statistics and without pressure on members to evangelize.

6. A commitment to being deeply involved in one another's lives, where people share openly and give encouragement and admonishment. Honestly, after seeing some abuses in this area, some churches are struggling to find the best way to implement biblical relationships but the practice of these is still a core value because it is believed to be a core value in Scripture.

7. An increasing emphasis on studying the Bible carefully in context. Many ministers have returned to school and are working on degrees

in biblical studies. The teaching ministry of Dr. Douglas Jacoby and the Athens Institute of Ministry has helped many churches and leaders embrace more scholarly study without losing a concern for practical application. Several leaders have earned doctorates in biblical or ministry studies.

8. Enthusiastic and expressive worship services with much response from the congregation in the form of participation in singing, playing instruments, in note taking, applause and "amens." The fellowship before a service begins is usually characterized by such animation that it can seem irreverent or disturbing to those used to a more formal experience of worship that is done with great solemnity. But in the ICOC fellowship is seen as a key and biblical component in the worship experience. With a heritage in acapella singing, the churches still have a great appreciation for this form of worship.

9. Special time almost always taken in the service where someone shares from Scripture or from his or her life to help prepare the congregation to take the Lord's Supper each week with thoughtfulness and gratitude.

10. A continuing commitment to women's ministry where women are teaching and leading women, while recognizing some of the mistakes made in asking for women to be over-committed to ministry as they were at home with their children.

11. Elders in most of the larger churches and a commitment to raise up other qualified men for this role.

12. A significant amount of money and time given to the support of churches in other countries. Normally in America you will find churches, because of earlier organization, that have some historic connection to a certain area of the world and continue to provide spiritual, physical and emotional support to those overseas. Seldom at this point do you find an American church sending Americans to lead in another country since the ICOC in its previous organizational format was successful in planting churches in most nations and in raising up nationals who lead there now.

13. A concern for the poor and the needy with support of both local programs and worldwide efforts to relieve suffering and want.

Appendix Sixteen
The Power of Humility

The following is an excerpt (Chapter Twenty) from The Prideful Soul's Guide to Humility *by Thomas Jones and Michael Fontenot. It is included here because of my conviction that this quality is crucial if we are to move forward with God's blessing.*

The most important question we can ask about anything is, "Does it please God?" Humility always passes that test and, for that reason, would be the right thing for our lives, whatever else we might say about it.

However, humility not only pleases God, but humility is powerful. Men and women who learn humility will experience victories and will see results that will never be present in the lives of prideful souls.

Prideful men and women are often powerful in a worldly sense, but their lives are devoid of spiritual and relational victory. One does not have to be humble to accumulate wealth, be successful in business, achieve political influence or be known for academic excellence. Prideful souls function quite well in all these and other arenas. But it is most common to find prideful people who have gained worldly success but have no clue about how to be happily married, how to be close to their children or how to have lasting friendships. They certainly have no walk with God.

The prideful soul can be successful—at all the things that ultimately do not matter. He will have no success where it really counts. What is missing in his life is the power of humility.

Humility should be our goal, whatever the apparent results, but the fact is that the results are dramatic. While humility sounds like an anemic word to some, in reality it unleashes divine power that can raise us to life on a new and higher plane.

God's Favor

First and foremost, humility is powerful because it brings to your life the favor of God. "God gives grace to the humble." That is the theme of this book. God is not detached and uninvolved in the lives of people. He is frequently described in the Scriptures as the God who wants to bless, and there is absolutely nothing that can stop him from blessing those with humble hearts.

When someone finds favor in the eyes of God, the things that really matter in his life will all be better. He will not have the finest car. She will not live in the biggest house. He will not be the most popular performer. She will not be the biggest vote-getter. But when someone finds favor in God's eyes, the things that count the most will be there in ever-increasing fashion. Humility will never mean an absence of problems. It will not mean comfort and ease, but it will bring an assortment of circumstances and experiences that God will blend together to make life rich and full of depth and meaning.

The Psalmist well understood how important it is to receive God's blessing, when he wrote:

> May the favor of the LORD our God rest upon us;
>> establish the work of our hands for us—
>> yes, establish the work of our hands. (Psalm 90:17)

Our greatest need is our need for God. We need his work on our behalf. We work, but we need him to "establish the work of our hands." We need him to take our efforts and then make them all they can be.

Life is far too complex and unpredictable for us to figure it out or to be able to manage it on our own. The humble soul deeply believes this. We need God shining his face on us, holding us in the palm of his hand, gently leading and guiding us. We need him to give us grace and to work in unseen ways behind the scenes for our good in all things. We need God to protect us and keep us safe.

Those who find this repugnant do so because they are prideful souls, unwilling to admit who man is and who God is. However, no disdain for these ideas changes the nature of reality. If you do not like it that you need air or water, what you like or do not like changes nothing. The same is true in relation to God: We need him. We need his blessing and his favor. Without those things from him, we miss what is most crucial in life.

Humility is powerful, above all, because it gets the attention of God. God is drawn to the humble heart. His radar picks up humility immediately. His squadrons of grace fly quickly and release their payloads of mercy on the lives of those with humble hearts. Show me a humble heart, and I will show you a person amazed at the way God has worked in his or her life. You will look at these people's lives and you will, of course, see that they have had trials, but you will see a peace in their eyes that says, "Yes, but God worked powerfully in all of these things." They will not be trying to *look* spiritual as they say this; they will be deeply convinced of it. They will be standing in awe of the difference God has made in their lives.

Humility is the most powerful attitude that can exist in the human heart because nothing else so brings to your life the might and power of the Almighty God.

Personal Growth

Nothing is really powerful, from a spiritual perspective, unless it changes people. The power of humility is seen in the way it brings change to every heart and every life in which it is found. Humble people are always changing. Their humility creates fertile ground in which growth thrives.

As the two of us writing this book look at our years of ministry, counseling and shepherding, we think of people who have changed dramatically. Without exception these were people who demonstrated humility. Prideful people do sometimes change, but not in ways that are righteous. What happens quickly with the humble does not happen at all with the prideful. This is unbreakable spiritual law. The two of us look at those times in our personal lives when change was the greatest and those times when change seemed to stop. Once again, we see clearly that there has always been a correlation between humility and growth, and a corresponding correlation between pride and stagnation.

Why did the Ethiopian in Acts 8 change? Because he was humble. Why did Saul of Tarsus undergo one of the most dramatic life changes in history? Because he was finally humbled. Why did a tough jailer in Philippi become a totally new man? Because he was humbled by his situation and by the word of God.

I remember one year in my life in which I probably changed more than any other. It all happened because of a specific decision I made to humble myself before God and before other spiritual people. I had gone through a year of diminishing spiritual strength. I was sinking deep into a pit where I was filled with negativity and discontentment. Pride had taken over in many areas of my life. Nothing in me was changing for the better. But when I humbled myself and very quickly got open about my life, I was amazed at how each day seemed to bring a fresh insight and growth. Others who knew me well were frequently commenting about changes that they saw in me. In the church atmosphere that I was in at the time, there were some tradition-bound souls who did not like the changes, but there was no doubt that they saw them.

From Year 1 when I was not changing, to Year 2 when I was, God had not changed. The Bible had not changed. My responsibilities had not changed. So what was different? My heart. Year 1: proud. Year 2: humble. Year 1: defensive about my life and my ministry. Year 2: eager to learn from others and quick to confess my sin. The power of humility was evident. I am deeply grateful for the events of that year and how God worked to humble me. It was in that year, now more than twenty years ago, that my convictions about the power of humility began to develop.

How much are you changing? Maybe you have blamed your lack of growth on a variety factors. There is one fundamental reason it does not happen: a lack of humility. Humility is powerful because humility will always bring change.

Unity

What people can achieve when they are united is remarkable. Unity is powerful. An army that is united can often defeat an opponent with superior skills when the opponent is plagued by division. The wise man certainly had it right when he said:

> Though one may be overpowered,
> two can defend themselves.
> A cord of three strands is not quickly broken. (Ecclesiastes 4:12)

Two people united can make a difference. Three people united will be hard to stop. A community of people united is a force to be reckoned with. A worldwide movement of disciples who are united will turn the world upside down (or right side up!). Unity is powerful, and whatever produces unity is powerful. It is no accident that when Paul charges the Ephesians to "make every effort to keep the unity of the Spirit" that the verse preceding that one calls us to "be completely humble" (Ephesians 4:2-3). Humility is essential to unity.

Put a group of people in a room, and let them start to work on a problem. The first thing you will notice is their diversity, not their unity. People see things in very different ways. Opinions are like noses: Everybody has one. When pride rears its ugly head, people will stubbornly hold to their positions, and the result will be a stalemate or paralysis. But if the people in this group are first of all humble before God and humble before his word, and then they are humble in their dealings with one another, their diversity will be transformed into unity. The best ideas from various people will be blended together to produce something better than any one person could have developed. When they unite behind the group consensus, you have a group ready to make a difference. Humility produces unity in marriages, in families, in churches and in spiritual movements.

I have always been impressed with the humility that characterized the relationship of Jesus and John the Baptist. These two, at the very beginning of the Christian movement, gave us an example that must be imitated. It would be hard to find two men more different in outward style. John arrived on the scene first and attracted great crowds. Jesus would come later and the stage was set for rivalry. But John eliminated the possibility of tension when he said: "After me will come one who is more powerful than I, whose sandals I am not fit to carry" (Matthew 3:11b). With Jesus not yet on the scene, John called people to not focus on himself, but on the one coming later. Humility in action. In another book, I have continued the story:

> But then here comes Jesus, and what is his first move with John? "Then Jesus came from Galilee to be baptized by John" (3:13). Jesus comes out, most likely stands in line with all the others, with the desire to place his body in John's hands for immersion. Humility in action.
>
> Then John responds. "But John tried to deter him, saying, 'I need to be baptized by you, and do you come to me?'" (3:13-14). Jesus, in so many words, says "This is the right thing. I need to humble myself and submit to your baptism" (3:15a). In humility, John then submitted to Jesus' submission (3:15b). Surely, Satan hated it. These two powerful men just kept humbling themselves before one another, and the bond of unity grew tighter and tighter. Such a pattern continued throughout their lives.*

Whenever you find division in a marriage, in a household, in an office, or in a church, you can be sure pride is alive and working. You can be sure that someone or several someones are not willing to humble themselves after the example of Jesus and John. You can be sure that people are much more concerned about holding on to what is theirs than they are about demonstrating humility.

Unity is always achievable, but a price must be paid. We must all take our pride up the hill of Calvary and let it be crucified with Christ. In writing to the Philippian church Paul made the same connection between humility and unity that we saw earlier in Ephesians:

> ...then make my joy complete by being like-minded, having the same love, being one in spirit and purpose. Do nothing out of selfish ambition or vain conceit, but in humility consider others better than yourselves. (Philippians 2:2-3)

Having said this, Paul then calls us to take this to the extreme. He says our attitude should be the same as that of Christ Jesus (v5) and that means going all the way to the cross (v8). When we follow Jesus to Calvary and crucify all our pride, unity will come—we will be one in spirit and in purpose. The process may take some time, but we will get there.

Division has always been Satan's primary objective. Humility thwarts his plans, brings about unity and empowers God's people to change their

---

*"Humility in Action" in *Jesus with the People* (Woburn, Mass: Discipleship Publications International, 1996, 14-16). See this chapter for a more detailed look at the interaction of Jesus and John.

communities and change the world. Humility must be practiced in every relationship and at every level of leadership because it always unleashes God's
power.

———

Final Thoughts

What is a healthy soul? It is one permeated with humility. It is a soul free
of pride. Pride is a soul pollutant. Pride prevents the soul from communing
with God—the One who gives life and wholeness to the soul. Pride keeps the
soul from communing with other souls and stops relationships that give richness to life.

When the soul is humble, it can soar. It can stand in awe of God and see
clearly the miracles of his grace. The humble soul is free to be grateful and free
to give praise. When the soul is humble, it can hear clearly the voice of God
and understand his will. When the soul is humble, it can touch the work of
God and become part of a great plan to change many lives. When the soul is
humble, it is liberated to accept challenge, and it will eagerly embrace adventure that will advance the kingdom of God.

Quite simply, when the soul is humble, it is emptied of self, and it can be
filled with the Spirit of God, the power of God and the wisdom of God.

O God, expose our pride.
Keep us always humble. Amen.

© 1998 by Discipleship Publications International
5016 Spedale Court #331, Spring Hill, TN 37174

Appendix Seventeen
The Writings of Reuel Lemmons

Reuel Lemmons (1912–1989) was the remarkable and legendary editor of the Firm Foundation for twenty-eight years. His weekly editorials may have been the most widely read articles in Churches of Christ during that period, but he was not one who tried to curry favor with others. He was a prophetic voice who spoke the truth as he believed he found it in Scripture. In so many ways he was a man ahead of his time. He spoke at a number of campus ministry seminars in the early days of the movement described in this book. Since most readers of this material have had no exposure to him, I have included excerpts from a number of his editorials. I want to thank my father, Thomas R. Jones, who had great appreciation for Reuel's editorials, kept them, and dug them out for me as I was writing this book. It was a treasure trove of material I have thoroughly enjoyed rereading.

Reuel Lemmons
Photo by Verdin Studio

"Either—Or" – October 23, 1973

Such a person almost always suddenly develops into one who has all the answers. Perish the thought that there isn't an "either—or" answer to everything! They are quite different from average men in that they cannot accept ambiguity and are totally lost in an area that calls for individual judgment. It must be totally black or totally white; completely right or completely wrong. And the way they do it is the only way that is completely right. This is a miserable kind of existence, yet a condition into which one can easily fall.

"Love the Brotherhood" – October 30, 1973

The world was to believe that Jesus had been sent from the Father because his disciples were undivided. Their unity was an indication of their love. If we can't love, we can't have unity. We don't have it today because we have not learned to love each other as we should. This lovelessness results in sectarian division and strife. The setting of brother against brother springs from the fact that we have not learned to love as we ought, rather from any difference in understanding of the Scriptures.

"The Value of an Open Mind" – November 18, 1975

About the only chance we have to grow is through association with brethren who differ from us in their opinions. If we associate only with those who think exactly as we think, what chance do we have of ever learning something we do not already know? When we thus measure ourselves by ourselves and compare ourselves to ourselves, we are not wise.

"What Are We Here For" – February 24, 1976

When God bombed history with the Holy Spirit on Pentecost, the result was three thousand conversions on a single day. Soon the number became five thousand and it multiplied until the chronographer simply lost count, and used the term "multitudes," to describe those who became obedient to the faith. We feel that the church has lost a lot of the deep and earnest consecration that marked the first-century church, and has become obsessed with its problems rather than its faith. It is losing its direction, and will continue to do so until we turn again to emphasizing evangelism. God forbid that the church should be frozen into a monolithic pattern that produces intellectualism and spiritual stagnation rather than converts.

"Ecumenicity" – April 6, 1976

Cutting across the sectarian lines that separate [denominations], religious people of all stripes are finding more fellowship in undenominationalism than they ever felt in denominationlism. We are of the strong conviction that it would well behoove us to strengthen contact with these people and engage in a little "dialogue" with them. And incidentally dialogue is ridiculed only by the extremely prejudiced and the extremely sectarian. How in the name of common sense can you reason with anyone without dialogue? We have insisted on monologue for too long. No sober soul wants to listen to that, and unless we can offer something better, we will always be preaching to ourselves.

We are convinced that the more we can multiply contacts and conversations with conservative religious elements of every kind the more will be our opportunities to extol New Testament Christianity in the midst of a willing audience. It is not necessary to compromise the truth to maintain at least a speaking acquaintance with others of a somewhat like mind.... Maybe the time is ripe to reach out to some who might even grasp our hand.

"Witnessing" – March 30, 1976

We are especially concerned with the opportunity we have of presenting an alternative to the sectarian world. We cannot do it in sectarian terms or in sectarian practices. In all our pronouncements and in all forms of public utterances we should make it crystal clear that our commitment is rooted in Biblical faith and not in sectarian pride. Let all claim that they and they alone are true to the Bible, as they will, but let our "witness" speak louder than our words. What we are will speak more forcefully than what we say. A Biblical base for our work and witness is absolutely essential if we are to present an alternative to the world.

"A Call for Reassessment" – January 25, 1977

All dictatorial systems work on a maze of indoctrination, Gestapo-type surveillance and witch-hunting, intimidation and punishment. Without these elements they cannot survive. And without these elements human religious societies cannot survive. Constant purging is essential to keeping such sects "pure." They become the "only local church" in a community this way.... Anytime we become a closed system, bent on "defending the faith" by purging the heretics, rather than an eager people hungry for truth, we doom ourselves. We must think as we go. To stop thinking is to die.

"A Reassessment of Legalism" – February 15, 1977

Legalists torture the word "fellowship." They twist it until it has little resemblance to the New Testament term. They also drive rebels to the opposite extreme and they, too, begin to mold the word to fit their private concepts. Perhaps the strongest weapon the legalist has is "withdrawal of fellowship." He uses it as a pruning hook to lop off all who can't pronounce his shibboleth. He uses it to instill fear, rejection, guilt, and worthlessness into the feelings of his brother. This attitude has nothing that we can see in common with the Restoration Movement.

"The Essence of Christianity" – April 19, 1977

Christianity is for real. It is God-serving in the likeness of Christ's example. It is as this-worldly as the incarnation. It cannot retire monastically into a cove or church building and content itself with counting its ecclesiastical beads or mumbling its ritualistic prayers. Christianity is revolutionary—as revolutionary as Jesus. It calls for violence in throwing the money-changers out of the temple. Christianity [also] calls for absolute aloneness—the kind of aloneness that Jesus experienced on the cross.... Without a total separation from the world, there can never be a total commitment to God. Into his hands alone we must commit our spirit.

"Mercy Not Sacrifice" – July 19, 1977

"We would be amazed at how relationships in the church would improve if we could just teach brethren the lesson of mercy. Sacrificial legalism [that is legalism that emphasizes giving the doctrinally correct sacrifice] has largely throttled mercy. Every brother running around with his own yardstick measuring everyone else is a ridiculous sight. And mark you, he deserves and gets plastered with yardsticks! The climate of unity will improve in direct proportion to our willingness to show mercy.

"The Restoration Principle" – October 11, 1977

The Restoration principle does not bind us to produce in the twentieth century the religion of the first century, but it does obligate us to return to the Source of our faith as they got their faith from the same Source. We do not produce in the twentieth century the church of the first century, but rather the *faith* of the first century church.... The legitimacy of the Restoration plea lies not in its restoration of historic relics, but in the recovery of unamalgamated truth and respect for it.

"The Mid-Continent Seminar" – April 18, 1978

Written after he spoke at our annual seminar in Springfield, Missouri, that was actually called the Mid-American Mobilization Seminar, but was a tough name and we forgave him! His idea may have been better.

If you are prone to worry about what is going to happen to the church when us oldsters who "guard the faith" are gone, you should have been in Springfield, Missouri, March 10-12. More than 1200 came from college campuses from one end of the land to the other. These were young college students—most of whom did not come from Christian college campuses.... Standing ovations were given to some of the most hard-hitting Bible-based messages.

We have been having a number of youth gatherings across the land. They attract a far greater number of young people than meetings a few years ago.... They are better trained and better motivated and better taught than were their predecessors. Those not fortunate enough to have opportunities like these should be neither envious nor suspicious of them. We are thankful for the opportunity of association with these fine young people, and for the privilege of making some contribution to their program.

"On Taking a Calculated Risk" – November 20, 1979

The church can risk anything that is not inherently evil. If we are going to get the job done, we surely must take risk…. Let's make plans that strain the resources, financially, morally and spiritually, of our people. Resting on what we have accomplished is not good enough. "We must stretch forth to those things that are ahead." We must dare to attempt the impossible. By the grace of God we just might accomplish it.

Christianity has always been a daring religion. The early Christians defied the Roman government, the hatred of the Jews, and scorns of pagans to become heroes in the faith and to possess a crown. It was a terrible risk, but the reward was worth it. May God help us if we are unwilling to take a calculated risk. Nothing worthwhile can be accomplished without risk. We believe it is better to have tried and failed than never to have tried at all. Too many churches, unwilling to risk anything have set down to "hold their own," and have sitting, died.

"The National Campus Ministers Seminar" – September 9, 1980

Written after he spoke at the seminar in Baton Rouge.

We sort of inherited the *Firm Foundation's* interest in campus evangelism. When an organization by that name appeared on the scene, we supported it. We still think it was a worthy effort. Mismanagement brought its criticism, and as is our custom, finally crucifixion. [He is talking here about CE that planned the 1968 Seminar.]

We would like to see congregations near every college or university in the land become interested in campus ministry. Just as with congregations, there are a few instances where they may not be doing the best work in the world, but in by far the greater number of them a really outstanding work is being done. It makes no more sense to throw a blanket indictment over them all because of a few bad experiences than it does to condemn all congregations because a few split. These campus ministries deserve and should have the support of brethren.

"The Crossroads Controversy" – November 17, 1981

We are appalled at the extent brethren will go to win a fight. They will brazenly enlist the assistance of the secular press when they know full well what the Holy Spirit said about that in the Corinthian letter. Paul shamed the church for doing this.

Did you ever notice that those who are eager to brand some groups a cult are themselves cultish to the hilt? They usually have henchmen who dutifully gather material and send it to their leader for publication.

Most of the criticism we have seen was purely rhetoric, by someone whose ox had been gored. When you boil out the inflammatory talk, and get right down to what is scripturally wrong with the congregation [at Crossroads], you may find a thimble full. You might find more in your own congregation.

"Revisiting Our Isolation Theology" – Undated

Found on the Web at http://www.geocities.com/nucmanchh/isolation_theology.htm

It is amazing how separated two groups can become in just twenty-five years. With our brethren it seems impossible to cross party lines without completely losing all fellowship with them. All our sects—every last one of them—are composed of fallible and imperfect human beings with incomplete and imperfect knowledge. The more imperfect our knowledge, the more we try to make up for it with judgementalism.

Salvation is in Jesus Christ alone. It is not in Jesus, plus the right branch of the Restoration Movement. Salvation itself creates the only right church. Why can't we let it stand that way? God's family is larger than any of our cliques.

It is strange, but true, that the very exalted view we hold of the Scriptures makes us especially vulnerable to extreme legalism. We all believe that the Bible is the inspired word of God. We are united in the belief that as originally given, it was, and is, inerrant.

We want to do Bible things in Bible ways and have a thus saith the Lord for every rule of faith and practice. But that produces a fear-dominated sense of law keeping that almost does away with grace entirely. We become almost Gnostic in our emphasis upon salvation by knowledge rather than by faith.

"Personal Discipleship" – April 26, 1983

Written four months before he ended his time with the Firm Foundation.

Cross-bearing is the measure of discipleship. A cross is not a burden as most of us think, nor is it the terrible weight under which we stumble. It is a symbol of our complete rejection of the world, and the world to us. It is the mark of the point of no return, where commitment is past the possibility of apostasy.

So long as we are satisfied with mediocre service or come to worship because we feel it is our duty, we ought to keep an ear open for triple crowing of the cock.

If Jesus had anything less than total commitment the world would never have had a Savior. Appreciation for our own salvation will demand total commitment from us. It is really tragic when we hear Christians making light of total commitment. The closeness with which we walk in the footsteps of Jesus is determined by our commitment. The greater our faith, the closer we walk. It is our lack of faith that allows us to follow afar off.

A new term is making its appearance among us. It is "discipling." Oh, the term is in the Bible alright, but we haven't used it much until lately. It is a good sign now that we are beginning to talk about "discipling" people. We could spend a lot more time than we do in molding and making people after his will.

"We could spend a lot more time than we do in molding and making people after his will."

Selected Bibliography

Bonhoeffer, Dietrich. *The Cost of Discipleship*. New York: Macmillan Publishing, 1949.

——. *Letters and Papers from Prison*. London: SCM Press, 2001.

Coleman, Robert. *The Master Plan of Evangelism*. Old Tappan, NJ: Fleming H. Revell, 1963.

Elliott, Elisabeth. *A Path Through Suffering*. Ann Arbor, MI: Servant Publications, 1992.

Ferguson, Gordon. *Romans: The Heart Set Free*. Spring Hill, TN: DPI, 2001.

Ferguson, Gordon, and Wyndham Shaw. *Golden Rule Leadership*. Spring Hill, TN: DPI, 2001.

Foster, Douglas A. (Editor), Paul M. Blowers (Editor), Anthony L. Dunnavant (Editor), D. Newell Williams (Editor). *Encyclopedia of the Stone-Campbell Movement*. Grand Rapids: Wm. B. Eerdmans, 2006.

Hughes, Richard T. *Reviving the Ancient Faith*. Grand Rapids: Wm. B. Eerdmans, 1996.

Jones, Thomas. *Deep Convictions*. Spring Hill, TN: DPI, 1994.

——. *Letters to New Disciples: Revised Edition*. Spring Hill, TN: DPI, 2007.

——. *Mind Change: Third Edition*. Spring Hill, TN: DPI, 2007.

——. *No One Like Him: Jesus and His Message*. Spring Hill, TN: DPI, 2002.

Jones, Thomas, and Michael Fontenot. *The Prideful Soul's Guide to Humility*. Spring Hill, TN: DPI, 1998.

Kriete, Henry. *Worship the King*. Spring Hill, TN: DPI, 2000.

Lewis, C.S. *Mere Christianity*. New York: Macmillan Publishing, 1943, 1945, 1952.

McIntosh, Gary L. and Samuel D. Rima. *Overcoming the Dark Side of Leadership: The Paradox of Personal Dysfunction*. Grand Rapids: Baker Books, 1998.

Olbricht, Thomas. *The Power to Be*. Abilene, TX: Hillcrest Publications, 2003.

Reese, Jack. *The Body Broken*. Abilene, TX: Leafwood Press, 2006.

Stanback, C. Foster. *Into All Nations: A History of the International Churches of Christ*. Spring, TX: Illumination Publications International, 2005.

Webber, Robert. *The Divine Embrace*. Grand Rapids: Baker Books, 2006.

Wright, N.T. *Simply Christian*. New York: HarperSanFrancisco, 2006.

Yancey, Philip. *Disappointment with God*. New York: Harper Paperbacks, 1988.

Web Sites

Churches of Christ News and Comment — www.christianchronicle.org

Christian Churches News and Comment — www.christianstandard.com

Christian Church General Information — www.christianchurchtoday.com

In Search of a City Web Site — www.insearchofacity.net

International Churches of Christ News and Comment —
www.disciplestoday.net

Mind Change Web Site — www.mindchangeonline.org

Restoration Movement, Scholarly Study of —
www.acu.edu/sponsored/restoration_quarterly.html

Restoration Movement Resources — www.mun.ca/rels/restmov

Stadia Church Planting — www.stadia.cc

Unity Efforts — www.connect4change.net

Index

Other Resources by Thomas A. Jones

Mind Change
A Biblical Path to Overcoming Life's Challenges

Helps you to transform negative thinking to positive, God-oriented thinking: "Yes...problems. But...God." www.mindchangeonline.org

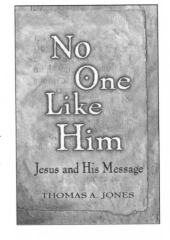

No One Like Him
Jesus and His Message

Unveils the heart, character and message of Jesus, presenting an oft-told narrative in a fresh and compelling way.

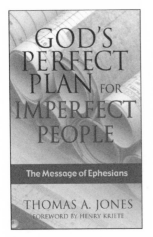

God's Perfect Plan for Imperfect People
The Message of Ephesians

Takes you through the book of Ephesians and convinces you that, even with your imperfections, God's plans involve you.

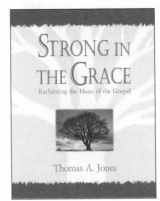

Strong in the Grace
Reclaiming the Heart of the Gospel

Shows that the grace of God must become the core of our faith and the deepest conviction from which all else flows.
A little book with a big message.

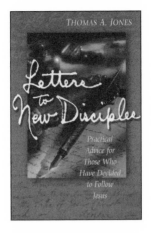

Letters to New Disciples

Practical Advice for Those Who Have Decided to Follow Jesus

Addresses new Christians, presenting principles that will help them have victory over their struggles and solidify their faith.

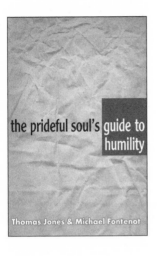

The Prideful Soul's Guide to Humility

Co-authored with Michael Fontenot

Helps you discover the power of a seldom-sought, but sorely-needed quality and shows that true humility is full of strength and passion.

To Live Is Christ

An Interactive Study of Philippians
Co-authored with his wife, Sheila Jones

Offers a month of inspiring daily devotionals focused on Paul's letter to the Philippians. Also includes insightful application questions.

Relationships: At the Center of the Target

A 4CD-set

Presents fresh insights regarding a topic that must always be front and center in churches that are focused on following Jesus and making disciples.